John Weiner

Effective Creativity in the Workplace

The role of ideas in formalized text mining and knowledge utilization

LAP LAMBERT Academic Publishing

Impressum/Imprint (nur für Deutschland/ only for Germany)
Bibliografische Information der Deutschen Nationalbibliothek: Die Deutsche Nationalbibliothek
verzeichnet diese Publikation in der Deutschen Nationalbibliografie; detaillierte bibliografische
Daten sind im Internet über http://dnb.d-nb.de abrufbar.
Alle in diesem Buch genannten Marken und Produktnamen unterliegen warenzeichen-, marken-
oder patentrechtlichem Schutz bzw. sind Warenzeichen oder eingetragene Warenzeichen der
jeweiligen Inhaber. Die Wiedergabe von Marken, Produktnamen, Gebrauchsnamen,
Handelsnamen, Warenbezeichnungen u.s.w. in diesem Werk berechtigt auch ohne besondere
Kennzeichnung nicht zu der Annahme, dass solche Namen im Sinne der Warenzeichen- und
Markenschutzgesetzgebung als frei zu betrachten wären und daher von jedermann benutzt
werden dürften.

Coverbild: www.ingimage.com

Verlag: LAP LAMBERT Academic Publishing GmbH & Co. KG
Dudweiler Landstr. 99, 66123 Saarbrücken, Deutschland
Telefon +49 681 3720-310, Telefax +49 681 3720-3109
Email: info@lap-publishing.com

Herstellung in Deutschland:
Schaltungsdienst Lange o.H.G., Berlin
Books on Demand GmbH, Norderstedt
Reha GmbH, Saarbrücken
Amazon Distribution GmbH, Leipzig
ISBN: 978-3-8433-9468-0

Imprint (only for USA, GB)
Bibliographic information published by the Deutsche Nationalbibliothek: The Deutsche
Nationalbibliothek lists this publication in the Deutsche Nationalbibliografie; detailed
bibliographic data are available in the Internet at http://dnb.d-nb.de.
Any brand names and product names mentioned in this book are subject to trademark, brand
or patent protection and are trademarks or registered trademarks of their respective holders.
The use of brand names, product names, common names, trade names, product descriptions
etc. even without a particular marking in this works is in no way to be construed to mean that
such names may be regarded as unrestricted in respect of trademark and brand protection
legislation and could thus be used by anyone.

Cover image: www.ingimage.com

Publisher: LAP LAMBERT Academic Publishing GmbH & Co. KG
Dudweiler Landstr. 99, 66123 Saarbrücken, Germany
Phone +49 681 3720-310, Fax +49 681 3720-3109
Email: info@lap-publishing.com

Printed in the U.S.A.
Printed in the U.K. by (see last page)
ISBN: 978-3-8433-9468-0

ın Weiner

Effective Creativity in the Workplace

Table of Contents

Chapter One – Learning and Team Creativity

Introduction

This book considers the process of continuing learning as an asset to team creativity. The idea – learning and team creativity – has been considered (e.g., Kipp 2007), but, the link hasn't been addressed in a formal way. The implications stemming from a relationship between learning and creativity form the basis for the material introduced in this book. The elements involved include:

1. Tools and techniques for effective learning of new information.
2. Enhancing the roles of specialists serving on creative teams.
3. Team actions to achieve rapid and effective solutions to problems.

Typically, the individuals chosen for the creative team are specialists in the various topics making up the subject. With such capability, the expectation is that new solutions can be rapidly produced. However, such progress is not the usual. The difficulties stem from the lack of a common language among the specialists and the differences in personalized knowledge, more accurately described as wisdom bases – a prioritized and filtered organization of the information. This organization of the existing information has been recognized as the epitome. However, is it the most effective in solving a new problem? What may be needed is a process that facilitates comprehensive and accurate identification and organization of all of the elements describing the topic. That type of knowledge base is filtered only by the contributions of the worlds' experts without further reduction. With that resource, missing and inconsistent findings can be identified. The experts can focus on the measures, procedures, criteria, and decision-structures needed to flesh out the new information structure leading to innovation.

The development of the comprehensive knowledge resource can be accomplished by eliminating the fatigue and clerical/mechanical barriers associated with manual text mining. To perform this function, pertinent data must be identifiable. The idea has been recognized throughout time as the powerful element facilitating communication and action. In order for software to perform accurately, an operational definition of the idea was required. That definition was *a pair of informative terms within the authors' sentences*. With that definition, the process of identifying, extracting, and organizing the authors' ideas is made feasible. The software can segregate the sentences within the text. It can identify informative terms by using attributes of specific types of words (i.e., nouns, verbs, adjectives). This list constitutes the authors' vocabulary used in describing the subject. The software can identify pairs of these informative terms within a sentence and prepare data records containing the ideas and associated identifying data.

The ideas prepared in this fashion will constitute a larger set than would be considered manually. The computer's set would include ideas that were considered important by the authors (as determined by frequency of use) as well as those that were relatively low in frequency. The latter make up two groups. One consists of ideas that are fading from use over time. The second consists of ideas that are increasing in use through time.

There is a third group in this low frequency category. That is the 'missing idea'. That is, an idea that has not yet been introduced in a subject, but, might have relevance once included in the body of knowledge. The missing idea is the desired one, albeit elusive. Finding such an idea and having it 'explain' a particular topic more effectively is the goal of investigators.

A computer-supported process [Weiner 1979] was used to identify the ideas and organize them together with the associated sentences and bibliographic data. The result is a comprehensive and accurate resource -- the Scholar's WorkStation -- containing the ideas as the building blocks for existing and new descriptions of the topic. This research tool is unique only in its focus on the idea. There are numerous ways of processing ideas and Idea Analysis^{tm} is one. Other approaches were described in Section 2. The resulting Scholar's WorkStation is a useful resource. It contains the ideas describing a subject and can be used by any number of investigators without repeating the tedious process of extraction and organization. The Scholar's WorkStation is an open-access repository available on request from learning@tutorghost.com.

The developed idea resource plus established algorithms can support rapid and effective preparation of syntheses and new research strategies.[Piniewski-Bond 2009] As such, 90% of the effort in dealing with an intellectual subject can be assigned to efficient and accurate computer and technical processing, freeing the individual to focus on the higher cognitive tasks requiring human experience and ingenuity.

The idea building blocks facilitate construction of new descriptions of the topic.[Piniewski-Bond 2001, Weiner 2005] These syntheses can be developed rapidly by allowing the authors to serve as mentors. They do this when the individual uses the authors' ideas. The frequency of ideas can be used to declare certain ideas as important. These higher frequency ideas form a type of consensus-description of the topic. The associated sentences provide initial text that can be edited and rewritten to form a new product. These idea structures also can be used to identify potentially interesting and innovative new studies. The low frequency ideas are sources of interest for that purpose.

The emphasis on using the ideas to construct and evaluate structures, consisting of concepts (swarms of ideas describing a specific attribute)[Eberhart 2001] and dimensions (clusters of concepts describing characteristics of the topic, helps shift the effort from data capture to knowledge utilization.[Weiner 2009] That transformation involves focus on measures useful in describing the attributes and characteristics of the topic as well as the processes used in managing them. There is a focus on criteria useful in classification and discrimination. There is a focus on decision structures enabling the individual to prioritize and select syntheses worthy of further use. The shift from the traditional study process, emphasizing memorization and recall, to one dealing with self-learning and critical thinking are natural consequences in adopting the full range of cognitive functions as the domain of interest.[Scriven 1987]

These intellectual behaviors are the primary reason for the selection of subject specialists for membership in the creative team. They are best equipped to build new syntheses and to employ the necessary measures, criteria, and decision-structures. This book provides a rationale and a process whereby the creative process can be systematized and accomplished effectively and

2

efficiently. However, the individuals must have the appropriate tools and the willingness to use those tools in dealing with the challenges.

The underlying premise is that the problem can be divided into specific tasks. Each of these tasks can be accomplished by assigning the best available capability to it. In general, there are three levels of task-capability matches:

1. Clerical, mechanical tasks can be assigned to software. The computer is capable of tirelessly carrying out specific tasks and can do so faster and more accurately.
2. Lower level cognitive tasks (e.g., recall, analysis and syntheses) can be assigned to technicians. These individuals can be trained to perform the necessary procedures and can do so with pride and diligence.
3. Higher level cognitive tasks (e.g., synthesis, comparison, evaluation, judgment, and application) can be assigned to individuals who appreciate and enjoy the challenge of developing measures, criteria and decision structures.

There are advantages to this separation of tasks. The obvious ones are speed in accomplishment, enhanced accuracy, and improved understanding. These, however, come with a cost. There is a long history of using techniques, designed around paper, in carrying out intellectual functions. These procedures are slow and often tedious, but, traditionally, represent intellectual prowess. Unfortunately, the assignment of the accolade of intelligent action must be based on the product of the effort. The process used is safely locked away in the brain of the individual. As a result, each generation of students must begin at the same starting point and hopefully will reach the same ends. Change in the body of knowledge is slow. Change in the methods employed is slow.

A Postmodernism Example? A philosophic theory describing the behaviors associated with the advent of the Information Age was called Postmodernism (see Chapter 7). That theory suggested the promise of more rapid discovery of new benefits to humans. Significant advances in the diagnosis and treatment of chronic diseases were promised. Improved communication and processing of information were heralded as no longer in the realm of science fiction. The computer and its associated technologies offered the promise of a 'paperless society' with the free and rapid flow of information into knowledge.

Some of these dreams have been realized in the management of numeric data. The mechanisms for capture, edit, storage, and retrieval of such data were developed, fine tuned and widely utilized. Contributions to utilization of the resulting information came from Statistics as well as from Information and Computer Sciences. The latter provided the tools and skills to manage the numbers and the former offered the mechanisms needed to make sense of them. That is, a highly formalized process, detailing each step of a specific path, allowed individuals to use the numeric data in order to develop new descriptions of topics and to formulate strategies for further study.

The same happy result was not observed with text. The computer's power was employed to produce images comparable to paper ones.[Weiner 2004] Text was considered to be a composite that might be called a page, a chapter, or a book. The ingredients making up this composite, namely, the words, sentences, and paragraphs were of obvious importance but mainly as a total unit. This attitude differs from that seen in numeric processing. There the emphasis is on the

3

individual number. It serves as a building block to formulate relationships and to illustrate differences.

Certainly, words are important in the management of text. There are different types of words with differing degrees of importance. One classification involves two groups – the informative terms and the rest. Informative terms are nouns, adjectives, or gerunds. They are instrumental in describing the topic. That is, they provide descriptors or measures of a particular characteristic, which, in turn, depicts a segment of the topic under consideration.

Words alone, however, are not necessary and sufficient. They must be linked with other informative terms in order to represent the author's thoughts. A simple sentence illustrates that assertion. The sentence is composed of a subject, a verb, and an object. The subject and object form the thought or idea provided by the author. The verb indicates the state of being or action associated with the idea, but does not alter the fact that the author combined the two terms in order to communicate a thought.

If words are considered as the primary elements in this textual universe, then the ideas are the essential molecules representing compounds that can be used to build new and bigger structures. Interestingly, by identifying informative terms and pairs of these within author-designated sentences, the processing of text can be made effective and efficient in a manner comparable to the well-established numerical processing experience.

The *tasks in this formalized knowledge utilization approach* are:
1. *Identification of existing information.* In essentially all cultures, information is synonymous with the use of nouns. By identifying those terms within each sentence and forming pairs of these terms, the analyst is able to consider the ideas provided by the author.
2. *Retrieval of existing information.* The data records prepared by the software can be easily retrieved by entering a search statement in the search and retrieval software. When the data records are designed as ideas (i.e., pairs of informative terms) and they are published, the analyst knows, *a priori*, the contents of the topic. The advantages in retrieval are apparent. Recognizing this, modern text mining and search engines display terms and/or phrases found in the text for enhanced development of retrieval statements. However, few of these use the authors' ideas as the source of the essential information.
3. *Analysis of these data.* Analysis involves processing of textual relationships and numeric representations of the associated attributes and characteristics to form new descriptions, make decisions, or provide estimates of values. The availability of computer software, to manage the data and to perform the calculations, makes the science of Statistics even more pertinent in knowledge utilization. The analyst deals with the selection of appropriate models in developing the findings necessary to better understand and interpret the conditions, ideas, and concepts describing the problem under study.
4. *Synthesis of basic elements.* Ideas can be arranged and organized to depict the dimensions and concepts making up the topic. These constructs can more closely match specialists' conceptual representations. Ideas and numeric results can be integrated to form new descriptions of a topic or phenomenon. These constructions provide facts and interpretations in a packaged fashion.

5. *Comparison of constructions.* The resulting information structures can be compared for similarities and differences. The informational content of each structure can be considered.

6. *Organization of these constructions using the established criteria.* Ideas can be arranged to conform to a study design. This type of organization is useful in considering possible knowledge generating strategies.

7. *Selection of the best of the constructions.* The analyst, using criteria, can select the appropriate construction and translate that into a text description of the topic or to a new investigative proposal designed to develop better understanding.

8. *Development of knowledge generating mechanisms.* This new study plan, when fleshed out with methods for capture, management, analysis and reporting of data, constitutes a knowledge generating mechanism.

What is the *value of the ideas*? The ideas take the words from the vocabulary and combine them to express relationships, meanings, and interpretations. The ideas are the experts' thoughts regarding the topic. They are critical in the construction of existing organizations of the information and in devising new descriptions. As such, ideas would be considered critical in the learning and use of a subject.

These sentences contain one or more of the three terms – cancer, breast, male. However, none of the sentences included the three. As such, while interesting, these sentences don't describe the specified condition.

To compare the gastric **cancer** (GC) patients by their family history with gastric and non-GC.

Of the 256 probands, 112 (76 **male**, 36 female) were incorporated into familial GC (FGC) group: at least two GC members; 144 (98 **male**, 46 female) were included in the non-FGC group (relatives only affected with non-GCs).

Of 399 tumors in relatives (181 from FGC against 212 from non-FGC), GC was thmost frequent, followed by esophageal, hepatocellular, and colorectal **cancer**.

Nasopharyngeal **cancer** was next to lung **cancer** but prior to **breast** and urogenital **cancer**s.

The ratio of **male**s to females in affected first-degree relatives was usually higher in **male** probands.

Paternal history of GC was a slight risk for GC in **male**s (OR = 1.19, 95% CI: 0.53-2.69), while risk of GC by maternal history of non-GCs was increased in females (OR = 0.46, 95% CI: 0.22-0.97).

To develop understanding, these terms must be combined to form thoughts. The authors do that by including at least two informative terms (i.e., nouns, adjectives, or verbs behaving like nouns) in the sentence. These sentences contain all of the three terms. The first two sentences

5

illustrate the authors' intent to describe the specific condition. This linking confirms the authors' focus on describing characteristics of the disease.

Due to its rarity, **male breast cancer** is not widely reported, especially in the Asian population.
The presentation of **breast cancer** in a **male** as a solitary axillary mass is very unusual.

These sentences also contain the three terms. The authors appear to be discussing other conditions and not the specific one of interest. However, a more extensive analysis of the literature would show that these seemingly unrelated ideas are part of the picture represented by the triad – cancer, breast, and male. A frequent innovative action is the establishment of links between sites and disease.

For other sites, positive associations were observed only for specific metabolic factors, that is, high triglycerides and **male** colon **cancer** (HR = 1.71, CI = 1.11- 2.62), and obesity and female **breast cancer** (HR = 1.75, CI = 1.21-2.55).

Breast, prostate and bladder **cancer**s increase risk of second tumour in female genital organs [RR 4.78 (3.84-5.93)], urinary system [RR 3.69 (2.89-4.69)] and **male** genital organs [RR 3.76 (2.84-4.69)] respectively.

Enhanced Communication Capabilites: A significant barrier in developing new text descriptions is in getting started. The first draft does not come easy. However, once the text is written, editing, revising, redrafting are easier to accomplish and faster to complete. Traditionally, an outline would be constructed and then sentences and paragraphs would be formed to provide the flesh on this skeleton.

This drafting technique facilitates development of a strategy for enhancement of the text. Decisions can be made regarding expansion with additional data from the articles. Decisions also can be made regarding elimination of any references. Importantly, decisions can be made regarding expansion of any of the ideas by more in-depth search and retrieval. These decision structures – data acquisition, refining triaging of sources, and in-depth acquisition of additional ideas – can be formalized and tracked so cognitive functions involved can be made public and subjected to quality control.

The advantages to idea-driven text construction are reduced preparation time and improved intellectual effort. The establishment of a multi-phased approach to the text utilization process actually results in a faster, more effective end-product. Clearly, fatigue is minimized by reducing the mechanical tasks. Perhaps the most important result of the new process is the challenge and excitement associated with the discovery and transformation of new information into knowledge. By focusing effort on the cognitive tasks, the success can be felt that is associated with effectively developing products indicative of academic prowess.

Phases of Discovery: Consider the phases of discovery in dealing with a new topic. The first phase would include identification, extraction and organization (as knowledge bases) of pertinent data from the text. These tasks are appropriately performed by software because of the tedious nature and mechanical operations involved. Using manual methods leads to significant error, although the hundreds of years of experience in doing these tasks have led to a perception that such acts are part of the intellectual process.

The second phase involves construction of descriptions of existing idea structures. The simplest of these descriptions is a table or map depicting important terms (i.e., nodes) and the connections between these nodes. These have been described as networks and depict representations of terms and their interrelationships. The network describes the conceptual issues inherent in the topic. Building these descriptions of existing knowledge is a technical procedure and can be performed by following defined algorithms.

The third phase involves real intellectual functions consisting of synthesis, comparison, evaluation, judgment and application. These activities are the province of the subject specialist and acquiring skills in using them is a challenge faced by each student. By having the products and results from the first two phases available to the student, the cognitive functions can be initiated earlier and can be accomplished more effectively and efficiently. This is evident simply by the elimination of the enormous amount of replication involved in identifying, extracting and organizing data items from literature.

However, there is a more compelling reason. That is, the contrast between document management and information utilization. In document management, the intent is to provide a label enabling retrieval. Once documents are retrieved, subsequent analysis of the text is performed manually. In information utilization, the pertinent data from the document are stripped and organized in order to develop new descriptions. The intent is to build new rather than simply retrieve. The document source is less important than the informational elements contained in it. If the approach was completely successful, retrieval of documents would be obsolete. Instead, retrieval of pertinent data would be the standard.

Conceptual Architecture: The focus on ideas allows easy translation of the cognitive functions associated with intellectual activity from privately held mental black boxes to open procedures. That shift allows the student to study the intellectual process as well as the result of the effort. As such, the starting place for each generation of students would be the final place reached by the previous group. The question is one of deciding how to reach the promised land of continual learning in an effective, efficient way. If one decides that this is the desired goal, then the tools, attitudes, and behaviors involved must necessarily change to improved, systematic assignment of capabilities to the tasks.

This focus on cognitive functions in building new descriptions is called Conceptual Architecture. [Weiner 2006] It is the application of computer-supported techniques in the analysis of text. The intent is to provide a historically accurate and comprehensive accounting of the issues considered by subject specialists as they investigated a particular topic. With that knowledge properly displayed, the time and energy associated with developing new descriptions and new research strategies can be focused on the higher cognitive tasks of synthesis, comparison, evaluation, judgment, and application.

The essential element in the conceptual structure is the idea. Developing conceptual structures involves identifying the nouns, adjectives, and verbs behaving as nouns, within a sentence and the authors' combinations of these as ideas. These terms are organized in a matrix or graph. In the latter, lines are drawn connecting the identified existing pairs, i.e., the ideas. To facilitate identification of ideas missing from the existing literature, dashed lines are drawn connecting the involved terms. The methods in conceptual architecture are different but should lead to duplication of the results obtained by the specialist using traditional approaches.

Processing Text – Enhanced Team Creativity? The hope of the future is that everything will be digitalized. Until that happens, is there an efficient way of dealing with text? There are at least two. The first identifies and processes the topic sentences from each paragraph of the text. The second identifies the sentence(s) containing the specific idea of interest.

The topic sentence approach uses the included ideas to construct an information structure. The information structure serves a comparable role to the numeric database in that the structure contains all of the data of interest. Individual analysts could select specific subsets of the data records in order to build new descriptions of the topics contained within the subject.

These subsets of information can be depicted using a variety of display formats. One such is the information network. This consists of terms and lines connecting the terms. The terms represent nodes within the network and the lines represent paths between the nodes. Nodes can be prioritized in terms of importance by the number of times the terms are used in describing ideas or relationships with other nodes.

The information network can be further enhanced by subdividing the associated nodes in terms using meaning and/or function. Categories can be created representing major segments of the total topic. These categories are called dimensions. Within each dimension, sub-divisions can be constructed by clustering ideas describing a common attribute. These sub-categories are called concepts.

The network, the dimensions, and the concepts help to organize the information relevant to the topic so that effective and innovative descriptions of the information can be constructed.

A second approach, One-Stop Learning, deals with a specific idea within a sentence and represents a major shift in processing. It combines the search process with the analysis of the ideas within the retrieved sentences. The entire document used to be the vessel containing the information of interest. This filtering method restricts the domain to those sentences that actually contain the search idea. This form of note-taking is similar to highlighting specific sentences or copying blocks of text for rewriting.

A third approach, Idea Analysis, deals with each of the sentences in a text. The informative terms and ideas from each sentence are identified, extracted, and organized as a repository. These ideas, representing those that the author considered pertinent in describing the topic, as well as others included in an incidental fashion, constitute the complete set of ideas dealing with the topic. These ideas – important and less so – represent the potential for effective

8

description of the current understanding as well as possible changes associated with new situations.

These technical capabilities enhance the individual's understanding of the subject and as such, bring a different attitude and function to team science. With the information network established, the individuals in the team can focus on the important elements – measures to be studied, criteria dealing with management of the data and procedures, and decision-structures leading to interpretations of the results with effective dissemination via reports and manuscripts. This form of team science is efficient and effective, once the attitudes of the past are laid to rest.

To address the issues, the book is divided into four sections. These are:

1. Effective Learning of New Topics.
2. Efficient Extraction and Organization of New Information.
3. Formalized Approaches in Information Generation.
4. Tracing Creativity.

Section 1 – Learning New Topics

This section provides examples of the use of ideas in learning new topics. The process is:
1. Identify and retrieve electronic versions of documents and use software to extract and organize the informative terms (vocabulary) and ideas contained in the authors' sentences. Alternatively, use computer-supported manual methods to extract and organize the data. In either case, the objective is to develop a repository containing the ideas and associated identifiers.
2. Determine the frequency of occurrence of ideas involving each of the informative terms used by subject specialists.
3. Select the higher frequency ideas and build information networks describing the interrelationships among the terms having the larger number of ideas.
4. Retrieve documents containing identified ideas and extract the sentence(s) containing those ideas.
5. Organize those sentences. This initial draft of the authors' sentences can be edited and rewritten to form a new description.

The advantage of this approach, for the individual, is that the bulk of the effort is spent using the higher cognitive functions of synthesis, comparison, evaluation, judgment, and application. The advantage for the creative team is a rapidly developed perspective of the informational network with its important terms (i.e., nodes) and relationships among the nodes.

Chapters 2 – 5 illustrate the learning approach associated with using ideas as the basis. This form of on-demand, self-discovery learning matches the needs realized when a new problem is to be solved. Chapter 2 deals with learning about the ideas and concepts making up breast cancer. Idea constructions involving three (triadic ideas) and four (quadrupletic ideas) term arrangements all from the same sentence are illustrated. The specific example describes the higher frequency ideas involved in studying breast cancer mitochondria. The mitochondria are relevant in breast cancer because of a relationship between this cellular component and cellular death (apoptosis).

The example in this chapter deals with developing insights into the relationships involving the central triadic idea – breast & cancer & mitochondria – with other terms. This example is of interest in that the study of mitochondria in breast cancer is infrequent even among specialists.

Chapter 3 describes the roles of simple paired ideas, triadic ideas and quadrupletic ideas in determining differences and similarities between breast and ovarian cancers. The major question is associated with surveillance and relationships between that term and others linking with the triadic idea – breast & cancer & surveillance or ovarian & cancer & surveillance. One explanation might be the transfer of approaches from one disease to another where similarities have been identified in occurrence, performance, or outcome. Breast cancer is an extensively studied disease and findings from that effort could be explored in other situations. Ovarian cancer surveillance might be an example of that exploratory approach.

Chapter 4 presents ideas involving prostate cancer and metabolic terms. The assignment deals with the question of how metabolic terms are used in the study of a cancerous condition. An exploratory process is illustrated using the options in excel to identify, extract, and organize subgroups of ideas related to a specific central term or idea. With those tasks managed in an efficient, relatively simple way, the in-depth study of rare events can be considered. The results could lead to a new description of the topic. This example also explores issues that are not universally studied.

Chapter 5 explored the use of procedures and related issues in physiology during the 50 year period – 1960 to 2009. The terms analyzed were those used by authors of the 2,533 articles published in the journals of the American Physiologic Society during 2009. The abstracts were retrieved from PubMed and analyzed using the text mining software – Idea Analysis^{tm}. The use of physiologic procedures can be measured using two indicators. The first is the number of articles containing a particular term or theme. The second is the number of ideas associated with the same central term. This example was part of a study intended to determine the relevance of instruction in physiology as practiced at the present time. Comparing the vocabulary and concepts in this example with the tables of content of text books provides insights into the differences between the wisdom and knowledge base approaches.

These chapters lay the foundation for the creative activities associated with developing new descriptions of subjects and the construction of strategies to capture new data leading to new interpretations of the existing knowledge. These results lead to the desired new solution anticipated by forming teams to perform creative acts.

Section Two – Ways to Identify Ideas

This section explores the various methods used to identify vocabulary and ideas. The methods described include:

1. *Topic Sentence Focus* – The topic sentence for each paragraph is extracted from the text and the informative terms identified. These terms are entered into an excel file and ideas built. Each idea would describe the primary and related terms making up the authors' idea, the chapter identifier, the book or article analyzed, and the paragraph identifier. This combined manual and computer-supported

method is efficient in building a repository that can be maintained and updated to provide easy access to the ideas in a topic.

2. ***One-Stop Learning*** -- This approach combines search using ideas presumably involved in the topic with extraction of sentences containing the specified idea. These sentences are used to identify and extract informative terms and these are entered into excel. Ideas involving those terms are constructed together with identifiers describing the year, the identification number for the document, and the sentence number. This method offers an effective and efficient way of dealing with digitized material involving a topic new to the individual.

3. ***Total Idea Extraction*** – This is a computerized method that reads the text, separates sentences, identifies informative terms, builds idea records, and stores them in excel files. The repository of ideas is designed to address more rapid learning of existing knowledge and to develop strategies to acquire new information.

The software used in this example is a system called Idea Analysis[tm]. This research tool was constructed in order to study the implications of using ideas in higher cognitive functions. The essential requirement was the ability to identify, extract, and organize the ideas from each sentence. These ideas are stored as data records and contain identification information as well. With these ideas in an accessible repository, the analyst can focus on building new descriptions and study strategies.

Section Three – Developing New Text

Chapter 8 shows the building of new text beginning with the authors' sentences from the One-Stop Learning exercise shown in Chapter 7. Additional examples are shown dealing with ideas from various topics. The methodology involving ideas as building blocks has been effective in developing new descriptions of topics and in developing new research strategies. The Idea Analysis[tm] software identifies, extracts, and organizes the authors' ideas as a comprehensive, accurate resource, the Scholar's WorkStation. These are open-access repositories available at learning@tutorghost.com. Analysis can focus on organizing clusters of ideas (i.e., idea swarms) [Eberhart 2001] rather than clusters of documents. The method yields a high degree of accuracy in retrieving precisely the documents of interest and of greater importance is the reduced need to retrieve documents in order to extract needed information. A significant benefit associated with the Scholar's WorkStation is the reduction in need and effort to repeatedly process original documents to extract data. The Idea Analysis software strips the ideas from the text. With those ideas in the Scholar's WorkStation, the retrieval of subsets of ideas for new purposes is a simple exercise. The real work can then be directed toward using the higher cognitive tasks to build a new result.

In learning a new topic, the higher frequency ideas represent those ideas considered most important by the authors. Alternatively, individuals seeking to develop new research might seek low frequency ideas, particularly those recently entered into the literature. Such ideas could represent new issues of interest. Finally, individuals seeking to develop new research could focus on the ideas that were missing from the literature. The identification of those ideas is not difficult or taxing. Indeed, when the information is properly organized, missing links are obvious. Given that set of ideas, the challenge facing the investigator is one that is exclusively private and important. Namely, the challenge is one of identifying the most important of those missing ideas for inclusion in new research.

Chapter 9 considers the research process and its various phases. This formalized, data-driven approach to learning is the most effective in developing consensus related to a given concept. The missing idea, as the focus for possible research studies, is discussed.

Chapter 10 introduces an algorithmic approach to developing models used in simulation studies. Much of the investigative process dealing with complex problems is costly and time consuming. The application of modeling and simulation offers an effective and economically feasible way to consider the different possible outcomes before investing real dollars, personal, equipment, and time in scenarios which appear to be interesting but without data support.

The research process leading to a creative act depends on the quality performance of predecessors in the form of:
1.   Development of an informative knowledge base of the elements making up the subject under study.
2.   Utilization of that knowledge base to identify missing ideas or inconsistencies clouding interpretation of the existing information structure.

This section deals with the details of developing a research program and the advantages associated with using algorithms in the construction of models representing actual situations.

Chapter 11 focuses on cognitive functions to assist in developing a gestalt perspective. The example uses health financial literature. With that approach, the process of developing the measures, criteria, and decision-structures needed in accomplishing each of the cognitive functions can be performed. These constructions are examples of syntheses. With those in place, the individual can learn to develop measures helpful in performing comparisons. These measures and associated decision criteria provide evidence needed in evaluating the findings. The measures, criteria, and decision-structures used in evaluation will prioritize the findings so that a judgment can be made as to the best, or most effective, or most economical. Based on that decision, a new structure can be considered to report findings and/or to build a new knowledge-generating scheme.

Section Four – Case Studies

Chapter 12 presents case studies using funded research proposals as the critical documents. The Scholar's WorkStations are used to trace the development of the funded research showing that this creative process can be traced through time. In addition, these studies illustrate the feasibility of introducing new ideas designed to enhance understanding of the topic. Case studies deal with emergency medicine and geriatrics, gynecologic oncology, chronic renal failure, substance abuse, endometriosis, and epidemiology. These examples show the feasibility of developing new research investigations based on the ideas previously studied and those that appear promising.

Scholar's WorkStation

The Scholar's WorkStation is a text processing and knowledge utilization system. The intent is to enable the analyst to focus essentially full attention on the problems and issues associated with the topics involved, while retaining insights with respect to the details involved in the processing. The focus is on the authors' ideas, as presented in sentences in the text. As a result, the individual is able to devote more attention and effort on the higher cognitive functions of synthesis, comparison, evaluation, judgment, and application. The actions involved are similar to those in building and using numeric databases. In that situation, the first phase involves construction of an accurate and comprehensive repository for the data. The second phase involves retrieval of selected subsets of the data for use in various analytic efforts. The third phase involves expenditure of intellectual effort in interpreting and reporting the results.

One advantage of this structured process is in having resources that can be shared, with confidence, by a relatively large number of interested investigators. Another is in the use of standard, accepted analytic techniques to determine trends and relationships among observations and measurements. Finally, the individual can demonstrate his/her intellectual prowess by producing interpretations of the findings and/or by identifying new knowledge generating strategies. The Scholar's WorkStations are open-access resources available on request from learning@tutorghost.com.

Chapter Two – Learning About Breast Cancer

Continued learning using effective methods represents an important element in team creativity. The problem requires a new, comprehensive presentation of the ideas related to the problem. This, in turn, suggests that creativity is a consequence of learning. In addition, that learning must be rapid, complete, and effective. The combination of a knowledge base containing relevant data plus software to eliminate or minimize the clerical/mechanical aspects of text mining offers a modern capability to make the team more effective. This and other chapters illustrate the importance of just-in-time, self-discovery learning in transforming a monumental project into a feasible, rapidly accomplished one.

The ideas and associated reference data have been extracted from scientific reports entered in PubMed for the years 2006 – 2010 and dealing with breast cancer. This resource (i.e., the Scholar's WorkStation for Breast Disease) contains the ideas from the breast disease literature, and is updated periodically to ensure that current ideas are available for consideration. The current resource covers 2006 – 2010. [*available at* learning@tutorghost.com]

Example Analysis

Assume that a student wishes to learn about breast cancer. Further, assume that the student has no prior background in the topic but is required to develop sufficient understanding of the disease to prepare a description of a major component. Further assume that the component deals with breast cancer, mitochondria, and related terms. Lastly, assume that the student has access to the Scholar WorkStation dealing with breast disease. That open-access resource is based on the assumption that the subject specialists have special insights, experiences, and knowledge that can be identified, extracted, and organized. These data can be used to guide a student interested in learning a new subject.

The instructor can serve as an effective coach in assisting the student to develop insights and understanding of a new subject. Self-learning and self-discovery are valued approaches as the student becomes motivated and involved in the learning process. These efforts emphasize higher cognitive skills such as syntheses of existing information to form new descriptions. In addition, the student can be encouraged to formulate measures and criteria for assessment of the new organizations. These efforts reinforce the long term memory of the facts and relationships making up the concepts in the subject as well as identify gaps and inconsistencies that might be corrected with new data.

The following example traces an exploration of author-guided learning using the scientific reports in the Breast Cancer 2006 Scholar WorkStation.

Idea Files

The ideas are separated by year. A preliminary analysis using the recall programs built into the Scholar WorkStation system was performed to construct excel files containing the breast cancer related ideas for each of the involved years. In addition, vocabulary files describing the terms related with the breast cancer were prepared.

Table 1. Excerpt from Breast Cancer Triadic Ideas – 2006 – File.

Cancer	Breast	Triads	Year	Ident	Sentence
cancer	breast	bronchial	2006	15657729	5
cancer	breast	chronic	2006	15657729	5
cancer	breast	gastric	2006	15657729	5
cancer	breast	hepatitis	2006	15657729	5
cancer	breast	infection	2006	15657729	5
cancer	breast	kidney	2006	15744540	3
cancer	breast	lung	2006	15744540	3
cancer	breast	metastases	2006	15744540	3
cancer	breast	life-threatening	2006	15852406	1
cancer	breast	ovarian	2006	15876481	1
cancer	breast	suppressor	2006	15876481	1
cancer	breast	tumour	2006	15876481	1
cancer	breast	apoptotic	2006	15878797	1
cancer	breast	phenol	2006	15878797	1
cancer	breast	preventive	2006	15878797	1
cancer	breast	proliferative	2006	15878797	1
cancer	breast	emotion	2006	15880627	1
cancer	breast	gene	2006	15880627	1
cancer	breast	repression	2006	15880627	1
cancer	breast	suppression	2006	15880627	1
cancer	breast	ovarian	2006	15880639	1
cancer	breast	risk	2006	15880639	1

These terms form triadic ideas (breast & cancer & related term). An excerpt is given in Table 1. The idea records are arranged by sentence for each identification number. This organization shows the ideas considered by each author. Each record represents a single idea composed of a pair of informative terms, the central idea – cancer & breast -- plus a third term. The third terms are shown in the column labeled triads. These triadic ideas are of interest in that they approximate preliminary concepts provided by subject specialists.

Review of these would indicate that some may be more important than others. The intent of the software is to capture the total set of ideas irrespective of importance. The rationale is based on the realization that ideas change in importance with time. As such, an analysis would show the currently important ideas, those that are fading, and those that are emerging.

Table 2 shows an excerpt of the vocabulary representing the triadic terms. As seen, the terms are ranked in order of the frequency of occurrence of the triadic idea involving each. The idea – breast & cancer & risk – occurred 1347 times in the 2006 breast literature. The ideas involving genetic characteristics, treatment, and outcomes including survival were in the higher frequency set. Of interest, the triadic idea linking breast cancer and the site – ovary – also was in the higher frequency group. The topic assigned – breast & cancer & mitochondria – occurred 50 times in 2006. This relatively low frequency idea could be an example of an idea that is growing in popularity with time or diminishing. The idea also could represent the emerging interest in translational research in cancer.

Table 2. Excerpt from Breast Cancer Triadic Idea Vocabulary – 2006.

Terms in Breast Cancer Triads	Freq
risk	1347
women	1291
tumor	886
gene	846
expression	840
receptor	522
estrogen	493
data	468
protein	433
inhibit	402
survival	372
metastatic	368
primary	361
growth	348
chemotherapy	344
node	339
detect	330
ovarian	328
invasive	323
stage	323
mutation	316
screening	306
menopausal	302
etc.	**etc.**
Total triads	**30160**

This analysis illustrated the information provided by more complex idea formations. Breast cancer ideas involve over 800 individual *informative terms*, selected by author-specialists to describe the subject. These terms were linked with the central term – breast -- more than 68,000 times in 2006 to form ideas. These are defined as a pair of informative terms, presented by the authors, within the domain of the sentence. Of these individual ideas, in 2006, 30,160 ideas involved the combination of the central idea – breast & cancer – with a third term. The number of ideas per year specifically linking a third term to the central idea of breast cancer is shown in Figure 1. The median frequency was about 40,000 per year. These triadic ideas were considered in determining the relationship between breast cancer and mitochondrial function.

Figure 1. Number of Breast Cancer Triadic Ideas Per Year – 2006-9.

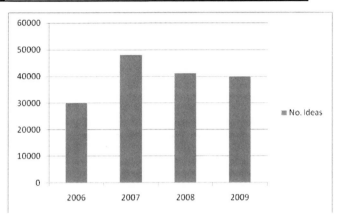

Information Networks: Quadrupletic ideas more closely approximate the concepts from specialists. The term – concept -- is defined as -- *an idea of something formed by mentally combining all its characteristics or particulars; a construct.* To qualify as a quadrupletic idea, the four terms involved must come from the same sentence. The terms – apoptosis, apoptotic, cellular, death, DNA, protein, tumor, and expression – all link with the central triadic idea to form a concept dealing with death of cancer cells based on alterations of mitochondrial function.

Developing New Text Descriptions: The Idea Analysis[tm] approach involves identifying sentences from authors' idea sets that show selected idea interrelationships. The steps in building new text are:

1. Select higher frequency ideas.
2. Define unfamiliar terms.
3. Determine how authors used the ideas by selecting representative idea sets depicting specific sentences.
4. Build an idea path using the frequencies of the selected ideas.
5. Construct new sentences using the ideas in the form of questions.
6. Convert the question format to a statement if the ideas were used in the stated way by one or more author.
7. Prepare references showing the authors using specific ideas.

To illustrate the process, consider the relationships between informative terms and mitochondria, the critical term of interest. Two identification numbers were considered and the selected sentences in the form of idea sets are shown in Table 3. The first document was **16361073.** The involved sentence contained 9 triadic ideas and the first of those was – mitochondria & cancer & apoptosis. The second idea set was from document **16546963** and contained 7 triadic ideas.

18

The dictionary definitions for four unfamiliar terms are:

Apoptosis – programmed cell death.
Caspase – one of a group of proteases that mediate apoptosis.
Mitochondria – energy factory in cell.
Proteases – a group of proteins.

The higher frequency ideas can be arranged as a frequency path as follows:

Mitochondria → cancer → breast → apoptosis → expression → protein → DNA → inhibit → caspase → oxygen → polymorphism → regulation → superoxide → tumor

The linking of higher frequency ideas with the ways that the authors used those ideas offers insights in developing a new set of sentences describing the subject.

Table 3. Ideas From Sentences in Two Reports – PMID 16361073 and PMID 16546963.

Mitochondria	Cancer	Related	Year	Ident
mitochondria	cancer	apoptosis	2006	16361073
mitochondria	cancer	apoptotic	2006	16361073
mitochondria	cancer	breast	2006	16361073
mitochondria	cancer	caspase	2006	16361073
mitochondria	cancer	death	2006	16361073
mitochondria	cancer	expression	2006	16361073
mitochondria	cancer	growth	2006	16361073
mitochondria	cancer	immunoblot	2006	16361073
mitochondria	cancer	inhibit	2006	16361073

mitochondria	cancer	apoptosis	2006	16546963
mitochondria	cancer	apoptotic	2006	16546963
mitochondria	cancer	breast	2006	16546963
mitochondria	cancer	caspase	2006	16546963
mitochondria	cancer	inhibit	2006	16546963
mitochondria	cancer	protein	2006	16546963
mitochondria	cancer	regulation	2006	16546963

Such sentences might be as follows:

Apoptosis expression in breast cancer involves an effect on the mitochondria. Caspase is defined as a group of proteases (proteins) that mediate apoptosis or programmed cell death. Mitochondrial function is studied using caspase inhibitors in the regulation of the apoptotic process. The method used in studying the function was immunoblot.

19

The terms from the example idea sets are shown in red. These newly constructed sentences first may be considered as questions. For example, the first sentence might be changed to the question -- *Does apoptosis expression in breast cancer involve an effect on the mitochondria?* If the authors studied the relationship between apoptosis, breast cancer, and mitochondria, then the question could be changed to a statement. The fact that author-specialists employed the ideas adds credibility to the new arrangement. Each such statement could be properly referenced. As seen in Table 3, both authors considered this relationship. In addition, the second author made the connection between caspase, mitochondria, and apoptosis. The idea path suggested by these authors might be – Caspase → mitochondria → apoptosis → breast cancer.

The higher frequency ideas in Figure 3 can be expressed as paths, then questions or statements depending on the confirmation by author-specialists. The paths are:

Breast cancer → mitochondria → apoptosis
Breast cancer → mitochondria → tumor
Breast cancer → mitochondria → DNA
Breast cancer → mitochondria → apoptotic
Breast cancer → mitochondria → death

Breast cancer mitochondria verb apoptosis?
Breast cancer mitochondria verb tumor?
Breast cancer mitochondria verb DNA?
Breast cancer mitochondria verb apoptotic?
Breast cancer mitochondria verb death?

Exhibit 1. Sentence containing Quadrupletic Idea – Breast & Cancer & Mitochondria & Apoptosis – PubMed Identifier PMID: 16546963 [Liu et al 2006]

> In conclusion, these studies show that inhibition of PI3K can sensitize cerulenin-induced **apoptosis** in MBA-MB468 **breast cancer** cells via activation of caspases, down-regulation of antiapoptotic proteins, such as XIAP, cIAP-1 and Akt, and possibly, activation of Bak in **mitochondria**.

Exhibit 1 shows a sentence containing the four terms in the first quadrupletic idea above. As such, the question involving these terms can be changed to a statement. Similarly, Exhibit 2 contains a sentence involving the quadrupletic idea – breast cancer & mitochondria & death. That idea can be expressed as a statement.

Exhibit 2. Sentence containing Quadrapletic idea – Breast & Cancer & Mitochondria & Death – PubMed Identifier PMID: 16603054 [van der Kuip et al 2006]

> To visualize viability, cell **death**, and expression of surface molecules in different compartments of non-fixed primary **breast cancer** tissues we established a method based on confocal imaging using **mitochondria**- and DNA-selective dyes and fluorescent-conjugated antibodies.

The exhibits illustrated how authors incorporated those ideas to provide specific information. The value of ideas is that they are dimensionless and can be combined in any number of ways to build new concepts. This flexibility is the advantage of working with the ideas. The analyst can arrange the ideas in various ways. Some will be new. Others will be replicates of those used in scientific reports. As the complexity of the idea increases (i.e., from the simple pair to the triad to the quadruplet), the likely use of the idea by a specialist also increases, substantiating the transformation of the idea in question form to a statement.

Figure 2. Interrelationships between Terms Linked with the Central Triadic Idea – Breast & Cancer & Mitochondria.

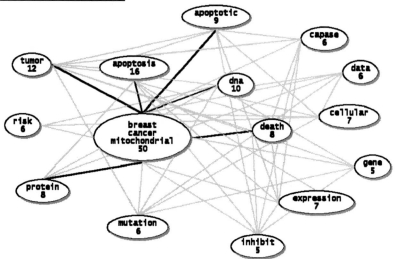

The network structure, in Figure 2, shows the idea links favored by the author-specialists and those that are less frequently used. This separation into higher and lesser frequency groups can be used to recognize different degrees of knowledge. The more frequent represent a type of consensus among the author-experts and implies that these ideas are well accepted within the fabric of the subject.

The less frequent ideas may represent those previously favored and now disappearing. Alternatively, these low frequency ideas may be the ones that are emerging as potentially important. Temporal analysis of these lesser frequency ideas can be used in considering potentially new and important strategies in generating new knowledge.

Summary

This analysis of the relationships among the ideas involved a triadic idea (breast & cancer & a third term) and a quadrupletic idea (breast & cancer & mitochondria & a fourth term). These ideas were used to show the development of concepts as well as the formation of new text. The generation of new text involves the identification and definition of unfamiliar terms appearing in higher frequency ideas. This information, together with the frequency of ideas, leads to the development of idea paths depicting the chain of ideas based on frequency of occurrence. Those ideas are used to retrieve representative idea sets depicting sentences incorporating these higher frequency ideas. These data contribute to the construction of statements in the form of questions. By forming a question, the analyst is considering the possibility that the idea is relatively new and may be of interest for further study. If author-specialists have studied the idea within each question, conversion to a statement is justified. The transformation confirms that, using their expertise, the specialists also have considered the idea identified by the analyst. This simple confirmation shows that the individual, studying a new topic, has matched findings provided by the specialists in the discipline.

Building new text by using ideas allows the individual to rapidly acquire the vocabulary, the ideas, and methods used in the study of the subject. This accelerated learning is of value in meeting the demands of continual learning.

Chapter Three -- Surveillance in Ovarian and Breast Cancers

Introduction

This chapter considers the role of surveillance in two cancers affecting women. The analysis employs information networks in describing how surveillance is incorporated in management of these diseases. The networks consist of ideas presented by the author-specialists. The ideas of interest are composed of four informative terms contained within a sentence. These quadrupletic ideas consist of a central triadic idea – *breast & cancer & surveillance* or *ovarian & cancer & surveillance*. This idea is linked with a fourth term from the same sentence forming the complex idea.

Syntheses of Ideas: These quadrupletic ideas can be organized into major components or dimensions representing segments of the total information in the topic. Generic dimensions would be:

1. Personal factors.
2. Environmental factors.
3. Subject matter factors.
4. Intervention factors.
5. Outcome factors.
6. Methods.

Figure 1. Generic Dimensions Arranged as a Clinical Study Model.

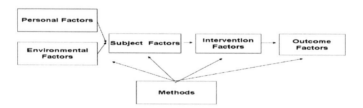

Figure 1 shows an arrangement of these generic dimensions as used in clinical trial research. The model shows the relationships between the dimensions describing a topic. The personal and environmental factors describe the attributes and characteristics of the study subjects. The subject factors represent the informational elements comprising the topic. The interventional factors represent the actions designed to change subject factors and the results of those changes are called outcome factors. Influencing each of these dimensions in various ways are the methods employed in observing, deciding, and applying.

Various Idea Formations: Table 1 shows an excerpt of the simple paired ideas. Each idea is shown as a separate record. In addition to the pair of informative terms forming the idea, the record includes the year that the article was entered into PubMed, the Identification Number assigned to the document by PubMed, and the number of the sentence in the abstract containing the idea.

Table 1. Excerpt of Ovarian Ideas in 2009 Resource.

Primary	Related	Year	Ident	Sentence
ovarian	abdominal	2009	19537883	9
ovarian	acetylation	2009	19935792	4
ovarian	adhesion	2009	19574774	1
ovarian	adhesion	2009	19574774	4
ovarian	adhesion	2009	19363681	3
ovarian	age	2009	19305347	2
ovarian	age	2009	19261323	5
ovarian	age	2009	19201457	5
ovarian	age	2009	19751997	4
ovarian	amplification	2009	19370966	5
ovarian	amplification	2009	19370966	9
ovarian	amplification	2009	19370966	13
ovarian	analysis	2009	19854497	7
ovarian	analysis	2009	19125205	6
ovarian	analysis	2009	19636370	7
ovarian	analysis	2009	19636370	13
	etc		etc	

Table 2. Excerpt of Ovarian Triadic Ideas in 2005.

Primary	Cancer	Triads	Year	Ident	Sentence
ovarian	cancer	breast	2005	10915918	1
ovarian	cancer	evidence	2005	10915918	1
ovarian	cancer	risk	2005	10915918	1
ovarian	cancer	apoptosis	2005	11319608	4
ovarian	cancer	cell	2005	11319608	4
ovarian	cancer	apoptosis	2005	11319608	9
ovarian	cancer	benign	2005	11809106	2
ovarian	cancer	expression	2005	11809106	2
ovarian	cancer	polymerase	2005	11809106	2
ovarian	cancer	tumor	2005	11809106	2
ovarian	cancer	benign	2005	11809106	3
ovarian	cancer	expression	2005	11809106	3
ovarian	cancer	tumor	2005	11809106	3
	etc		etc		

Table 2 shows an excerpt of the triadic ideas involving the central paired idea – ovarian & cancer. The idea record also contains the third term from the same sentence and the identifiers described in Table 1.

Table 3. Excerpt of Quadrupletic Ideas with the Central Triad – ovarian & cancer & surveillance.

Primary	Cancer	Surveillance	Quadruplets	Year	Ident	Sentence
ovarian	cancer	surveillance	age	2008	17892451	2
ovarian	cancer	surveillance	age	2008	18558577	5
ovarian	cancer	surveillance	analysis	2008	17986243	2
ovarian	cancer	surveillance	antigen	2005	15333188	5
ovarian	cancer	surveillance	antigen	2009	19820365	1
ovarian	cancer	surveillance	behavior	2009	19273395	1
ovarian	cancer	surveillance	behavior	2009	19273395	8
ovarian	cancer	surveillance	BRCA	2008	18208856	1
ovarian	cancer	surveillance	BRCA	2008	18208856	11
ovarian	cancer	surveillance	BRCA	2008	18413372	10
ovarian	cancer	surveillance	BRCA	2008	19105530	1
ovarian	cancer	surveillance	BRCA	2009	19273395	1
ovarian	cancer	surveillance	BRCA	2009	19273395	10
ovarian	cancer	surveillance	BRCA	2009	19035463	3
ovarian	cancer	surveillance	breast	2005	15333188	5
ovarian	cancer	surveillance	breast	2006	16531042	7
ovarian	cancer	surveillance	breast	2006	16549852	4
ovarian	cancer	surveillance	breast	2006	16736286	6
		etc		etc		

Table 3 shows an excerpt of the quadrupletic ideas. The first three columns show the triadic idea and the fourth column gives the related terms. The other columns give the identifiers – year, identification number, and sentence number.

Information Network in Ovarian Cancer: An information network consists of nodes (frequently used terms or ideas) linked with related terms (expanding on the meanings of the nodes). These terms are connected by lines or paths demonstrating the presence of relationships. This configuration is similar to a geographic display featuring, for example, a major city and its suburbs. Figure 2 is an example of an information network involving one principal node, the triadic idea. Linked with it are numerous terms. These terms have been classified into the generic dimensions to illustrate a more complete picture of ovarian cancer surveillance.

Figure 2. Terms Linked with the Central Triadic Idea – ovarian & cancer & surveillance.

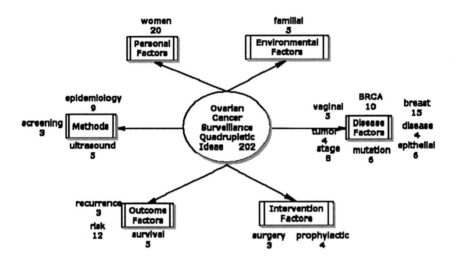

There were 202 quadrupletic ideas involving the central triad of ovarian cancer surveillance. Added to that idea were terms provided by the author-specialists in the same sentences. One such was – women. This quadrupletic idea (ovarian & cancer & surveillance & women) was cited 20 times by the authors. In contrast, the quadrupletic idea involving surgery was cited 3 times. There were eight terms classified as Disease Factors (Subject Factors in Ovarian Disease). These terms describe attributes representing anatomic sites (breast and vaginal), genetic characteristics (BRCA and mutation), tissue types (epithelial), disease descriptors (disease, stage, and tumor).

Authors' Use of Quadrupletic Ideas: These terms, when linked with the central triadic idea, provide an enhanced description of the role of surveillance in this cancer. To illustrate that, Exhibit 1 shows how Bermejo-Perez et. al. used the quadrupletic idea – ovarian cancer surveillance plus BRCA.
In addition, this sentence contained other quadruplets:

        Ovarian cancer surveillance plus imaging
        Ovarian cancer surveillance plus breast
        Ovarian cancer surveillance plus women
        Ovarian cancer surveillance plus mutation
        Ovarian cancer surveillance plus gene

Exhibit 1. Sentence showing the Author's use of the Quadrupletic Idea plus additional complex ideas.

We have systematically reviewed the literature focusing on the performance of **surveillance** programmes and **imaging** techniques for the early diagnosis of **breast** and **ovarian cancer** in **women** carrying **mutations** in **BRCA1/2 genes.**

[Bermejo-Pérez MJ, Márquez-Calderón S, Llanos-Méndez A. Cancer surveillance based on imaging techniques in carriers of BRCA1/2 gene mutations: a systematic review. Br J Radiol. 2008 Mar;81(963):172-9. Epub 2008 Jan 21.]

Exhibit 2 shows another sentence containing the quadrupletic idea. The additional terms in that sentence were: behavior, women, risk, hereditary, breast, and susceptibility. The authors combined a number of simpler sentences to form the complex one presented. In addition, they repeated a number of the informative terms within the sentence.

Exhibit 2. Sentence showing the Author's use of the Quadrupletic Idea plus additional complex ideas.

PURPOSE/OBJECTIVES: To investigate cancer surveillance behaviors of women at risk for hereditary breast and ovarian cancer (HBOC) who presented for clinical BRCA cancer susceptibility testing, specifically to describe cancer surveillance behaviors and reasons for not engaging in behaviors, compare surveillance behaviors with existing surveillance guidelines, and evaluate associations of cancer surveillance behaviors with BRCA results. [Loescher LJ, Lim KH, Leitner O, Ray J, D'Souza J, Armstrong CM. Cancer surveillance behaviors in women presenting for clinical BRCA genetic susceptibility testing. Oncol Nurs Forum. 2009 Mar;36(2):E57-67.]

The Idea Analysis[tm] software, used in developing the Scholar's WorkStation, avoids capturing multiple copies of the idea contained within the sentence. The identification and extraction focuses on the simple pair, i.e., ovarian & cancer, ovarian & surveillance, etc. These simple ideas were combined in the synthesis first to triadic ideas and then to quadrupletic ideas.

Exhibit 3. Sentence showing the Author's use of the Quadrupletic Idea plus Additional Complex Ideas.

Annual surveillance by transvaginal ultrasound scanning and serum CA-125 measurement in women at increased familial risk of ovarian cancer is ineffective in detecting tumors at a sufficiently early stage to influence prognosis. [Stirling D, Evans DG, Pichert G, Shenton A, Kirk EN, Rimmer S, Steel CM, Lawson S, Busby-Earle RM, Walker J, Lalloo FI, Eccles DM, Lucassen AM, Porteous ME. Screening for familial ovarian cancer: failure of current protocols to detect ovarian cancer at an early stage according to the international Federation of gynecology and obstetrics system. J Clin Oncol. 2005 Aug 20;23(24):5588-96.]

Exhibit 3 shows the quadrupletic idea together with additional informative terms. Those informative terms were: vaginal, scanning, familial, risk, and stage. The same investigative group published a second report in 2008 stating the same negative finding associated with ultrasound.

Comparison of Information Networks: Figure 4 compares the two information networks. The terms forming quadrupletic ideas in both networks are highlighted in red. The ideas in common involved: women, BRCA, stage, breast, ovarian, risk, screening, and survival. Building new text can be accomplished by identifying the higher frequency ideas and arranging them in various ways. The path of ideas, in terms of frequency of use by the authors, would be – ovarian → cancer → surveillance → women → breast → risk → BRCA → stage → survival → screening. Sentences involving these ideas would begin with declarative ones such as:

> Ovarian cancer surveillance verb women.
> Ovarian cancer surveillance verb breast.
> Ovarian cancer surveillance verb risk.
> Ovarian cancer surveillance verb BRCA.
> Ovarian cancer surveillance verb stage.
> Ovarian cancer surveillance verb survival.
> Ovarian cancer surveillance verb screening.

These sentences require the choice of an appropriate verb to depict state of being or action. Once the simple sentences are constructed, more complex ones can be developed by combining the simple ones.

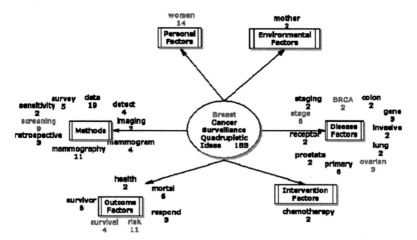

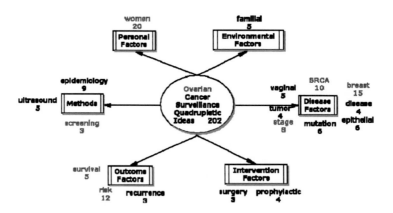

29

<u>**Exhibit 4. Sentences showing the Inclusion of the Quadrupletic Ideas.**</u>

Women at high risk of ovarian cancer are currently offered two options: either surveillance or prophylactic bilateral salpingo-oophorectomy.

Cancer genetic counseling has multiple repercussions, such as identification of a deleterious genetic mutation associated with a high probability of developing breast and/or ovarian cancer, the implementation of preventive measures ranging from close surveillance to the decision to perform mutilating prophylactic surgical procedures, or the impact of the information on the other members of the counselee's family also concerned by the genetic risk.

To investigate cancer surveillance behaviors of women at risk for hereditary breast and ovarian cancer (HBOC) who presented for clinical BRCA cancer susceptibility testing, specifically to describe cancer surveillance behaviors and reasons for not engaging in behaviors, compare surveillance behaviors with existing surveillance guidelines, and evaluate associations of cancer surveillance behaviors with BRCA results.

The purpose of this report on breast cancer and ovarian cancer genetics is to review the evidence for the efficacy of surveillance for early detection, bilateral prophylactic mastectomy, prophylactic oophorectomy, and chemoprevention in preventing breast cancer and improving survival of BRCA1 and BRCA2 carriers.

Analysis of Quadrupletic Idea Paths: Exhibit 4 shows selected sentences containing quadrupletic ideas and associated paths. The first sentence shows the combination of the declarative sentences – *ovarian cancer surveillance verb women and ovarian cancer surveillance verb risk.* As seen, the authors elected to arrange the ideas using the following path – **ovarian cancer surveillance → women → risk.** The second sentence used the path – *ovarian cancer surveillance → breast → risk.* The third sentence used the path – *ovarian cancer surveillance → women → risk → BRCA.* The fourth sentence used the path – *ovarian cancer surveillance → breast → survival → BRCA.*

Summary

These sentences and related synthesis paths illustrate the power of the idea as a building block in constructing concepts, issues, and topics. By arranging the ideas in various ways, a text can be formed that reflects the individual's interpretation of the knowledge base of ideas. The result is comparable to ones obtained using previous, less transparent methods. The difference is in the objective construction of the data resource. All of the ideas presented by authors – important and less so – are captured by the Idea Analysis^{tm} software. This factual presentation enables any number of analysts to select subsets of the ideas for secondary analyses.

The advantages associated with using ideas as building blocks are numerous and include:
1. Faster completion time.
2. Increased accuracy.
3. Enhanced monitoring by third-parties.
4. Improved learning.

This analysis of breast and ovarian cancer showed interesting similarities in informational structures associated with surveillance. One explanation might be the transfer of approaches from one disease to another where similarities have been identified in occurrence, performance, or outcome. Breast cancer is an extensively studied disease and findings from that effort could be explored in other situations. Ovarian cancer surveillance appeared to be an example of that translational and exploratory approach.

An alternative explanation would suggest that a set of ideas comprise the role of surveillance irrespective of the disease involved. As such, when comparing breast and ovarian cancer surveillance, this set of common ideas is evident.

Chapter Four – Learning About Prostate Cancer

Introduction

Assume that a student wishes to learn about the metabolic conditions in prostate disease. Further, assume that the student has no prior background in the topic. Finally, assume that the student has access to the Scholar's WorkStation dealing with prostatic disease. [learning@tutorghost.com] These data can be used to guide a student interested in learning a new subject.

Self-learning and self-discovery are valued approaches as the student becomes motivated and involved in the learning process. These efforts emphasize higher cognitive skills such as syntheses of existing information to form new descriptions. In addition, the student can be encouraged to formulate measures and criteria for assessment of the new organizations. These efforts re-enforce the long term memory of the facts and relationships making up the concepts in the subject as well as identify gaps and inconsistencies that might be corrected with new data.

To accomplish this form of learning, different types of resources and procedures are helpful. One is a focus on the authors' ideas. The dictionary definition of an idea is – "any conception existing in the mind as a result of mental understanding, awareness, or activity, a thought, conception, or notion." A more realistic representation of the idea is the subject and object in a simple sentence. That pair of nouns, adjectives, and/or gerunds provides the thought considered by the author. The verb, used to complete the sentence, provides information relative to action or state of being associated with that idea.

Using this definition, the computer can perform the following tasks. Sentences can be separated. Within each, the nouns, adjectives, and/or gerunds can be identified. These terms, when combined to form pairs, represent the ideas provided by the author in the sentence. Those ideas can be extracted and organized as a database. The sentences making up the document can be stored and used for quality control analyses. The result is the Scholar's WorkStation.

The Importance of Ideas? To accomplish this form of learning, different types of resources and procedures are helpful. For example, what are the basic building blocks used in formulating new descriptions of a subject? What constitutes a primary thought? The answer to such questions has been known for centuries. It is the idea. A more realistic representation of an idea is the **subject and object in a simple sentence**. That pair of nouns, adjectives, and/or gerunds provides the thought considered by the author. The verb, used to complete the sentence, provides information relative to action or state of being associated with the idea.

Why are they important? Ideas are dimension-free and can be organized to form any number of different conceptual structures. Ideas also can be arranged to describe a type of consensus across subject-specialist-authors. The ideas form a structure showing the terms involved and the links between these terms. This idea network is called an information structure.

33

Why are they useful? By focusing on the process of constructing these informational networks, learning complex topics can be accomplished and stored in long term memory. The process involved is helpful in recalling the components and the way those are combined. The Scholar's WorkStation approach concentrates on identifying and organizing the ideas together with arranging these ideas to form descriptions of existing topics and construction of new knowledge generating strategies.

What is Idea Analysis[tm]? Idea Analysis[tm] is a form of text mining that takes advantage of the accuracy and speed associated with computerized pattern recognition. In addition, the domain considered, in identifying the terms and relationships, is the author's sentence. The major strength and difference is the focus on the authors' ideas. These ideas are defined as *pairs of informative terms presented, by the author, in the sentence.*

The software performs the following operations:

1. Identifies and separates each of the author's sentences.
2. Identifies and extracts each of the informative terms within each sentence. An informative term is a noun, adjective or gerund.
3. Prepares all pairs of these informative terms.
4. Links each of these ideas with the identification data depicting the document.
5. Organizes these ideas as a data file for subsequent processing.

This system prepares the input for the Scholar's WorkStation.

Step 1. Identifying possible metabolic terms.

The task of identifying possible metabolic terms could be accomplished by considering the suffixes that might represent alcohols, salts, acids, and minerals. Those endings would include – ase, –ate, -ble, -ean, -ein, -ic, -id, -ide, -in, -ine, -ite, -oe, -ol, -one, -ose, -oy, -um, -xyl, and –yde. Using the search capability in excel, the vocabulary could be scanned to identify those with these endings. The accuracy of this initial list can be determined using information provided by the authors who used the terms in sentences.

Table 1 shows an excerpt from the excel file of possible metabolic terms linked with prostate in 2009. These ideas – prostate & metabolite – are ranked in order of frequency of occurrence. Protein was linked with prostate 264 times in 2009. Vitamin and prostate occurred 56 times while kinase was linked 50 times. These terms are general ones applying to any number of different situations. The first term that might have metabolic significance is – **kinase**.

34

Table 1. Higher Frequency Ideas Involving Prostate and 'Metabolic' Terms – 2009.

Terms	2005	2006	2007	2008	2009
protein	249	260	175	259	264
vitamin	111	93	71	75	56
kinase	101	122		112	50
peptide	86	84		64	37
insulin	46	44	35	41	28
selenium	45	48	22	50	29
phosphatase	32	48	29	28	
estramustine	28	3	14	12	2
protease	27	13	16	27	12
soy	25	11	25	22	10
lycopene	24		28	23	4
flavone	23	22	34	36	17
keratin	23	21		15	5
serine	23	13	13	24	10
proteinase	23	9	13	22	7
choline	23	4	17	34	20
cyclin	23	1	31	14	10
acetate	22	27	23	34	13
calcium	22	12	26	20	10
isoflavone	22		34	32	16
	etc.		etc.		etc.

This organization shows the degree of emphasis placed by authors on each idea. That focus suggests that the authors can provide guidance in understanding the meaning of each term as well as how the authors used the term to describe the conditions related to prostate.

The exploration process is as follows:

1. Using the idea records in excel, search for the term kinase and change it by coloring it red.
2. Sort the records using the Ident, Sentence, and Related columns.
3. Search for the term kinase and color the other records with the same Ident and sentence numbers.
4. Use the Sort/Filter option and sort the records on the basis of color. The kinase related records in red will be at the top and the other records will follow.
5. Extract the kinase related records and store in a new excel file.
6. Sort the records using the Related Column and then the Subtotal function in the Data Edit section.
7. Select the 'metabolic' terms linked with kinase and analyze those ideas using steps 1 – 5.
8. Continue this selection-analysis process until new terms are not evident.

Table 2. Terms Forming Ideas with the Term – kinase -- in 2009.

Kinase with:	Freq
inhibit	54
protein	52
prostate	48
inhibitor	42
cancer	38
expression	38
cell	35
dependent	31
phosphorylation	**27**
receptor	26
growth	23
activity	20
tyrosine	**20**
cellular	19
apoptosis	18
regulation	17
tumor	17
activator	16
mitogen	16
inositol	**13**
phosphatidylinositol	**13**
adhesion	11
androgen	11
inhibition	11
transcription	11
binding	10

Table 2 shows the higher frequency terms linking with the key term -- **kinase**. The possible metabolic terms linked with this central term were: phosphorylation, tyrosine, inositol, and phosphotidylinositol. Outcome factors associated with – **kinase** – included inhibitor, receptor, growth, apoptosis, regulation, adhesion, transcription, and binding.

Table 3 shows the terms linked with phosphorylation, inositol (and phosphatidylinositol), and tyrosine. The terms coded in orange were previously identified. There were no additional 'metabolic' terms identified.

Table 3. Terms Forming Ideas with the Terms –Phosphorylation, Inositol, and/or Tyrosine -- in 2009.

Phosphorylation	Freq	Inositol	Freq	Tyrosine	Freq
inhibit	27	kinase	26	kinase	20
kinase	27	protein	10	receptor	17
expression	25	prostate	8	prostate	11
prostate	19	apoptosis	6	inhibit	10
apoptosis	16	cell	6	cancer	8
cell	15	family	6	growth	7
cancer	13	inhibit	6	inhibitor	7
protein	13	inhibitor	6	cell	6
dependent	12	cancer	4	phosphorylation	4
treatment	11	genesis	4	adhesion	3
human	10	growth	4	expression	3
cellular	9	phosphorylation	4	molecule	3
receptor	9	regulation	4	proliferation	3
ability	6	tumor	4	tumor	3

The presumed metabolic relationship associated with the idea – **prostate & kinase** -- involves an organization of -- prostate → kinase → phosphorylation → tyrosine → inositol (phosphatidylinositol). This organization would involve results including: inhibition, apoptosis, regulation, or proliferation associated with the metabolic factors interacting with cell receptors.

Step 2. Sort the Ideas Related to Prostate.

Table 1 showed an excerpt of the terms linked with prostate for each year. Protein was linked with prostate 249 times in 2005 and 264 times in 2009. Estramustine shows a decrease in prostate related ideas from a high of 28 in 2005 and 2 in 2009.

Step 3. Select Higher Frequency Terms Related to Prostate Across Time.

Table 4 shows the higher frequency terms linked with prostate each year. The terms occurring in 4 of the years are coded in red. Those occurring in 3 of the 4 years are coded in purple. Those occurring in 2 of the 4 years are coded in green. Those occurring in single years are in black. Acetate, insulin, phosphatase, protein, selenium, and vitamin were linked with prostate across the 4 years.

Table 4. Higher Frequency Terms Linked with Prostate.

prostate 2005	prostate 2006	prostate 2007	prostate 2008
acetate	acetate	acetate	acetate
calcium	calcitriol	cadherin	cadherin
choline	caspase	calcium	calcium
cyclin	cholinergic	cyclin	caspase
estramustine	clodronate	dutasteride	catenin
flavone	dutasteride	flavone	cholesterol
insulin	endonuclease	insulin	choline
keratin	flavone	isoflavone	dutasteride
kinase	insulin	luciferase	flavone
lycopene	integrin	lycopene	insulin
metalloproteinase	interleukin	phosphatase	interleukin
peptide	keratin	protein	isoflavone
phosphatase	kinase	selenium	kinase
protease	lipid	soy	lipid
protein	peptide	vitamin	lycopene
proteinase	phosphatase		metalloproteinase
selenium	phosphate		peptide
serine	protein		phosphatase
soy	selenium		protease
sterol	telomerase		protein
vitamin	vitamin		proteinase
			selenium
			serine
			soy
			sterol
			vegetable
			vitamin

Step 4. Comparison of High Frequency Ideas in 2009.

The higher frequency ideas involving prostate with metabolic terms in 2009 were added to the previous list. In addition, the terms occurring only once in the 5 year period were eliminated. Table 5 shows the higher frequency terms linked with prostate for each of the years. The higher frequency terms for 2009 (Jan-Oct) are included for comparison. Of the eight higher frequency terms in 2009, 4 were observed in the previous 4 years as higher frequency terms. Two of the terms occurred in three prior years and one in two previous years. Integrin occurred in 2006 and then again in 2009.

Table 5 Reducing the List of Higher Frequency Terms and Comparing with those in 2009.

prostate 2005	prostate 2006	prostate 2007	prostate 2008	prostate 2009
acetate	acetate	acetate	acetate	**choline**
calcium	dutasteride	cadherin	cadherin	**insulin**
choline	flavone	calcium	calcium	**integrin**
cyclin	insulin	cyclin	choline	**kinase**
flavone	integrin	dutasteride	dutasteride	**peptide**
insulin	interleukin	flavone	flavone	**protein**
keratin	keratin	insulin	insulin	**selenium**
kinase	kinase	lycopene	interleukin	**vitamin**
lycopene	lipid	phosphatase	kinase	
metalloproteinase	peptide	protein	lipid	
peptide	phosphatase	selenium	lycopene	
phosphatase	protein	soy	metalloproteinase	
protease	selenium	vitamin	peptide	
protein	vitamin		phosphatase	
proteinase			protease	
selenium			protein	
serine			proteinase	
soy			selenium	
sterol			serine	
vitamin			soy	
			sterol	
			vitamin	

Step 5. Prostate-Choline Related Triads.

The higher frequency ideas related to prostate in 2009 can be used to develop an initial description of metabolic relationships in prostate disease. The first term in the reduced list of potentially important terms was choline. Table 6 shows an excerpt of the triadic terms linked with the central idea – prostate & choline. The ideas suggest that choline is used in imaging methods to detect cancer. As seen, the triads of interest were prostate-choline with, respectively, tomography, positron, imaging, detection, and fluorocholine. The diseases were cancer and benign tissue. Prostatectomy was a frequently linked treatment.

39

Table 6. Prostate-Choline Triadic Ideas.

Prostate-Choline-Triads	Freq 2005-9
cancer	36
tomography	19
emission	18
positron	18
imaging	17
radical	16
carcinoma	15
prostatectomy	14
detection	12
treatment	10
fluorocholine	9
tissue	9
benign	8
adenocarcinoma	7
citrate	7

etc.

The perspective obtained by using the authors' ideas is sufficient to provide a preliminary understanding of the role of choline in prostate disease. This perspective is different from the one offered by the medical dictionary – *"a base $C_5H_{15}NO_2$ that occurs as a component of phospholipids especially in animals, is a precursor of acetylcholine, and is essential to liver function"*. The English dictionary definition is – *"A natural amine, $C_5H_{15}NO_2$, often classed in the vitamin B complex and a constituent of many other biologically important molecules, such as acetylcholine and lecithin."*

Step 6. Prostate-Insulin Related Ideas.

Another relevant idea would be prostate and insulin implying the conditions associated with cancer as well as diabetes. The interaction between hormonal treatments for the cancer and insulin for the diabetes is suggested by these ideas. These ideas suggest that the authors were concerned about the management of the combination of cancer and diabetes.

Table 7 shows the terms linked with this central idea. Growth was observed in 93 ideas, cancer in 79, and diabetes in 9. Included in the list linked with insulin are the hormonal terms – androgen, hormone, gonadotropin, estrogen, and testosterone. If these ideas suggest the complexities of managing the combination of cancer and diabetes, there should be ideas that show the conditions involved. The first column has terms such as risk, binding, resistance, expression, receptor, dependent, and progression. The second column has sensitivity, aggressive, agonist, and inhibitor. The third column has inhibit and relationship. The triads can

40

be classified into three basic dimensions – disease conditions, treatment factors, and outcomes of the interaction between the two other dimensions.

Table 7. Prostate-Insulin Triads Ranked by Frequency of Occurrence.

Prostate-Insulin Triads	No. Idea	Prostate-Insulin Triads	No. Idea	Prostate-Insulin Triads	No. Idea
growth	93	sensitivity	8	bone	4
cancer	79	apoptosis	7	cardiovascular	4
risk	39	control	7	cohort	4
binding	30	glucose	7	epithelial	4
resistance	20	prospective	7	estrogen	4
breast	19	psa	7	genesis	4
androgen	18	stage	7	glyceride	4
expression	18	cholesterol	6	inhibit	4
receptor	18	colon	6	interleukin	4
tumor	17	death	6	leptin	4
antigen	14	epidemiologic	6	lipid	4
development	14	lung	6	mass	4
progression	14	polymorphism	6	metastasis	4
marker	13	aggressive	5	mitogen	4
protein	12	agonist	5	prevent	4
cell	11	carcinoma	5	promoter	4
hormone	11	deprivation	5	protective	4
dependent	10	dietary	5	relationship	4
obesity	10	gonadotropin	5	supplement	4
rectal	10	inhibitor	5	testosterone	4
data	9	tissue	5	triglyceride	4
diabetes	9	vascular	5	vitamin	4
colorectal	8	weight	5	etc.	
proliferation	8				

Step 7 – Prostate-Integrin Triad Ideas Ranked by Frequency of Occurrence.

Table 8 shows the terms linked with the prostate-integrin idea. The entries in the table can be classified in four primary groups or dimensions. The results are listed as outcome factors. The tissues studied are identified. The sites studied and the chemical factors are shown. These entries suggest that integrin has a number of functions involved in the regulatory processes.

Table 8. Prostate-Integrin Triadic Ideas Organized by Frequency of Occurrence.

Prostate-Integrin Triads	No Ideas	Prostate-Integrin Triads	No Ideas	Prostate-Integrin Triads	No Ideas
cancer	46	breast	4	antibodies	2
expression	38	endothelial	4	behavior	2
cell	31	invasive	4	benign	2
adhesion	16	malignant	4	biologic	2
growth	12	MRNA	4	brca	2
receptor	12	organization	4	clonal	2
carcinoma	11	proliferation	4	colon	2
dependent	11	sarcoma	4	colorectal	2
tumor	11	skeleton	4	cox-2	2
androgen	10	transfection	4	cyclooxygenase	2
metastasis	9	angiogenesis	3	cysteine	2
protein	9	collagen	3	density	2
tissue	9	data	3	endothelium	2
binding	8	death	3	hepatocellular	2
invasion	8	epithelial	3	histidine	2
activity	7	family	3	immunohistochemistry	2
bone	6	gland	3	kidney	2
gene	6	glycoprotein	3	leuprolide	2
inhibit	6	ligand	3	luminal	2
migration	6	lung	3	magnetic	2
stroma	6	marker	3	measure	2
transcription	6	modulation	3	monoclonal	2
kinase	5	molecular	3	morphology	2
progression	5	prevent	3	muscular	2
regulation	5	reduction	3	mutation	2
		survival	3	neoplastic	2
		therapy	3	oxygen	2
		vascular	3	phosphorylation	2
				secretory	2
				suppressor	2
				tyrosine	2

Summary

This example illustrates the use of the Scholar's WorkStation in Prostate Cancer (2009) in developing an initial understanding of the ideas and relationships involved. The Scholar's WorkStation is based on the assumption that the subject specialists have special insights, experiences, and knowledge that can be identified, extracted, and organized. These data can be used to guide a student interested in learning a new subject.

The premise is that the individual has no prior knowledge of the disease and its management. The Appendix shows the flow of information from the ideas in the Scholar WorkStation to the original abstracts. The sentences containing the triadic idea of interest are highlighted and then extracted together with the title of the document. These data are used to build new sentences containing the original authors' text together with minor editing changes. The final step involves the development of new text reflecting the individual's intent.

The final sentences for the triadic idea – prostate & cancer & choline – are shown below to illustrate the end result of this text building process. The sentences were constructed in conformance with usual literature review format, i.e., statement followed by references cited.

> *[(11)Cl]choline PET/CT is an established imaging approach in detecting changes in staging of prostate cancer following treatment.[Rinnab 2009, Picchio 2009, Muller 2009, Pascali 2009]   The choline related imaging also was effective in detecting risk of prostate cancer.[Johansson 2009]*

Appendix – Building New Text

The abstracts containing the prostate & cancer & choline triadic ideas in the PubMed repository for 2009 are indicated by the highlighted identification numbers. The Ident can be used to retrieve the original documents from PubMed.

Table 1 – Prostate Cancer Choline Triadic Ideas – 2009.

Primary	Related	Triads	Year	Ident	Sentence
prostate	cancer	choline	2009	**19234708**	1
prostate	cancer	choline	2009	**19234708**	13
prostate	cancer	choline	2009	**19293771**	9
prostate	cancer	choline	2009	**19352653**	2
prostate	cancer	choline	2009	**19352653**	3
prostate	cancer	choline	2009	**19423531**	7
prostate	cancer	choline	2009	**19520298**	3

The abstracts for the identified numbers are shown below. The three terms – prostate, cancer, and choline – were highlighted and the sentences containing the triad were bolded.

World J Urol. 2009 Oct;27(5):619-25. Epub 2009 Feb 21.

[(11)C]*choline* PET/CT in *prostate cancer* patients with biochemical recurrence after radical *prostate*ctomy.

Rinnab L, Simon J, Hautmann RE, Cronauer MV, Hohl K, Buck AK, Reske SN, Mottaghy FM.

Department of Urology, University of Ulm, Ulm, Germany. ludwig.rinnab@uniklinik-ulm.de

Abstract

OBJECTIVE: To evaluate [(11)C]*choline* positron emission tomography/computed tomography ([(11)C]*choline* PET/CT) for the detection of a biochemical recurrence of *prostate cancer* after radical *prostate*ctomy.

METHODS: Retrospective analysis of [(11)C]*choline* PET/CT performed in 41 consecutive *prostate cancer* patients with a rising PSA. The mean time to biochemical relapse was 24 months. PSA levels were determined at time of examination, and patients received either a targeted biopsy or surgery. Histopathology reports served as reference for the evaluation of the [(11)C]*choline* PET/CT findings.

RESULTS: Mean PSA in [(11)C]*choline* PET/CT positive patients was 3.1 ng/ml (median 2.2 ng/ml, range 0.5-11.6 ng/ml) and 0.86 ng/ml in [(11)C]*choline* PET/CT negative patients (median 0.83 ng/ml, range 0.41-1.40 ng/ml). Six of 12 patients with PSA < 1.5 ng/ml [(11)C]*choline* PET/CT revealed a pathological uptake. Histopathology was positive in 6/12 patients in this group. At PSA levels ranging from 1.5 to 2.5 ng/ml all [(11)C]*choline* PET/CT were positive (n = 16), a positive histology was found in 12/16 patients (75%) and at PSA 2.5-5 ng/ml [(11)C]*choline* PET/CT was positive in 8/8 patients, confirmed by histology in 7/8 patients. Finally, at PSA higher than 5 ng/ml [(11)C]*choline* PET/CT identified 5/5 patients positive all confirmed by histology. The sensitivity of [(11)C]*choline* PET/CT for the detection of recurrence at PSA < 2.5 ng/ml was 89% with a positive predictive value of 72%.

CONCLUSION: [(11)C]*choline* PET/CT is useful for re-staging of *prostate cancer* in patients with rising PSA even at levels below 1.5 ng/ml. Our study confirms results from other published studies on [(11)C]*choline* PET/CT in *prostate cancer* relapse.

PMID: 19234708 [PubMed - indexed for MEDLINE]

Q J Nucl Med Mol Imaging. 2009 Apr;53(2):245-68.

PET-CT for treatment planning in *prostate cancer*.

Picchio M, Crivellaro C, Giovacchini G, Gianolli L, Messa C.

Nuclear Medicine, Scientific Institute H San Raffaele, Milan, Italy. picchio.maria@hsr.it

Abstract

Molecular imaging techniques, such as positron emission tomography (PET), may be of help in management treatment planning. In particular, in *prostate cancer* patients, PET and PET-computed tomography (PET-CT) can be successfully used in treatment planning at different steps, including: 1) tumor characterization and staging, to define the most appropriate primary treatment; 2) re-staging, to define a second line therapy on the site of possible recurrences; and 3) monitoring the disease and the efficacy of treatment. Although the most commonly used PET tracer, [(18)F]Fluorodeoxyglucose ([(18)F]FDG), presents limitations in imaging *prostate cancer* patients, several alternative PET tracers have been proposed to evaluate by PET these patients, with promising RESULTS: Optimal treatment for *prostate cancer* depends on the accuracy in tumor characterization and staging. In fact, localized primary tumor can be treated with radical *prostate*ctomy, while metastatic tumor is usually treated with systemic therapeutic regimen. Different PET tracers, including [(11)C]*Choline*, [(18)F]*Choline* and [(11)C]Acetate, have been successfully reported. However, further studies in large population of patients are still necessary to establish their final clinical role in the primary detection and staging of *prostate cancer*. The information on the site of possible recurrences is also important for therapeutic strategies. Several PET tracers have been proposed to re-stage *prostate cancer* patients. **In particular, [11C]*Choline* PET has now been established as a clinical procedure to non-invasively re-stage, in a single session, *prostate cancer* patients presenting an increase of *prostate* specific antigen (PSA) after radical treatment.** The role of PET and PET-CT in monitoring the disease and the effects of treatment are under investigation and still to be defined.

In the present review, we focused on the use of several PET tracers in different clinical indications aimed at the treatment planning of *prostate cancer* patients.

PMID: 19293771

Eur J Nucl Med Mol Imaging. 2009 Sep;36(9):1434-42. Epub 2009 Apr 8.

Characterization of *choline* uptake in *prostate cancer* cells following bicalutamide and docetaxel treatment.

Müller SA, Holzapfel K, Seidl C, Treiber U, Krause BJ, Senekowitsch-Schmidtke R.

Department of Nuclear Medicine, Technische Universität München, Ismaninger Strasse 22, Munich, 81675, Germany.

Abstract

PURPOSE: *Choline* derivatives labelled with positron emitters are successfully used for PET imaging of *prostate cancer* patients. Since little is known about uptake mechanisms, the aim of this study was to characterize *choline* uptake in *prostate cancer* cells, also following anti-androgen treatment or chemotherapy.

METHODS: *Choline* uptake in *prostate cancer* cells (LNCaP, PC-3) and Michaelis-Menten kinetics were analysed using different concentrations of (3)H-*choline* via liquid scintillation counting. Inhibition of (3)H-*choline* uptake was assayed in the presence of hemicholinium-3 (HC-3), unlabelled *choline*, guanidine and tetraethylammonium (TEA), an inhibitor of the organic cation transporter (OCT). Changes in *choline* uptake triggered by bicalutamide and docetaxel were evaluated and *choline* transporters were detected via Western blotting.

RESULTS: Michaelis-Menten kinetics yielded a saturable transport with K(m) values of 6.9 and 7.0 micromol/l *choline* for LNCaP and PC-3 cells, respectively. Treatment of cells with bicalutamide and docetaxel caused an increase in total *choline* uptake but had no significant effect on K(m) values. Uptake of (3)H-*choline* was NaCl dependent and 4.5-fold higher in LNCaP cells than in PC-3 cells. (3)H-*Choline* uptake was reduced by 92-96% using HC-3 and unlabelled *choline*, by 63-69% using guanidine and by 20% using TEA. The high-affinity *choline* transporter was detected via Western blotting.

CONCLUSION: *Choline* uptake in *prostate cancer* cells is accomplished both by a transporter-mediated and a diffusion-like component. Results of inhibition experiments suggest that uptake is mediated by a selective *choline* transporter rather than by the OCT. Bicalutamide- and docetaxel-induced changes in total *choline* uptake could affect PET tumour imaging.

PMID: 19352653

Cancer Epidemiol Biomarkers Prev. 2009 May;18(5):1538-43.

One-carbon metabolism and *prostate cancer* risk: prospective investigation of seven circulating B vitamins and metabolites.

Johansson M, Van Guelpen B, Vollset SE, Hultdin J, Bergh A, Key T, Midttun O, Hallmans G, Ueland PM, Stattin P.

Unit of Genetic Epidemiology, IARC, Lyon 69372 Cedex 08, France. JohanssonM@fellows.iarc.fr

Abstract

PURPOSE: Components of one-carbon metabolism are believed to influence *cancer* development with suggested mechanisms, including DNA methylation and DNA repair mechanisms. However, few prospective studies have investigated one-carbon metabolism in relation to *prostate cancer* risk, and the results have been conflicting. The aim of this study was to do a comprehensive investigation of the components of one-carbon metabolism in relation to *prostate cancer* risk. A panel of seven circulating B vitamins and related metabolites was selected, most of which have not been studied before.

MATERIALS AND METHODS: We analyzed plasma concentrations of betaine, *choline*, cysteine, methionine, methylmalonic acid (MMA), vitamin B2, and vitamin B6 in 561 cases and 1,034 controls matched for age and recruitment date, nested within the population-based Northern Sweden Health and Disease Cohort. Relative risks of *prostate cancer* were estimated by conditional logistic regression.

RESULTS: Positive associations with *prostate cancer* risk were observed for *choline* and vitamin B2, and an inverse association was observed for MMA. The relative risks for a doubling in concentrations were 1.46 [95% confidence interval (95% CI), 1.04-2.05; P(trend) = 0.03] for *choline*, 1.11 (95% CI, 1.00-1.23; P(trend) = 0.04) for vitamin B2, and 0.78 (95% CI, 0.63-0.97; P(trend) = 0.03) for MMA. Concentrations of betaine, cysteine, methionine, and vitamin B6 were not associated with *prostate cancer* risk.

CONCLUSION: The results of this large prospective study suggest that elevated plasma concentrations of *choline* and vitamin B2 may be associated with an increased risk of *prostate cancer*. These novel findings support a role of one-carbon metabolism in *prostate cancer* etiology and warrant further investigation.

PMID: 19423531

Nucl Med Biol. 2009 Jul;36(5):569-74. Epub 2009 Mar 26.

Optimization of automated large-scale production of [(18)F]fluoroethyl*choline* for PET *prostate cancer* imaging.

Pascali G, D'Antonio L, Bovone P, Gerundini P, August T.

University of Pisa, Italy. giancarlo.pascali@bioclinica.unipi.it

Abstract

INTRODUCTION: PET tumor imaging is gaining importance in current clinical practice. FDG-PET is the most utilized approach but suffers from inflammation influences and is not utilizable in *prostate cancer* detection. Recently, (11)C-*choline* analogues have been employed successfully in this field of imaging, leading to a growing interest in the utilization of (18)F-labeled analogues: **[(18)F]fluoroethyl*choline* (FEC) has been demonstrated to be promising, especially in *prostate cancer* imaging.** In this work we report an automatic radiosynthesis of this tracer with high yields, short synthesis time and ease of performance, potentially utilizable in routine production sites.

METHODS: We used a Modular Lab system to automatically perform the two-step/one-pot synthesis. In the first step, we labeled ethyleneglycolditosylate obtaining [(18)F]fluoroethyltosylate; in the second step, we performed the coupling of the latter intermediate with neat dimethylethanolamine. The final mixture was purified by means of solid phase extraction; in particular, the product was trapped into a cation-exchange resin and eluted with isotonic saline.

RESULTS: The optimized procedure resulted in a non decay corrected yield of 36% and produced a range of 30-45 GBq of product already in injectable form. The product was analyzed for quality control and resulted as pure and sterile; in addition, residual solvents were under the required threshold.

CONCLUSION: In this work, we present an automatic FEC radiosynthesis that has been optimized for routine production. This findings should foster the interest for a wider utilization of this radiomolecule for imaging of *prostate cancer* with PET, a field for which no gold-standard tracer has yet been validated.

PMID: 19520298

The sentences containing the triad were extracted along with the authors' titles. These text were used in forming new sentences using the format – Author → title of document → extracted sentences. The minor editing used in building these sentences is indicated in red. Essentially, the editing was designed to provide transitions from the titles to the authors' sentences.

49

Rinnab et al studied (11)C]choline PET/CT in prostate cancer patients with biochemical recurrence after radical prostatectomy. These authors evaluated (11)C]choline positron emission tomography/computed tomography in the detection of recurrent prostate cancer after prostatectomy.

Picchio M, reported PET-CT for treatment planning in prostate cancer. They stated that (11)C]choline PET/CT was useful in staging of prostate cancer. They suggested that the procedure was effective in patients with rising PSA in the normal range.

Muller et al reported study of the characterization of choline uptake in prostate cancer cells following bicalutamide and docetaxel treatment. They suggested that choline PET was established in staging prostate cancer patients presenting with an increase in PSA following treatment. Choline uptake in prostate cancer cells was studied.

Johansson et al studied one-carbon metabolism and prostate cancer risk: prospective investigation of seven circulating B vitamins and metabolites. They suggested that prostate cancer risk was linked with levels of choline and vitamin.

Pascali et al reported the results of optimization of automated large-scale production of [(18)F[fluoroethylcholine for PET prostate cancer imaging. They stated that choline was useful in prostate cancer imaging.

The final step involves preparation of new sentences containing the information provided by the authors. This last step can vary with each individual depending on the emphasis and intent of the new description.

[(11)Cl]choline PET/CT is an established imaging approach in detecting changes in staging of prostate cancer following treatment.[Rinnab 2009, Picchio 2009, Muller 2009, Pascali 2009] The choline related imaging also was effective in detecting risk of prostate cancer.[Johansson 2009]

Chapter Five – Learning Procedures and Relationships in Physiology

Introduction

This chapter explored the use of procedures and related issues in physiology during the 50 year period – 1960 to 2009. There were 2,533 articles entered in PubMed during 2009 from the journals published by the American Physiological Society. This analysis was intended to characterize the realistic and current use of concepts and procedures dealing with physiological issues. By restricting attention to articles from the Society's journals, the accuracy of retrieval could be assured. That is, each of the articles published was reviewed by peer-reviewers and was considered to be an appropriate contribution to the physiologic literature. That degree of judging ensured that the articles retrieved from the bibliographic database, using the journal as part of the search statement, were appropriate representatives of the field.

The software matches a median of 80% of the terms employed by the specialists and over 90% of the terms specific to the topic. As such, this vocabulary, when combined as ideas and concepts, can be used to enhance the dictionary definition of the term – physiology – by providing the procedures, conditions, and results of the scientific inquiries performed.

Table 1. Terms in the 2009 Physiologic Literature and the Number of Ideas Associated with Each.

Primary	Freq	Primary	Freq
induce	5234	promote	939
protein	4371	gene	896
inhibit	4341	genesis	861
receptor	3092	glucose	853
mice	2757	model	844
activation	2446	chronic	825
activate	1626	oxygen	776
regulation	1614	proliferation	775
regulate	1506	animal	759
kinase	1479	formation	710
endothelial	1437	agonist	691
phosphorylation	1432	peptide	686
cardiac	1374	report	676
stimulate	1291	peroxide	673
mitochondria	1221	binding	672
ester	1139	stimulation	661
measure	1034	secretion	658
epithelial	1022	analysis	635

Table 1 shows the informative terms identified in this literature, together with the number of times each was used in an idea. Overall, there were 815 terms identified and 107,102 ideas involving pairs of these words. **Induce** was included in 5,234 ideas, **protein** in 4,371, and

inhibit in 4,341. These terms illustrate the vocabulary employed by investigators in their scientific reports.

The frequencies of use of informative terms and ideas can be used to explore the question of theme or term use over time. That is, *have investigators changed their use of particular procedures as the field progressed from 1960 to 2009?*

Figure 1. Percent of Articles Containing Selected Terms in Articles Published by the American Physiological Society in Specific Years.

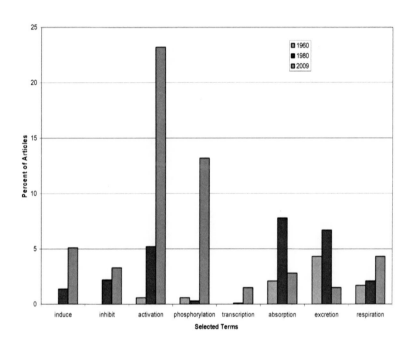

Figure 1 shows selected terms and the percent of articles containing the procedures for the years 1960, 1980, and 2009. The terms represent those **frequently involved** in ideas during 2009 including: **induce, inhibit, activation, phosphorylation, transcription,** and **absorption.** Two others -- **excretion** and **respiration** -- represented **relatively infrequent use** in 2009. The higher frequency terms showed increase from 1960 to 2009. Activation (about 20%) and phosphorylation (about 15%) showed the largest increases in use from 1960 to 2009. Absorption showed a different pattern with the most frequent use in 1980 and relatively the same use in 1960 and 2009. This pattern might represent the expected increase early on with a resulting decline as the emphases and applications changed. Excretion also showed the larger use in 1980 with considerable decline in 2009. Respiration showed the increase over time similar to the higher frequency terms. This analysis of frequency of articles offers insight into what might be considered a thematic approach to the dissemination of information. As such, specific themes appeared to have changed during the time period considered.

Table 2 shows the high frequency terms and two of the low frequency terms from Figure 1. The ideas involving each term are given. There are three principal observations illustrated:

1.   **Each term has a specific set of related terms and the conglomerate agrees with the definition of a concept.** The concept expands the definition of the central term. For example, the definition of **activation** is the act of exciting or making the entity more reactive. The ideas involving activation had terms as follows:

a.	endothelial [tissue]
b.	induce
c.	inhibit
d.	kinase
e.	mice
f.	phosphorylation
g.	proliferation
h.	promote
i.	protein [tissue]
j.	receptor
k.	regulation
l.	secretion
m.	stimulate

Of these ideas, activation with, respectively, induce, inhibit, promote, regulation, and stimulate, depict the act of exciting or making the target more reactive. The idea – activation with kinase – describes the use of an enzyme employed to accomplish the desired result. The ideas – activation with, respectively, phosphorylation, proliferation, and secretion – represent the resulting change. These three components – **meaning, procedure, result** – make up the concept represented by the term – activation.

2.   **Comparison of concepts.** The ideas involving activation, induce, inhibit, and phosphorylation show similarities and differences. The terms showing agreement across these four high frequency central terms are highlighted in red. Those terms were: activate, endothelial, induce, inhibit, kinase, mice, phosphorylation, proliferation, protein, receptor, regulation. In 2009, these **terms** and their **relationships** formed gateways to understanding the subject.

3. **Different Structures for High and Low Frequency Ideas.** Table 2 also showed the terms forming ideas with absorption and excretion. These central terms were relatively low frequency in 2009 and showed different patterns of use across time when the measurement was -- number of articles.

Table 2. Comparison of Ideas Associated with High and Low Frequency Terms In Ideas – 2009.

A.   Terms – A through E

Terms	Activation	Induce	Inhibit	Phosphorylation	Absorption	Excretion
activate	**xxxxxxx**	**57**	**68**	**32**		
adaptation					3	
agonist		55				3
apoptosis		66				
binding				13		
butyrate					3	
carbachol						2
cardiac	31	90		15		
catabolic					3	
cholesterol					4	
choline						2
chronic		52				
collagen						2
constriction		48				
contraction				13		
creatinine						4
cystic					4	
digestion					3	
endothelial	**43**	**113**	**51**	**19**		
epithelial	26	48			6	
ester			54		5	

The ideas involving these two central terms showed minimal agreement with the structures associated with the higher frequency terms. The terms linked with absorption, from the central set, were induce, inhibit, protein, and regulation. Protein was the only term linked with excretion from that same set.

B. Terms – F through O

Terms	Activation	Induce	Inhibit	Phosphorylation	Absorption	Excretion
fibrosis					4	
filament				17		
filtration						3
gene	24					
gestation						2
glucose					4	
induce	197	xxxxxxx	382	119	5	
infusion					3	
inhibit	151	382	xxxxxxx	111	6	
injection						2
kinase	72	71	125	69		
kinetic					3	
marker						2
measure					5	
metabolism					7	
mice	29	171	68	16		11
mitochondria		71				
model		50				
nitrogen						2
nuclear				14		
nutrient					5	
oxidative				12		2

C. Terms – P through T

Terms	Activation	Induce	Inhibit	Phosphorylation	Absorption	Excretion
perfusion						5
phosphate					4	
phosphatase				15		
phosphorylation	75	119	111	xxxxxxxx		
potassium						2
proliferation	23	48	63	22		
promote	27		48	14		
protein	105	212	180	78	9	4
receptor	107	131	140	38		4
regulation	41	84	52	22	8	
secretion	21				10	
sodium					5	18
stimulate	29		84	50		
synthase		47				
transport			46		12	
tyrosine				30		

Table 2 shows the similarities and differences in information potential between articles (i.e., themes) and ideas (i.e., concept structures). The theme information is more general and would require additional analysis of the documents once the theme is selected and the corresponding articles retrieved. In addition, an article could contain a number of themes. A user could select any one of these to be the more important and that selection may or may not agree with the authors'. In contrast, the idea approach provides concepts. Each of these offers specific information found in the document as well as the organization of these ideas across documents.

The relationships between the original article, the idea repository, and the organization of the ideas to describe a specific author's statement are shown in Figure 3. The sentence and the informative terms are shown together with the idea records from the repository for this sentence/document (19091957). The graphic relationship of these ideas also is given. The connecting lines indicate that each term was linked with the others to form the full set of ideas presented by the author in this sentence. These data also suggest the simplicity of retrieving a specific document from PubMed by using the identification number provided by the idea record. Article 19091957 was retrieved and the sentence extracted. The value of this retrieval approach is the preciseness and the accuracy of the retrieval, since the content of the document is known by considering the ideas.

Figure 2. Terms Linked with the Activation Concept – Physiology 2009.

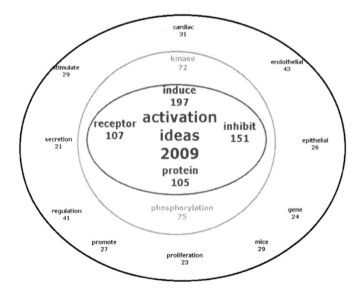

Graphic Descriptions of Selected Concepts: Table 2 showed that the central terms considered were linked with many of others. The concepts shown in Figures 2 – 5 underscore this interconnectedness.

Figure 2 shows the ideas making up the activation concept. The first tier shows the two action terms – induce and inhibit. The tissues involved were protein and receptor. The second tier depicts important ideas in accomplishing the activation process. The third tier includes additional effect descriptors – proliferation, promote, regulation, secretion, and stimulate.

Figure 3. Terms Linked with Induce - Concept in Physiology 2009.

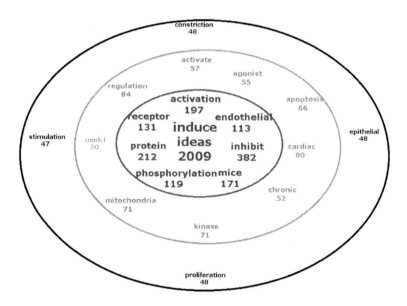

Figure 3 shows the ideas making up the induce concept. The first tier includes three effects – activation, inhibit, and phosphorylation. Three ideas represent the tissues studied – endothelial, protein, and receptor. The final idea described the study subject. The second tier includes effects, tissues, and the enzyme – kinase. The third tier included epithelial tissue and three effect descriptors – proliferation, stimulation, and constriction.

Figure 4 shows the ideas in the inhibit concept. Comparing the first tier in this concept with the one in the induce concept shows the comparability between these two opposite actions. The inhibit ideas involving kinase and stimulate were the only ones that didn't match with the first tier in induce. In that concept, the non-matching ideas were induce with endothelial and mice. In the inhibit concept, both endothelial and mice were second tier ideas.

Figure 4. Terms Linked with Inhibit Concept – Physiology 2009.

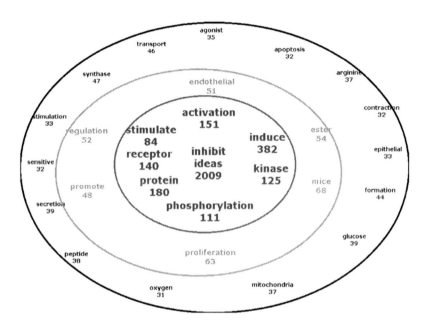

Figure 5 describes the ideas in the phosphorylation concept. The majority of the ideas were the same as in previous concepts. Tyrosine and phosphorylation is the only one of the higher frequency ideas unique to this concept. In the third tier set, cardiac, endothelial, promote and stimulation were the terms linked with the central term common to previous concepts.

Figure 5. Terms Linked with Phosphorylation Concept – Physiology 2009.

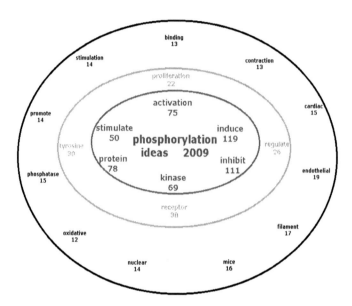

Figure 6 shows the absorption concept. The first tier involved four ideas – absorption with, respectively, protein, regulation, secretion, and transport. The second tier contained the high frequency central terms – induce and inhibit. The map underscores the difference between absorption and the higher frequency central terms. Terms are introduced that were not considered in the other maps.

Figure 6. Terms Linked with Absorption Concept – Physiology 2009.

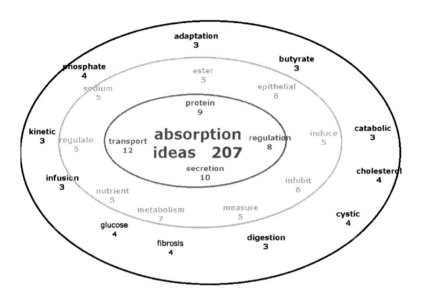

The excretion concept in Figure 7 re-enforces the distinction between high and low frequency concepts. The first tier terms consisted of mice and sodium. The second tier includes protein and receptor. These also were linked with the high frequency central terms. The third tier contained the term – agonist. This was involved in ideas with induce and inhibit.

Figure 7 Terms Linked with Excretion Concept – Physiology 2009.

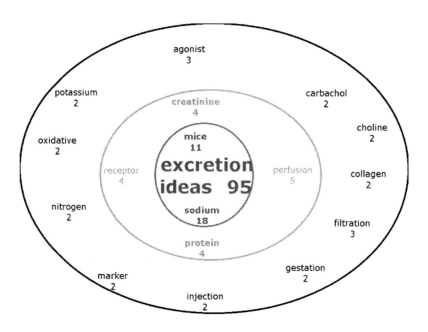

Summary

The abstracts were retrieved from PubMed and analyzed using the text mining software – Idea Analysis[tm]. The advantage of using software is that the necessary tasks can be performed in an efficient and accurate fashion with quality control procedures in place. The software can recognize and segregate sentences in the text. Eight hundred and fifteen terms were identified as the vocabulary used by these authors. The terms were combined by the authors to form ideas and the software identified these. The term – induce – was used in 5,234 ideas. Protein was used in 4,371 ideas and inhibit in 4,341 ideas. Other high frequency terms included activation (and activate) with 4,172 ideas, regulation with 1614 ideas, and phosphorylation with 1,432 ideas.

Any of these terms could have been considered to be themes representing the contents of the articles. Using this measure of usage, the higher frequency terms showed increase for the time period 1960, 1980, 2009. Activation and phosphorylation showed the largest increases. Excretion ideas occurred with a low frequency in 2009 and the number of articles containing the excretion theme showed a decrease in use between 1960 and 2009.

Traditionally, articles have been classified using thematic descriptions. Using important terms as an indicator of a potential theme, each article could contain 20 or more of these. As noted above, the terms also can be characterized by the number of ideas involving each. These ideas form a configuration in agreement with the definition of a concept.

The concept offers more specific insights regarding the meaning of the central term. The dictionary provides a succinct statement of the meaning of the word. The ideas, when combined to form a concept, provide information regarding the definition of the term, procedures involved, and results of the combination.

Comparison of the concepts involving activation, induce, inhibit, and phosphorylation showed that a common set of terms were related to each central term. The term – excretion – showed different patterns using either the number of articles or the number of ideas as the measure. The measure based on the number of articles suggested that usage decreased from 1960 to 2009. The terms forming ideas with excretion were different from those paired with the four higher frequency terms.

This preliminary analysis presented data suggesting that the two measures of investigator behavior agreed. The measure using number of articles, containing a specific theme, showed that usage of terms representing procedures or results changed with time. Activation and phosphorylation increased in usage while excretion decreased. Absorption showed an increase from 1960 to 1980 and then a decrease at 2009.

The measure using number of ideas forming concepts provided more specific information about the three components associated with learning. Those were:

1. **The meaning of the central term**. The dictionary provides a succinct statement. The concept expands that definition by providing additional attributes.
2. **The procedures involved**. The concept provides terms representing the procedures involved in dealing with the central term.
3. **The results of the combination** – meaning and procedures. The concept provides terms representing the results of employing procedures to elicit changes in the terms representing the meaning of the central one.

The concept approach expanded on this general usage by providing information regarding the vocabulary in a subject, and, how the specialists combined those terms to provide meaning, procedures, and results. That combination provides essential ingredients to enhance learning.

Chapter Six – Topic Sentences

Introduction

A typical situation faced by students is the reading and learning of information from a single document. This document, often in the form of a text book, provides the vocabulary, ideas, methods, and interpretations needed by the student in acquiring understanding of the subject. The problem, however, is how to identify, organize, analyze, and interpret the information provided, in a relatively short time and in the most efficient way? This chapter considers a formalized, quality controlled approach to the capture and use of information from this single source document.

Documents are represented by topic sentences and supporting sentences in each paragraph. In turn, the paragraphs, collectively, provide a description of the topic. The intent of an analysis of the single document is to capture sufficient data to develop an accurate version of the information structure considered by the author. To illustrate the process, the text used is given in the Appendix. This text consists of paragraphs each with an identified topic sentence.

The topic sentence is used as a filter in learning a new topic. The topic sentences were identified and the ideas included were extracted and organized. The process of using these ideas to develop an understanding of the topic is shown. An important consideration in using any filter is the information obtained. In addition, the lost information must be considered. The trade-off between savings in time and effort and awareness of a new topic must be balanced with the deficits associated with having a less than complete awareness of the elements making up the topic. Another relevant consideration involves the criteria used in assessing the efficacy and efficiency of a filter. With effective information processing methods in place, the individual is freed of the tedious, mechanical tasks and can focus more attention and effort on the higher cognitive functions involved in intellectual acts. The development and use of criteria and algorithms are important components in this activity.

In order to develop an effective, accurate representation of the information structure considered by the author, a filtering process is needed that will reduce the scope of work associated with effectively acquiring and organizing the information contained in the text book. One such filter is the emphasis on topic sentences and the ideas contained in each. The topic sentence is constructed by the author to provide an insight into the information provided in the paragraph.

Building an Information Network: Information networks are composed of terms serving as nodes and the paths (lines) connecting them. A node is a word used more frequently by the author, with other terms, to present ideas. These nodes are connected to other nodes or to individual terms. Each pair of terms represents an idea presented in a sentence. As such, the information network would be composed of terms frequently coupled with other terms.

Table 1. Excerpt of Topic Sentence Ideas from Text in Appendix.

Primary	Related	Sentence
difference	learning	1
difference	linear	1
difference	non-linear	1
linear	learning	1
linear	non-linear	1
non-linear	learning	1
avatars	flash	2
avatars	interest	2
flash	interest	2
instruction	avatars	2
instruction	flash	2
instruction	interest	2
instruction	sound	2
instruction	streaming	2
multimedia	avatars	2
etc.		

Table 2. Excerpt from Topic Ideas with Summary Counts.

Primary	Related	Sentence
analysis	analyst	8
analysis	relationship	8
analysis	terms	8
analysis	theme	8
analysis count		**4**
analyst	relationship	8
analyst	terms	8
analyst	theme	8
analyst count		**3**
approach	advisor	11
approach	analysis	8
approach	analyst	8
approach	data	8
approach	instructor	11
approach	qualitative	8
approach	relationship	8
approach	role	11
approach	terms	8
approach	theme	8
approach count		**10**
etc.		

An excerpt of the topic sentence ideas is shown in Table 1. These ideas are arranged by sentence, and primary term within each sentence. Each topic sentence represents a paragraph. As such, sentence 1 is the topic sentence for paragraph 1. Sentence 2 is the topic sentence for paragraph 2.

Table 2 shows the location of each idea in the sentence as well as the total number of ideas involving each primary term

Table 3. Nodal Terms in Information Network.

Primary	Freq	Primary	Freq	Primary	Freq
computer	20	analysis	4	author	1
data	9	mining	4	program	1
method	8	technician	4	relationship	1
approach	7	analyst	3	team	1
links	6	knowledge	3		
qualitative	6	option	3		
terms	6	statistical	3		
calculation	5	statistics	3		
text	5	traditional	3		
		assistance	2		
		expert	2		
		supported	2		

Table 3 shows the number of ideas involving each of the terms from the topic sentences. The term, computer, was involved in 20 ideas. In contrast, the term, team was involved in 1 idea. This table is a simplified representation of the information network showing the terms making up the nodes. This summary is useful in determining possible nodes for study. It does not show the paths established by authors among the nodes.

Figure 1. Terms Linked with the Node – Computer.

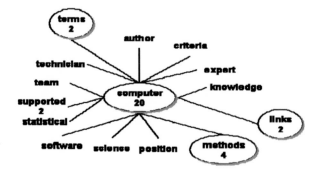

Figure 1 shows the activity involving the node, computer. As seen, that term was linked with 3 other nodes. In addition, the term was linked to individual words. The combination of nodes and related terms depicts the 20 ideas involving the term, computer.

The following shows the process involved in building an information network, using the ideas in the *topic sentences* beginning with the two nodes – non-linear and learning.

Figure 2. Non-Linear and Learning Nodes and Relationships.

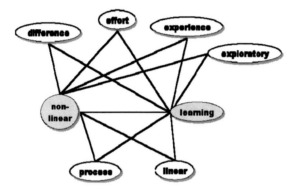

Figure 2 shows the network involving learning and non-linear together with the terms related to both from the ideas given in Table 4. As seen, this structure consists of 8 nodes. One of the nodes linked with both non-linear and learning was process.

Table 4 shows the ideas involving non-linear and/or learning from the topic idea file. The records are arranged so that agreement with primary and related terms is evident. For example, non-linear was linked with difference, effort, experience, exploratory, process, and linear. Learning also was linked with these terms. The transitive property of equality would suggest that since non-linear and learning were, respectively, linked with those terms, the idea – non-linear & learning – also should be observed. That idea was present and the involved paragraphs were identified. In addition, there were ideas involving – learning -- that were not linked to non-linear and ideas linked with non-linear that were not linked with learning. For simplicity, this example focuses on the terms forming nodes in the network. To be classified as a node, the term must be involved in at least two ideas.

66

Table 4. Ideas Involving Non-Linear and/or Learning.

Primary	Related	Paragraph	Primary	Related	Paragraph
			learning	activity	9
non-linear	approach	2			
			learning	aspect	20
			learning	assurance	9
			learning	design	20
non-linear	difference	1	learning	difference	1
			learning	discipline	20
			learning	discovery	21
non-linear	effort	7	learning	effort	7
non-linear	experience	4	learning	experience	4
			learning	experience	20
non-linear	exploratory	7	learning	exploratory	7
			learning	exploratory	9
			learning	findings	20
			learning	goal	21
			learning	investigative	20
			learning	just-in-time	21
			learning	lifelong	21
non-linear	linear	1	learning	linear	1
			learning	management	20
non-linear	matter	2			
			learning	methodology	9
			learning	methodology	21
non-linear	new	2			
non-linear	learning	1	learning	non-linear	1
non-linear	learning	4	learning	non-linear	4
non-linear	learning	7	learning	non-linear	7
			learning	on-demand	21
			learning	procedure	20
non-linear	process	7	learning	process	7
			learning	process	9
			learning	quality	9
			learning	requirement	9
			learning	study	20
non-linear	subject	2			
			learning	thought	9

Figure 3. Evolving Information Network Consisting of Non-Linear, Learning, and Process Nodes.

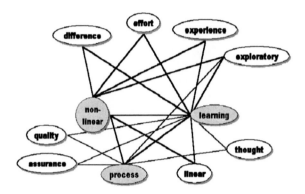

Comparing Figures 2 and 3, the addition of the process node identified assurance, quality, and thought as nodes. These terms were related to learning in Table 4 and qualified as nodes by being linked to the term – process -- two or more times. The adding of nodes can be extended by considering the ideas related to assurance, quality, and thought.

The ideas involving the terms related to the nodes – assurance, quality, and thought -- are shown in Figure 4. The lines linking nodes indicate the popularity of a term as a node. The more frequently used nodes are color coded to help clarify the increasingly complex picture of relationships being portrayed.   This example focused only on those terms that were involved in ideas occurring at least twice. The excel files describe all of the ideas and serve as resources in determining other syntheses that might be of interest.

Based on these ideas and associated text, the relationships between the non-linear node and the others could be clarified. If this possible gap was confirmed, an interested investigator could develop a research program for a better understanding of the ideas and associated concepts involved with this presumably important modification of the learning process. In this way, a rapid and formalized approach in developing descriptions of existing knowledge helps to identify potential directions for obtaining new information.

Figure 4. Information Network following Addition of Ideas involving Assurance, Quality, and Thought.

Information Structure Yields Information Networks: An information structure is a comprehensive array of the ideas and related data describing the topic. That structure can be used to develop any number of informational networks depending on the analysts' interests. In forming informational networks, the nodes and related terms selected can be organized into dimensions and concepts. The related terms are used in this classification process. They are categorized based on meaning and/or function.

Table 5 shows an excerpt of the records from the topic sentence idea file. These records were sorted using the primary and related terms. The related terms are used to classify the ideas into dimensions and concepts. A dimension is a major segment of the information contained in the topic. A concept is a sub-segment of the dimension and describes a particular characteristic. By assigning the ideas to dimensions and concepts, a detailed picture of the information network can be constructed.

69

Table 5. Terms in Topic Sentences in the Intervention Dimension and Method Concept.

Primary	Related	Sentence	Dimension	Concept
computer	team	15	intervention	method
expert	team	15	intervention	method
instruction	sound	2	intervention	method
instruction	streaming	2	intervention	method
instruction	talking	2	intervention	method
knowledge	team	15	intervention	method
multimedia	sound	2	intervention	method
multimedia	streaming	2	intervention	method
multimedia	talking	2	intervention	method
sound	talking	2	intervention	method
streaming	sound	2	intervention	method
streaming	talking	2	intervention	method
technician	team	15	intervention	method
video	sound	2	intervention	method
video	talking	2	intervention	method

The terms for the intervention dimension and the method concept are given. The intervention dimension deals with ideas designed to introduce change. The ideas shown illustrate this emphasis. For example, instruction is linked with sound, streaming, and talking. This implies that change is accomplished using those effects. Instruction, multimedia, streaming, and video, respectively, have more than one related term. Terms involving more than one idea serve as focal points or nodes.

Table 6. Terms in Topic Sentences with Outcome Dimension and Cognitive Concept.

Primary	Related	Sentence	Dimension	Concept
artificial	intelligence	14	outcome	cognitive
computer	knowledge	15	outcome	cognitive
flow	knowledge	16	outcome	cognitive
formalization	intelligence	14	outcome	cognitive
formalization	knowledge	14	outcome	cognitive
information	intelligence	14	outcome	cognitive
information	knowledge	14	outcome	cognitive
information	knowledge	16	outcome	cognitive
knowledge	intelligence	14	outcome	cognitive
processing	intelligence	14	outcome	cognitive
processing	knowledge	14	outcome	cognitive

70

Table 6 shows ideas representing the outcome dimension and the cognitive concept. This table summarizes the ideas presented by the author dealing with the terms – intelligence and knowledge – when they are linked with primary terms.

Table 7. Ideas with Learning as the Primary Term.

Primary	Related	Sentence	Dimension	Concept
learning	assurance	6	outcome	result
learning	difference	1	outcome	result
learning	exploratory	6	outcome	result
learning	goal	17	outcome	result
learning	lifelong	17	outcome	result
learning	linear	1	outcome	result
learning	methodology	6	outcome	result
learning	non-linear	1	outcome	result
learning	non-linear	3	outcome	result
learning	non-linear	5	outcome	result
learning	process	6	outcome	result
learning	quality	6	outcome	result

Table 8. Ideas Classified in the Methods Dimension and Structure Concept.

Primary	Related	Sentence	Dimension	Concept
learning	process	5	method	structure
non-linear	process	5	method	structure
assurance	process	6	method	structure
quality	process	6	method	structure
requirement	process	6	method	structure
computer	links	9	method	structure
method	links	9	method	structure
author	position	10	method	structure
computer	links	10	method	structure
computer	position	10	method	structure
links	position	10	method	structure
method	links	10	method	structure
method	position	10	method	structure
terms	position	10	method	structure
calculation	program	12	method	structure
data	program	12	method	structure
option	program	12	method	structure
statistical	program	12	method	structure
formalization	processing	14	method	structure

Table 7 shows the ideas with a common primary term – learning. Those ideas also have a common dimension – outcome – and a common concept – result. The orientation shown here illustrates the building block notion associated with ideas. These ideas come from sentences scattered throughout the block of text. However, when brought together in a simple alphabetic arrangement using the related term as the sort characteristic, a picture of learning involves exploration, thought, assurance, lifelong process, etc.

Table 8 shows the ideas from the Methods dimension and the Structure Concept. The records are arranged by sentence. Comparing the topic sentences in the Appendix with the entries in Table 4 shows where the ideas came from.

Table 9 shows the same data records now arranged by related term. The term, links, is related to computer and method. The term, position, was related to 5 words. The term, program, was linked with 4 others. These tables, showing different organizations of data records, illustrate the synthesis function. These constructions can be performed by technicians following specific algorithms using the data operations built into the Excel software. The findings can be presented to the analyst for comparison, evaluation, and interpretation. Those tasks are examples of higher cognitive functions.

Table 9. Ideas Classified in the Methods Dimension and Structure Concept – Oriented by Related Terms.

Primary	Related	Sentence	Dimension	Concept
computer	links	9	method	structure
computer	links	10	method	structure
method	links	9	method	structure
method	links	10	method	structure
author	position	10	method	structure
computer	position	10	method	structure
links	position	10	method	structure
method	position	10	method	structure
terms	position	10	method	structure
assurance	process	6	method	structure
learning	process	5	method	structure
non-linear	process	5	method	structure
quality	process	6	method	structure
requirement	process	6	method	structure
formalization	processing	14	method	structure
information	processing	14	method	structure
calculation	program	12	method	structure
data	program	12	method	structure
option	program	12	method	structure
statistical	program	12	method	structure

Summary

This chapter focused on using the topic sentence ideas to construct an information structure. That organization of information represents the totality considered relevant in describing the subject when the information is filtered using the important sentence in each paragraph. In this example, that totality consists of the ideas contained in the topic sentences. The information structure serves a comparable role to the numeric database in that the structure contains all of the data of interest. Individual analysts could select specific subsets of the data records in order to build new descriptions of the topics contained within the subject. These subsets of information can be depicted using a variety of display formats. One such is the information network. This consists of graphs or tables consisting of important terms (or nodes) plus the terms connecting them to each other. The terms represent nodes within the network and the lines represent paths between the nodes. Nodes can be prioritized in terms of importance by the number of times the terms are used in describing ideas or relationships with other nodes.

The information network can be further enhanced by subdividing the ideas using meaning and/or function of the related term in each idea. Categories can be created representing major segments of the total topic. These categories are called dimensions. Within each dimension, sub-divisions can be constructed by clustering ideas describing a common attribute. These sub-categories are called concepts. The network, the dimensions, and the concepts help to organize the information relevant to the topic so that effective and innovative descriptions of the information can be constructed.

<u>**Appendix – Formalized, Objective Analysis of Text**</u>

The following text is an example of a single document. The challenge faced by the analyst is to rapidly summarize the information provided. One approach is to focus on the topic sentences. Topic sentences are typically the first sentence in each paragraph. By considering just those sentences and the ideas contained, an explicit description of the topic can be constructed. The topic sentences are highlighted.

There is a difference between linear and non-linear learning. Linear learning is a sequential, incremental approach relying on an organization of the material by the instructor. The student is expected to acquire the information by following the sequence of steps provided by the instructor. Non-linear learning is best described by a network of nodes and links, of informational clusters and connections. The student can consider the total network and decide the order of learning by selecting nodes and related paths of interest. This type of selective learning has a number of labels – discovery, on demand, or just-in-time learning. In each of these learning venues, the student takes charge of the learning process. S/he decides the material to be considered and the methods of learning to be used. In this setting, the instructor becomes an advisor. The result is intended to stimulate enthusiasm for learning and create an environment wherein lifelong learning is a reality.

However, how does this non-linear approach work when the subject matter is new to the analyst? How can the student select useful informational segments without some understanding of the subject? When the subject is new to the student, the feasibility of successfully picking and choosing insightful components seems remote.

What would constitute a non-linear learning experience? Figure 1 shows the informational network in terms of dimensions and concepts making up non-linear learning and objective analysis. Using that graph, or one similar, the student would identify the parts that are considered most interesting. The specific terms forming ideas with the central term or phrase would be sources for further exploration. The meaning of the terms and the implications of the linked terms would be of interest in developing an understanding of the topic. The student would continue to explore links between the selected node and adjacent ones until a cohesive new network was developed.

This approach sounds random and chaotic with low probability of selecting useful instruction. However, the power of the informational structure cannot be dismissed. The student is presented with the display of nodes and connections. Like its counterpart, the geographic map, recognition of 'important' nodes depends on the paths leading to each. In selecting instructional nodes, the student must consider the advice offered by the subject specialists, whose work contributed in forming the structure. In this way, the student is aided and guided by the observations and insights of the world's experts in the topic. The informational structure represents a comprehensive picture of the accepted, the possible and

75

the unlikely. While the student has control of the sequence of learning, advice and guidance are available.

The new description of the topic, developed by the student, may or may not agree with the teacher's preconceived one. That's the danger associated with exploratory learning. New issues may be uncovered. Previously uninteresting links may attain prominence. If the new description changes the existing information structure sufficiently, new paradigms might be introduced. This is the nature of creativity and that result is the stimulus that drives the scientific process.

Now, suppose that one is interested in non-linear learning but wanted to establish a process so that the meanderings of the exploratory effort could be traced. This process, if effective, would be like putting road signs in the maze to show the path from start to end. The subject specialists have provided their insights in terms of frequencies of use of specific nodes and paths. The challenge, then, is to develop a procedure for demonstrating the investigative process used by the analyst.

The motivation for this would be quality assurance or simply a desire to communicate a thought process. Quality assurance involves development of an information network with defined paths so that observations, decisions, and results can be validated. While thought processes are less apparent, assume that by mapping the involved ideas, a coherent representation of those thoughts can be developed. That is, the student can show the choice of nodes and links and the sequence used.

This requirement for a quality assurance process or a defined thought process that can be replicated by others introduces the need for a methodology to support the exploratory learning activity. That method is the subject of this text and involves the integration of previously separate and independent procedures. The primary elements are:

1. Text mining to identify the vocabulary, ideas, and related data from text.
2. Data processing to acquire, edit, store, and retrieve information.
3. Statistics to translate the intended explorations into meaningful and interpretable numeric results.

Text Mining: Text mining can be accomplished using traditional or computer-supported methods. The traditional ones involved identifying possible information sources, screening those for content, and selecting the pertinent ones. Each of these documents would then be read and notes prepared describing the analyst's perceptions of the important issues presented in the text. These would be organized and revised into a new document.

Computer-supported methods vary. A major approach is called qualitative data analysis and involves the analyst identifying pertinent terms and relationships in order to form themes. These are used to formulate a description of the phenomenon and particularly, the motivations for, or nuances of, performance. This method is dependent on the expertise of the analyst.

Another computer method involves identifying terms and forming links between these terms based on statistical criteria. These relationships are used to form themes for organizing documents, or developing groups of different types. The process is an extension of hyperlinking and is based on the assumption that the author emphasizes important terms and links between terms by presenting them in the *same document with increased frequency.*

A third computer method involves identifying terms and forming links between those terms based on the authors' positioning of the terms. The *domain of interest is the sentence* and the informative terms are nouns (e.g., survivor), adjectives (survival), or verbs behaving as nouns (surviving). The pairs of terms found in a sentence are operationally defined as ideas. These ideas form basic building blocks in developing informational networks.

This third approach is most in keeping with the role of the instructor as an advisor. The author of the document is best equipped to provide the essentials required by the student – the vocabulary relevant to the topic, the pertinent ideas, and appropriate methods involved. With these three components, the student can begin to think, and act, like the professional. As such, two computer-supported approaches – One-Stop Learning and Idea Analysis are presented. Idea Analysis is designed to provide a comprehensive knowledge base of ideas and related data for use by any number of analysts. One-Stop Learning is intended to provide a rapid overview of a new topic by focusing on sentences containing specific ideas.

<u>Data Processing:</u> **This function involves the development of data capture instruments, translation of the data to computer records, and organization of these records for different uses.** With the introduction of computer software, data management has progressed so that a 'natural' consequence of information use involves the construction and use of data resources. Once the design of the data records and their relationships to each other are defined, the process of entering, evaluating, and using the data is routine, enabling the analyst to focus on the more creative aspects of information processing.

<u>Statistics:</u> **Statistics has come a long way with the assistance of computer software.** Calculation of data now involves selecting options from statistical program menus. As such, the problem is choosing the appropriate method at the right time rather than adding, multiplying, or dividing.

That shift in operation also is commensurate with a change in emphasis. Earlier text books would emphasize the method and its calculation. With the software, the focus can be on the translation of the information network developed from the literature to a research design capable of providing the desired new information and insights. This design is executed, the data obtained, and findings developed. Those findings must be translated back to text and the body of knowledge updated. To illustrate this, case studies are presented that show the flow through the literature, research, analysis, interpretation processes. The studies also show the use of different types of data and the statistical methods involved.

Multifaceted Focus: The formalization of information processing and knowledge utilization is not an expression of artificial intelligence. Instead, the intent is to standardize those tasks that can be best accomplished by employing consistent, routine operations distinct from those requiring imagination and innovation. These operations are well accepted in most disciplines requiring adherence and compliance with methodology.

The fact that the computer, the technician and the knowledge expert must co-exist is a reality of modern team science. That sociologic phenomenon has increased as complex, multifaceted problems are addressed. A recent example is the Human Genome Project designed to characterize and formalize understanding of the human gene structure and function. That project was finished earlier than anticipated by the integrative efforts of scientists from different disciplines, biologic and information processing.

There are disciplines that deal with more general aspects of the learning experience including study design, investigative procedures and management of resulting findings. The typical approach is to provide an individual with an array of individualized courses and allow the person to integrate the knowledge according to need. There is little evidence that these separate disciplines have attempted to formalize the building of bridges in order to address a recognized problem from onset to conclusion. Non-Linear Learning and Objective Analysis is an attempt to accomplish this bridging. It is an essential approach in an information-rich, team oriented environment.

The overall goal is to enhance lifelong learning by offering methodology to facilitate on-demand, just-in-time, and discovery learning. In the 21st century, the concept of available information could be changed to one describing the abundance of information. Search engines can identify and retrieve millions of websites in fractions of a minute. Statistical software can perform complex arithmetic operations again in minutes. These technical capabilities require the expertise of the individual to determine which ones to use and when. In addition, the knowledge and skill of the person is necessary to interpret the findings. These technical improvements make the separation of tasks possible and feasible. As such, there are procedures that can be best performed by computer, by technician, and by subject specialist. The intent of Non-Linear Learning and Objective Analysis is to provide the tools and rationale that accelerate achievement in knowledge utilization.

Chapter Seven -- Identification, Extraction and Organization of Ideas

Introduction

Problems associated with investigation of text analysis procedures include the degree of effort involved in manually performing the searches and determining the consequences of each. This chapter presents three methods for the identification, extraction, and organization of ideas from retrieved documents. In the first two methods, the document retrieval is arbitrary and the methods deal with the sequential extraction of ideas. These methods combine manual and computer-support. In the third method, the search for documents is incorporated with the subsequent extraction of ideas from targeted sentences. These sentences contain the idea representing the search statement together with related terms. This method is primarily computer-supported but each step is controlled by the analyst.

Document identification and retrieval involves two basic approaches – *a posteriori* and *a priori* – search methods. In the *a posteriori* approach, the computer software performs the following tasks:
1. Reads the text.
2. Matches terms used in the search with those in the text.
3. Identifies the document containing the terms either singly or in combination.
4. Prepares a display of the selected data.

This approach takes milli-seconds of computer time to obtain the display and hours of manual processing time to identify the correct ones.

The *a priori* approach is associated with a different strategy. Here, the authors provide the terms and combinations to be used and the user chooses from those for inclusion in search and retrieval statements. The computer software performs the following tasks: Reads the text.
1. Identifies the sentences.
2. Identifies the informative terms (authors' vocabulary) within each sentence.
3. Identifies the couplets of these informative terms within each sentence.
4. Links each couplet with the associated sentence.
5. Links each couplet and sentence with the appropriate bibliographic data.
6. Stores the extracted data in a knowledge resource.

These strategies are springboards in processing text. The strategy differs based on the format of the original text (i.e., paper or digital) and the availability of software to perform post-processing analyses. In this chapter, the text is assumed to be digitized so that different post-processing software can be considered. The intent, however, is the same. Namely, to build an information structure that can be used to build new descriptions of the topic.

Knowledge utilization is the end result of an intellectual process in every discipline. If creativity in the workplace is to be real, a first step is the development of a comprehensive and accurate body of knowledge in usable form. Traditionally, the effective identification and use of information was acquired by a long program of study. The more sophisticated the subject, the longer the period of study. The instructional process involved designation of topics to be learned and the sequence to be used in learning them. This process was called *linear learning.*

An alternative approach has emerged with the introduction of computer-supported technologies. This is called *non-linear learning* and has the potential to enhance intellectual achievement. The student is responsible for picking the topics to learn and the order in which these are considered. This flexibility encourages enthusiasm and a desire for learning. Is desire sufficient? There is evidence that combining non-linear learning with a formalized method of knowledge utilization provides the student with the capability to excel in the transformation from novice to professional. The method considered deals with the *ideas* provided by the authors in their sentences. The rationale for focusing on ideas is based on the expertise of the authors, their inclusion of ideas in their sentences, and the ease of computer software in identifying, extracting, and organizing these ideas.

Suppose for argument sake that the intellectual process was divided into three important segments. The first is truly mechanical and involves the search and retrieval of articles presumed to contain information of interest for a particular problem. The second is mostly low level intellectual processing and can be performed by computers or trained technicians. That task involves the identification and organization of: the sentences in the text; the informative terms in each sentence; *and* the ideas involving those informative terms in each sentence. Sentences can be identified by ending punctuation. Typically, periods, exclamation points or question marks identify the vast majority of sentences in scientific text. With sentences identified, the informative terms are essentially nouns – names of persons, places or things. Given the list of informative terms, the next and most important task associated with this exercise is to identify the ideas provided by the author in the sentence.

A computer or a technician can perform this identification by recording the links between informative terms actually employed by the author. Alternatively, all of the pairs of informative term combinations within the sentence can be generated, organized and stored for future use. Factorial arithmetic can be used to define the total number of ideas within a sentence by counting the number of informative terms. The formula is the number of informative terms times that number minus 1 divided by 2. If the number of informative terms in the sentence was 10, the number of ideas would be $10(9)/2 = 45$.

The *combination of words, ideas, and methods* constitute the essential components in describing and using a subject. By focusing on the ideas as the primary data record, the text processing method incorporates the three elements in the most efficient way. In addition, by instituting defined algorithms, computer software can perform the task of identifying the words, constructing copies of the ideas presented by the authors, and storing those data in a repository that facilitates utilization of the information to form knowledge.

The *knowledge repository* consists of the ideas from the authors' sentences, the bibliographic data used to retrieve the full document, and the sentences containing the identified ideas. The latter are important in quality validation.

The *ideas are retrieved* from the resource and used to construct descriptions of the existing knowledge. These constructions are called syntheses. These can be assessed and the most useful selected based on established decision criteria and procedures. The result of this process is a new description of the topic together with the individual's assessment of gaps and/or inconsistencies. If of interest, correction of these existing flaws could be accomplished using information from new knowledge generating strategies and studies. This process is the essence of an objective analysis of information:

1. Idea Knowledge Resource
2. Syntheses of the existing ideas.
3. Comparison and evaluation of these syntheses.
4. Development of a new description of the topic.
5. Identification of a new course of action.

By using an accurate and comprehensive information repository as the source of the data to be considered, the bulk of the usual work is eliminated. That frees the individual to focus exclusively on the relationships described by the expert authors and the gaps or inconsistencies that might exist at any point in time.

These *relationships can be classified,* using the frequency of occurrence, into those representing agreement across the world of investigators and those that may not have reached that status. The latter may be emerging ideas and if so, may represent new areas of exploration.

In addition, the *condition placed on each idea* by the authors is of importance. This condition might be:

1. The idea is not yet established as real, i.e., inconclusive findings.
2. The idea is of definite value in describing the subject, i.e., positive findings.
3. The idea is not of value in describing the subject, i.e., negative findings.

Within each sentence, the informative term pairs, sequentially, are identified and extracted. These *sequential links* are recorded in a usable resource (say, an excel file). The format of each entry is shown in Table 1.

Table 1. Format of Ideas in Excel File.

Term	Term	Location	Sentence	Document
A	B	1	1	1
B	C	2	1	1
C	D	3	1	1
D	E	4	1	1

The sentence providing this information would contain the informative terms -- *A* ..... *B* .... *C* .... *D* .... *E*. The spaces between informative terms would be occupied by other terms – verbs, adverbs, conjunctions, prepositions, namely, all of the words in the language other than nouns, pronouns, adjectives, or gerunds. The location column identifies the sequential occurrence of the idea in the sentence. The first pair would be denoted as one. The second pair as two, etc.

As this file is expanded by entering more and more ideas, simple alphabetic sorting of columns 1, 2 or both can organize the data so that all of the ideas involving a particular term are together. This common term can be considered as a node in a system description of the topic. By identifying the nodal terms that depict the largest number of ideas, and by showing the terms that relate to each nodal term, the systemic description of the information can be presented. The source of each idea is evident from the location, sentence and document data. As such, a link is established between the original document and the critical data.

With text organized in this fashion, sequential identification and extraction of ideas assists in developing the swarm of terms associated with each central term as well as the links between these terms. This method would be called *sequential idea identification.*

Excel software is used to manage the resulting data and Inspiration[tm] is used to prepare graphs. The text analysis relies heavily on accurate and complete identification and extraction of the ideas associated with one of the following strategies:

1. Identification of all of the informative terms in the sentence with the ideas extracted involving a single central term. The term is used frequently by the author. This method selects ideas as follows – A $\rightarrow$ C, B $\rightarrow$ C, D $\rightarrow$ C, E $\rightarrow$ C, etc, where C is the central term.
2. Identification of all of the informative terms in the sentence with subsequent identification and extraction of the ideas occurring sequentially through the sentence. This method selects ideas as follows – A $\rightarrow$ B, B $\rightarrow$ C, C $\rightarrow$ D, etc.

Two examples will be used to illustrate the computer-supported sequential idea analysis approaches. The first deals with the term – postmodernism – and its meaning. The second describes Einstein's views on radiation.

Deciphering Postmodernism

There are several phases considered in studying philosophical ramifications of human thought and behavior. The first is labeled – *antiquity* – and represents historical events prior to the late 1700s. The second, ranging from approximately 1750 to 1900, was labeled *modern*. The third began in the early 1900s and became more evident by the 1980s. That one was labeled – *postmodernism*. This theory, couched in the language of philosophers, offered the following challenge - how to translate the complexities of the philosophical description of postmodernism to one understandable by the student striving to learn how postmodernist theory impacts, if at all, on his/her discipline of interest.

A description of postmodernism was prepared and distributed by Dr. Mary Klages [Klages, 2003]. That discussion is provided here in a modified form. The individual sentences are separated and informative terms within each are highlighted.

Sentences from Klages' Description

1. **Postmodernism** is a complicated **term**, or **set** of **ideas**, **one** that has only emerged as an **area** of academic **study** since the mid-1980s. – **28 ideas**

2. **Postmodernism** is hard to define, because it is a **concept** that appears in a wide **variety** of **disciplines** or **areas** of **study**, including **art, architecture, music, film, literature, sociology, communications, fashion,** and **technology**. – **105 ideas**

3. Perhaps the easiest **way** to start thinking about **postmodernism** is by thinking about **modernism**, the **movement** from which **postmodernism** seems to grow or emerge. – **10 ideas**

4. **Postmodernism**, like **modernism**, follows most of these same **ideas**, rejecting **boundaries** between high and low **forms** of **art**, rejecting rigid **genre distinctions**, emphasizing **pastiche** (dramatic, literary, or musical **piece** openly imitating the previous **works** of other **artists**), **parody** (a literary or artistic **work** that imitates the characteristic **style** of an **author**), **bricolage** (something made or put together using whatever **materials** happen to be available), **irony** (the use of **words** to express something different from and often opposite to their literal **meaning**), and **playfulness**. – **231 ideas**

5. **Postmodern art** (and **thought**) favors **reflexivity** and **self-consciousness**, **fragmentation** and **discontinuity** (especially in narrative **structures**), **ambiguity**, **simultaneity**, and an emphasis on the destructured, decentered, dehumanized **subject**. – **55 ideas**

6. But--while **postmodernism** seems very much like **modernism** in these ways, it differs from **modernism** in its **attitude** toward a lot of these **trends**. – **10 ideas**

7. **Postmodernism**, in contrast, doesn't lament the **idea** of **fragmentation, provisionality**, or **incoherence**, but rather celebrates that. – **10 ideas**

8. Another **way** of looking at the relation between **modernism** and **postmodernism** helps to clarify some of these **distinctions**. – **6 ideas**

9. According to Frederic Jameson, **modernism** and **postmodernism** are cultural **formations** which accompany particular **stages** of **capitalism**. – **10 ideas**

10. The third, the **phase** we're in now, is **multinational** or **consumer capitalism** (with the emphasis placed on marketing, selling, and consuming **commodities**, not on producing them), associated with nuclear and electronic **technologies**, and correlated with **postmodernism**. – **21 ideas**

11. Like **Jameson's characterization** of **postmodernism** in terms of modes of **production** and **technologies**, the second **facet**, or **definition**, of **postmodernism** comes more from **history** and **sociology** than from **literature** or **art history**. – **78 ideas**

12. This approach defines **postmodernism** as the **name** of an entire **social formation**, or **set** of social/historical **attitudes**; more precisely, this **approach** contrasts "**postmodernity**" with "**modernity**," rather than "**postmodernism**" with "**modernism**." – **55 ideas**

13. **Francois Lyotard** (the **theorist** whose **works Sarup** describes in his **article** on **postmodernism**) equates that **stability** with the **idea** of "totality," or a **totalized**

system (think here of **Derrida's idea** of "totality" as the **wholeness** or **completeness** of a **system**). – **153 ideas**

14. **Postmodernism** then is the **critique** of grand **narratives**, the **awareness** that such **narratives** serve to mask the **contradictions** and **instabilities** that are inherent in any social **organization** or **practice**. **–36 ideas**

15. **Postmodernism**, in rejecting grand **narratives**, favors "mini-**narratives**," **stories** that explain small **practices**, local **events**, rather than large-scale **universal** or **global** **concepts**. – **36 ideas**

16. **Postmodern** "mini-**narratives**" are always **situational, provisional, contingent**, and **temporary**, making no claim to **universal**ity, **truth, reason**, or **stability**. – **45 ideas**

17. In **postmodernism**, however, there are only **signifiers**. – **1 idea**

18. Rather, for **postmodern societies**, there are only **surfaces**, without **depth**; only **signifiers**, with no **signifieds**. – **15 ideas**

19. Another **way** of saying this, according to **Jean Baudrillard**, is that in **postmodern society** there are no **originals**, only **copies**--or what he calls "**simulacra**." -- **28 ideas**

20. Finally, **postmodernism** is concerned with **questions** of the **organization** of **knowledge**. – **6 ideas**

21. This is the **ideal** of the liberal **arts education**. – **3 ideas.**

22. In a **postmodern society**, however, **knowledge** becomes **functional**--you learn **things**, not to know them, but to use that **knowledge**. – **15 ideas**

23. Not only is **knowledge** in **postmodern societies** characterized by its **utility**, but **knowledge** is also distributed, stored, and arranged differently in **postmodern societies** than in **modern** ones. – **28 ideas**

24. Specifically, the advent of **electronic computer technologies** has revolutionized the **modes** of **knowledge production, distribution**, and **consumption** in our **society** (indeed, some might argue that **postmodernism** is best described by, and correlated with, the emergence of **computer technology**, starting in the **1960s**, as the dominant **force** in all aspects of social **life**). – **105 ideas**

25. In **postmodern societies**, anything which is not able to be translated into a **form** recognizable and storable by a **computer**--i.e. anything that's not digitizable--will cease to be **knowledge**. – **10 ideas**

26. **Lyotard** says (and this is what **Sarup** spends a lot of **time** explaining) that the important **question** for **postmodern societies** is who decides what **knowledge** is (and what "**noise**" is), and who knows what needs to be decided. – **28 ideas**

27. There are lots of **questions** to be asked about **postmodernism**, and **one** of the most important is about the **politics** involved--or, more simply, is this **movement** toward **fragmentation, provisionality, performance**, and in**stability** something good or something bad? -- **36 ideas**

28. In fact, one of the **consequences** of **postmodernism** seems to be the rise of **religious fundamental**ism, as a form of **resistance** to the questioning of the "grand **narratives**" of religious **truth**. – **21 ideas**

29. This **association** between the **rejection** of **postmodernism** and **conservatism** or **fundamental**ism may explain in part why the **postmodern avowal** of **fragment**ation and **multiplicity** tends to attract **liberals** and **radicals**. – **55 ideas**

30. On another **level,** however, **postmodernism** seems to offer some **alternatives** to joining the global **culture** of **consumption,** where **commodities** and **forms** of **knowledge** are offered by **forces** far beyond any **individual's control.** -- **55 ideas**

31. By discarding "grand **narratives**" (like the **liberation** of the entire working **class**) and focusing on specific **local goals** (such as improved **day care centers** for working **mothers** in your own **community**), **postmodernist politics** offers a **way** to theorize **local situations** as **fluid** and unpredictable, though influenced by global **trends.** – **136 ideas**

Analysis of Sentences: The informative terms in each sentence were identified and the number of ideas recorded for each sentence. A quick review of these sentences shows that the term – postmodernism – was used frequently. With that term occurring in the bulk of the sentences, it is reasonable to consider an analysis of the ideas involving this term.

Let's begin the analysis of this text by considering the ideas involving the term – postmodernism -- in the sentence containing the largest number of ideas. This term was used by the author 36 times in the 31 sentences. In addition, analyzing the sentences in order of the total number of ideas contained in each facilitates tracing the ideas considered relevant by the author.

Processing of text involving identification of nouns as informative terms results in two groups included in the extraction. One group consists of terms that specifically serve as attributes of the central term. The other group consists of nouns that are general in description. The criterion to be satisfied is –

"Does the term specifically serve as an attribute of the central term?"

If so, the term is included in the list of filtered terms. If not, the term is ignored.

This decision process is one requiring intellectual efforts and cannot be performed in a rote fashion. Two functions are involved and must be separated. The first is the identification and extraction of all nouns contained in the sentence. Clearly, the author will use those terms for different purposes and assign them differing priorities.

The second function is to identify the terms considered pertinent. The definition of the word pertinent is -- *pertaining or relating directly and significantly to the matter at hand.* The analyst must use the dictionary to establish the meaning of each candidate term. In addition, s/he must consider how the term was used by the author. In essence, the author is the ultimate authority for the meaning and/or function assigned to each term. Deciding pertinence depends on the analyst's perception of the term's direct relationship or its significance.

In this situation, the data set consists of all of the nouns identified in each sentence. That list should be fixed and final. What is done with it to develop a new description is the province of the new analyst. The resulting filtered list will reflect the analyst's individuality and bring differences and diversity to the final result. Each analyst will develop appropriate rules for the selection of terms for inclusion in the filtered set. Depending on the intended use of those terms, the selected list will not be the same as each analyst performs his/her tasks.

Table 2. Selection of Terms Meeting the Pertinence Criterion Related to the Central Term -- postmodernism.

Related Terms Filtered Set	Related Terms Total Set
architecture	architecture
art	area
communication	art
concept	communication
discipline	concept
fashion	discipline
film	fashion
literature	film
music	literature
sociology	music
technology	sociology
	study
	technology
	variety

The filtering process is an important intellectual exercise but an even more important one is to ensure that an audit trail is established enabling verification and validation of the analytic tasks performed. The audit trail requires identification of:

1. Sentences by physically separating them.
2. Informative terms by highlighting them.
3. Number of ideas per sentence by using the factorial arithmetic formula – N x (N-1) / 2, where N is the number of informative terms in the sentence.
4. All of the ideas in each sentence by recording them in an excel file.
5. Selected filtered ideas by evaluating the role each term plays in describing the central term.
6. Categories of ideas that enhance the description of the conceptual structure associated with the central term.

Table 2 shows the total and filtered terms from sentence 2 linked with the central term – postmodernism. That sentence is duplicated here –

> **Postmodernism** is hard to define, because it is a **concept** that appears in a wide **variety** of **disciplines** or **areas** of **study**, including **art, architecture, music, film, literature, sociology, communications, fashion,** and **technology**. – 105 ideas

The terms – architecture, art, communication, fashion, film, literature, music, sociology and technology – were used by the author to describe the areas of study involved in postmodernism. As such, these terms were assumed to be attributes (***something belonging to a person, thing, group***) and included in the filtered list. In addition, the term – discipline – was used as a category label for these various areas of study. The terms – area, study and variety – do not specifically and directly enhance understanding of the central term. Accordingly, they were not included in the filtered list.

The decision regarding pertinence of terms may vary. The filtering process need not yield consistency from analyst to analyst. However, there should be no variation in the identification and extraction of all of the nouns (i.e., informative terms) in the sentence. This list of terms should be extracted and organized *once* and placed in a shared, easily available data file.

The use of excel files for this purpose has been illustrated. Excel is a readily available software program that offers sufficient processing capability to manage the text manipulations required. An important feature is its transparency in operation. The user can perform required functions in an easy and convenient manner.

Table 3 shows the filtered and total set of terms linked with postmodernism in sentence 13. The terms – article, stability, totalized and work – were excluded from the filtered set assuming that these were too general to add information regarding postmodernism. The words – Derrida, Francois, Lyotard, and Sarup – were excluded assuming that proper names did not contribute to understanding of the central term. This latter exclusion is different from the typical emphasis on authors in describing humanities' related phenomena. Authors are cited as authorities in guiding thinking. In the idea approach, the author of the idea is less relevant than the idea. This is particularly pertinent when the student is challenged to learn the ideas and concepts. By focusing on the ideas and obtaining an understanding of those, refinements including authors can be assigned a secondary priority.

Table 3. Ideas Involving Postmodernism in Sentence 13.

Primary Term	**Related Terms**	**Related Term**
Postmodernism	**Filtered Set**	**Total Set**
	completeness	article
	idea	completeness
	system	Derrida
	totality	Francois
	wholeness	idea
		Lyotard
		Sarup
		stability
		system
		theorist
		totality
		totalized
		wholeness
		work

The terms -- completeness, totality, and wholeness -- were included in the filtered set assuming that these terms did contribute to understanding of the central term. The terms – idea and system – were included because of importance in enhancing the meaning of the central term.

Assignment of terms to categories is an important classification function and one that doesn't have necessarily correct results. As in the filtration task, classification is an individualistic endeavor. In building a classification scheme, it is useful to incorporate author's terms where appropriate. In the scheme shown in Table 4, the category labels were – disciplines, culture, technology, politics, and concept. The remaining category labels chosen were – time, product and solution.

Assignment of terms to the time category was simplest. The author included two descriptions of time – 1960s and 1980s – in her text.

Table 4. Categories of Terms Related to Postmodernism.

Time	Disciplines	Product	Culture
1960s	architecture	ambiguity	attitude
1980s	art	completeness	consumption
	communication	copy	global
	fashion	discontinuity	life
	film	fragmentation	social
	history	imitation	society
	literature	irony	
	organization	playfulness	
	music	reflexivity	
	sociology	rejection	
		simultaneity	
		stability	
		totality	
		wholeness	

Technology	Politics	Concept	Solution
available			
materials	capitalism	goal	contingent
computer	commodities	idea	provisional
distribution	conservatism	knowledge	situation
		self-	
electronic	fundamentalism	consciousness	
functional	local	thought	
narrative	liberal		
production	trend		
system			

The terms included in the Product category were more challenging. As seen in Table 3, the terms describe the character of the products prepared in this postmodernism era. Terms such as -
- ambiguity, completeness, discontinuity, fragmentation, irony, playfulness, reflexivity,

simultaneity, stability, totality and wholeness – describe aspects of the art, music, or literature produced. Terms such as – copy and imitation – represent approaches in constructing the products.

The four categories – technology, politics, concept, and solution – describe most closely the characteristics representative of the term – postmodernism. The technologic issue relevant in this central term was the introduction of computers. With that technology in place, the notion of knowledge changed from "knowing" to "using". The political concept supporting postmodernism was global capitalism with application of local solutions to problems based on the conditions found at each site. The notion of centralized organizational structures with rules governing all situations changed to one where each situation required individualized solution so that the totality could move forward.

Einstein's Views on Composition and Essence of Radiation

The sentences that follow present the discussion by Albert Einstein.[Einstein 1909] If this document was considered to be a *secret message*, then the challenge would be in decoding it to determine what the message really said. Assuming that the document is written in a code that only physcists in the early 1900s could understand, the challenge is to explore the information provided by identifying and depicting the ideas. The informational terms in each sentence were highlighted and the number of ideas in each sentence determined. The sentences in Dr. Einstein's paper follow.

1. When **light** was shown to exhibit **interference** and **diffraction**, it seemed almost certain that **light** should be considered a **wave**. – **10 ideas**
2. A large **body** of **facts** shows undeniably that **light** has certain fundamental **properties** that are better explained by Newton's **emission theory** of **light** than by the **oscillation theory**. – **36 ideas**
3. The greatest **advance** in theoretical **optics** since the **introduction** of the **oscillation theory** was **Maxwell's** brilliant **discovery** that **light** can be understood as an **electromagnetic process**. – **45 ideas**
4. The **introduction** of the **electromagnetic theory** simplified the **elements** of theoretical **optics** and reduced the **number** of arbitrary **hypotheses**. – **21 ideas**
5. In both **theories**, **light** is esentially an **embodiment** of the **state** of a hypothetical **medium**, the **ether**, which exists everywhere, even in the absence of **light**. – **21 idea**
6. The main outstanding **question** was the following: does the **ether** participate in the **motions** of **matter**, or does the **ether** inside moving **matter** move differently or, perhaps, does the **ether** ignore the **motions** of **matter** and remain forever at **rest**? – **45 ideas**
7. This **experiment** demonstrated that **matter** does not completely carry along its **ether** but, in general, the **ether** is moving **relative** to **matter**. – **21 ideas**
8. This **relative motion** was expected to produce a visible **anisotropy** of **space**, i.e., optical **phenomena** were expected to depend on the **orientation** of the **apparatus**. – **21 ideas**
9. **Lorentz** showed that if the **ether** were taken to be at **rest** and did not participate at all in the **motions** of **matter**, no other **hypotheses** were necessary to arrive at a **theory** that did **justice** to almost all of the **phenomena**. – **36 ideas**

10. According to **Lorentz's theory**. a uniform translational **motion** of the **apparatus** of **optical experiments** does not affect **light's** progress, if we ignore **second-** and **higher-order terms** of the **quotient (speed** of **apparatus)/(speed of light)**. – **85 ideas**

11. **Michelson's experiment** suggests the **axiom** that all **phenomena** obey the same **laws relative** to the **Earth's reference frame** or, more generally, **relative** to any **reference frame** in unaccelerated **motion**. – **78 idea**

12. The **foundation** of the **ether hypothesis** is the experimentally based **assumption** that the **ether** is at **rest**. – **15 idea**

13. Then the **electromagnetic fields** that make up **light** no longer appear as a **state** of a hypothetical **medium**, but rather as **independent entities** that the **light source** gives off, just as in **Newton's emission theory** of **light**. – **39 ideas**

14. Thus, the inertial **mass** of an **object** is diminished by the **emission** of **light**. – **8 ideas**

15. The **energy** given up was **part** of the **mass** of the **object**. – **6 ideas**

16. **One** can further conclude that every **absorption** or **release** of **energy** brings with it an **increase** or **decrease** in the **mass** of the **object** under **consideration**. – **36 ideas**

17. **Energy** and **mass** seem to be just as **equivalent** as **heat** and **mechanical energy**. – **15 ideas**

18. Why does the **color** of **light**, and not its **intensity**, determine whether a certain **photochemical reaction** occurs? – **10 ideas**

19. Why is **light** of short **wavelength** generally more effective chemically than **light** of longer **wavelength**? – **6 ideas**

20. Why is the **speed** of photoelectrically produced **cathode rays** independent of the **light's intensity**? – **10 ideas**

21. Why are higher **temperatures** (and, thus, higher **molecular energies**) required to add a short-**wavelength component** to the **radiation** emitted by an **object**? – **21 ideas**

22. the **energy** of the **gas molecules** would be continuously transformed into the **energy** of **radiation**, until all the available **energy** had turned into **energy** of **radiation**. – **28 ideas**

23. There would be no **equilibrium** between **gas** and **radiation**. – **3 ideas**

24. In addition to the spatial **irregularities** in the **distribution** of **radiation's energy** that arise from the **oscillation theory**, there are also other **irregularities** in the same spatial **distribution** that completely dominate the first-mentioned **irregularities** when the **energy density** of the **radiation** is small. – **66 ideas**

25. the **manifestation** of **light's electromagnetic waves** is constrained at **singularity points**, like the **manifestation** of **electrostatic fields** in the **theory** of the **electron**. – **55 ideas**

Analysis of Ideas: The discussion consisted of 25 sentences. The ideas in the sentences ranged in number from 3 (sentence 23) to 85 (sentence 10). This article served as an example of the exploratory process concomitant with sequential identification of ideas. The first sentence in that text was -- *When light was shown to exhibit interference and diffraction, it seemed almost certain that light should be considered a wave.* The sequential ideas began with the idea – light → interference -- and continued with the ideas -- interference → diffraction, etc.

Considering all of the sentences, 169 ideas were entered into Excel and sorted. The results were 10 swarms of ideas with central terms as follows: energy, ether, light, mass, matter, motion, radiation, relative, theory, and wavelength. A central term is one included in each of the idea pairs and occurring in 3 or more ideas. The resulting swarms were filtered to eliminate ideas containing non-specific nouns as related terms.

Table 5. Filtered Idea Swarms – Light, Ether, Matter, Motion.

Light	Ether	Matter	Motion
diffraction	matter	motion	anisotropy
electromagnetic	motion	relative	matter
emission	relative	rest	ether
ether	rest		relative
intensity			rest
interference			
oscillation			
properties			
ray			
source			
speed			
theory			
wavelength			

The ideas involving, respectively, the central terms -- light, ether, matter, and motion – are shown in Table 5. In column 1, light was linked with diffraction, electromagnetic, ether, ray, speed, and wavelength, among others. Column 2 shows the ideas involving ether. Column 3 shows the ideas involving matter and column 4 involves those ideas linking with motion. The table also shows links between the idea swarms. The term – matter – is involved with the ether and motion swarms while ether is included in the light and motion swarms as well as heading its own swarm.

Table 6. Filtered Idea Swarms – Relative, Wavelength, Radiation and Energy.

Relative	Wavelength	Radiation	Energy
Earth	electromagnetic	energy	density
ether	energy	density	gas
matter	light	distribution	mass
motion		gas	mechanical
reference			molecule
			oscillation
			radiation
			release
			wavelength

Table 6 shows the ideas involving, respectively, the central terms – relative, wavelength, radiation and energy. Wavelength was linked to electromagnetic and light as well as energy. Oscillation was another term linked to light and to energy. Such terms serve as bridges connecting different swarms and illustrating the connectivity that results in the final conceptual structure.

Figure 1. Idea Swarms Summarizing Ideas in Einstein Paper.

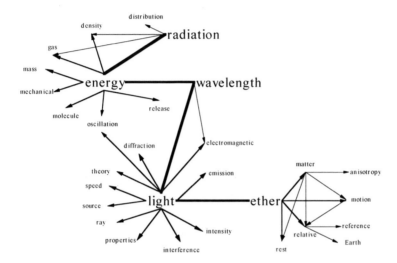

Figure 1 shows five central terms – light, ether, energy, wavelength, and radiation. When considering the central term – light – the author described attributes and extended that description to include the terms – electromagnetic and ether. Ether, in turn, introduced the link with the term – matter. The relationship between energy and mass was established. In addition, links between energy, radiation and wavelength were established.

The text and the graphic (Figure 1) indicated that light could be considered as a wave form and a mass. The relationship between light, mass, and energy was extended to include radiation.

A critique presented by the translator of this paper suggested that –

> *Light could be considered as a wave and a particle. The paper also indicated that particle and wave components of light produce pressure fluctuations in radiation.*

The two descriptions are similar suggesting that the decoding of the paper using sequential identification and organization of the ideas within each sentence was effective in developing a description of the conceptual issues considered by Dr. Einstein.

The Einstein article illustrated a different form of idea extraction. In addition, the author defines individual swarms of ideas and then links those to form a conceptual network. Table 7 shows the idea swarms associated with the central terms – light, ether, and wavelength.

Table 7. Connected Idea Swarms – Light, Ether, Wavelength

light			
	diffraction		
	electromagnetic		
	emission		
	ether	**ether**	matter
	intensity		motion
	interference		relative
	oscillation		rest
	properties		
	ray		
	source		
	speed		
	theory		
	wavelength	**wavelength**	electromagnetic
			energy
			light

Table 8 shows additional idea swarms and the links between them.

Table 8. Connected Ideas Swarms – Matter, Motion and Relative.

matter	motion	**motion**	anisotropy		
	relative		matter		
	rest		ether		
			relative		
			rest		
				relative	Earth
					ether
					matter
					motion
					reference

Table 9. Idea Swarms – Radiation and Energy.

radiation	energy	**energy**	density
	density		gas
	distribution		mass
	gas		mechanical
			molecule
			oscillation
			radiation
			release
			wavelength

The categories defined in Tables 7, 8, and 9 were shown by highlighting the terms used to characterize each idea swarm.

Figure 2. Example of Categories Defined by Central Terms in a Network – Backbone of Terms.

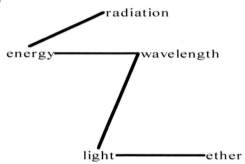

Figure 2 shows the backbone of the conceptual structure by highlighting the nodal terms. These terms also serve as the categories for defining the ideas in the conceptual structure.

Figure 3 shows the ideas comprising the light category and Figure 4 shows the category involving the central term – ether. Figure 5 shows the idea swarm involving energy and the links to the other central terms.

Figure 3. Expansion of Idea Swarm in the Light Category.

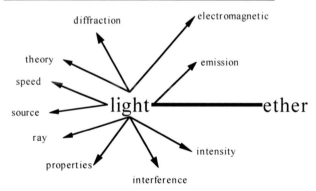

Figure 4. Expansion of Idea Swarm in the Ether Category.

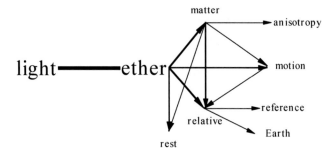

Figure 5. Expansion of Idea Swarm in the Energy Category and Related Backbone.

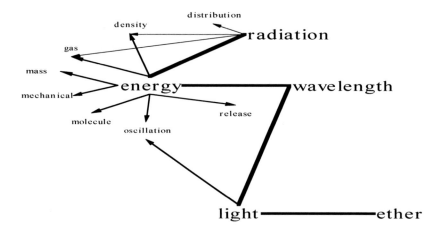

Given an accurate and complete database of ideas, selected ones can be retrieved and used in describing a new version of the information relevant to a topic. In retrieving ideas and in organizing them, clusters (i.e., categories) dealing with a common meaning and/or function can be formed. In the postmodernism example, these clusters could be labeled using author's terms or terms chosen by the analyst. In the Einstein example, the categories were defined by Dr. Einstein and the labels were his.

Other systems attempt to cluster *documents* based on a relatively small number of terms and describe those clusters as themes. The categorization considered here clustered *ideas* involving a common central term and related terms that were similar in meaning and/or function. Ideas can be combined and that combination is consistent with higher level cognitive functions. The two approaches would yield the same results if a document could be represented by a single idea. Since the average abstract contains approximately 100 ideas, collapsing to a single theme is neither accurate nor effective.

Combining Search Strategy and Idea Identification – One-Stop Learning

Another idea organization strategy focusing on sentences containing a specific idea. The search process takes each idea from the presenting text and expands by retrieving documents containing the idea. The specific sentences including the idea are used to develop the information structure. This process is illustrated using the following text:

> *An **ingredient** in **orange juice**, known as **agent X**, has been found to lessen the harmful effects of the **common cold**. **Researchers** found that the **common cold** could worsen and cause **pneumonia**. **Pneumonia** is an acute or chronic **congestion** of the **lungs** caused by **viruses**, **bacteria** or specific **chemicals**. **Scientists** believe that the active **ingredient** improves the **body**'s **defenses**, called **immune system**.*

As seen, this message begins with the sequence of ideas in the first sentence. The ideas are -- orange juice → agent X → common cold. Since we have no notion of what agent X might be, let's begin our search with the idea – orange juice → common cold.

What is the Relationship Between Orange Juice and Common Cold? The search statement – *"orange juice" AND "common cold"* was entered into the PubMed search engine. One article was retrieved. That one was published in 1979 and was the most recent observed. The sentence from the article is given in the Appendix and is repeated here.

> *A controlled **study** was made of the effects of **natural orange juice**, **synthetic orange juice**, and **placebo** in the **prevention** of the **common cold**; both **natural** and **synthetic** orange juices contained 80 mg of **ascorbic acid** daily.*

The sequential ideas in the sentence were:

1. study → natural orange juice
2. natural orange juice → synthetic orange juice
3. synthetic orange juice → placebo
4. placebo → prevention
5. prevention → common cold
6. common cold → natural
7. natural → synthetic orange juice
8. synthetic orange juice → ascorbic acid.

Note that phrases such as, *natural orange juice*, were included in the list. While terms such as, natural and synthetic, were used as adjectives in the sentence, considering each term individually would support the inclusion of these words as informative. In essence, the name of the 'noun' would be – *natural orange juice.*

The alternative way of viewing the ideas would involve considering the phrase, *common cold*, as central. Ideas in the sentence showing the link to this node would be determined. Those ideas would be:

1. common cold → study
2. common cold → orange juice
3. common cold → placebo
4. common cold → prevention
5. common cold → natural orange juice
6. common cold → synthetic orange juice
7. common cold → ascorbic acid.

Both of these lists are subsets of the total number of ideas in the sentence. That list would be:

1. study with, respectively, orange juice, placebo, prevention, common cold, natural, synthetic, and ascorbic acid.
2. orange juice with, respectively, placebo, prevention, common cold, natural, synthetic, and ascorbic acid.
3. placebo with, respectively, prevention, common cold, natural, synthetic, and ascorbic acid.
4. prevention with, respectively, common cold, natural, synthetic, and ascorbic acid.
5. common cold with, respectively, natural, synthetic, and ascorbic acid.
6. natural with, respectively, synthetic and ascorbic acid.
7. synthetic with ascorbic acid.

In the list of ideas involving the phrase – common cold – as the node, two ideas matched with those from the first sentence. The matching ideas from the retrieved sentence were – common cold with, respectively, orange juice and ascorbic acid. Reviewing these ideas suggests the possibility that *agent X* could be *ascorbic acid* (also called *Vitamin C*).

Is there a Relationship Between Vitamin C and Common Cold? The search statement – *"vitamin C" AND "common cold"* – was entered into PubMed. Six current reports were retrieved. Each of these contained one or more sentences describing the idea – vitamin C → common cold. Twenty-five terms were linked with Vitamin C. For example, Vitamin C was linked with, respectively, artic, community, and population.

Table 9. Ideas Involving Vitamin C from Search – Vitamin C and Common Cold.

environment	treatment	Outcome
artic	diet	Duration
community	dose	Failure
population	placebo	Immunity
species	prevention	Incidence
virus	prophylaxis	Protection
	therapy	Response
disease	treatment	
common cold	zinc	**Metabolic**
flu		Oxidative
infection		Redox
inflammatory		

Table 9 shows these terms, arranged into categories. The categories were: environmental, disease, treatment, outcome and metabolic factors. As seen, the investigators emphasized treatment and outcome factors as they considered the role of Vitamin C in studies of common cold management. A link between Vitamin C, common cold and influenza also was described in these studies. That suggests that the next question could involve common cold and respiratory disease.

Is there a Relationship Between Common Cold and Respiratory? Six articles included the idea – common cold and respiratory.

Table 10. Ideas Involving Respiratory from Search – Common Cold and Respiratory.

disease	metabolic	site
acute	antioxidant	airway
common cold	replication	olfactory
disease		tract
illness	**environment**	
infection	bacteria	**treatment**
influenza	probiotic	antibiotic
sinusitis	viral	antihistamine
symptom		antitussive
tonsillitis	**outcome**	consumption
URTI	incidence	drug
	prevention	nonsteroidal
	response	treatment

Table 10 shows the terms related to the term – respiratory – from the search using the idea – common cold → respiratory. The first idea, shown in the table, involved the idea -- respiratory → acute. The second idea was respiratory → common cold. The categories were disease, metabolic, environmental, outcome, site, and treatment factors. The investigators emphasized disease and treatment. Of interest, treatments linked with respiratory did not include Vitamin C.

Is there a Relationship Between Vitamin C and Respiratory? Two articles were retrieved from this search. The terms linked with respiratory from this search are shown in Table 11.

Table 11. Ideas Involving Respiratory from the Search – Vitamin C and Respiratory.

metabolic	outcome	disease	environment
antioxidant	duration	symptom	species
		common	
burst	protection	cold	
inhibition	response	damage	**treatment**
integrity		infection	suppression
oxidative	**cellular**	inflammatory	Vitamin C
oxygen	cell		zinc
reactive	neutrophil		
redox			

For example, the ideas were -- respiratory with, respectively, antioxidant, duration, and symptom. Categories developed were metabolic, outcome, cellular, disease, environmental, and treatment factors. Metabolic and disease categories were the most prominent.

The idea – antioxidant → respiratory – was observed in Table 11. This is the first occurrence of the term – antioxidant. This search and resulting sentence also showed an interesting gap as well. While respiratory was linked with infection and inflammatory, the principal disease – influenza – was not included. This table shows the presence of a new idea and the omission of another. Two searches are relevant. The first would involve antioxidant → common cold. The second would involve Vitamin C → influenza.

Table 12. Ideas Involving Common Cold from the Search – Antioxidant and Common Cold.

metabolic	outcome
antioxidant	risk

behaviors	environment
physical	
activity	people
work	
leisure	**treatment**
	Vitamin E
	beta-carotene

What is the relationship between antioxidant and common cold? The search statement – *"antioxidant"* AND *"common cold"* was entered into PubMed. One article was retrieved. Table

99

12 shows the informative terms from the sentence. The terms were arranged in categories and each term described an idea involving common cold as the central node. This search pointed to behavioral factors – physical activity, work, and leisure – as the most frequently occurring category. The antioxidants considered by these authors were Vitamin E and beta-carotene.

What is the Relationship Between Influenza and Vitamin C? The search of PubMed using the idea, influenza and Vitamin C, retrieved one article with three sentences containing the search idea. .

Table 13. Ideas Involving Influenza
from the Search – Influenza and Vitamin C.

disease	outcome
deficiency	response
immune	
infection	**environment**
pathology	virus

site	treatment
lung	Vitamin C

The involved ideas are shown in Table 13. Influenza was linked with new terms – immune, pathology, and virus. The authors of this report explored the sequence of ideas-- *Vitamin C* → *deficiency* → *lung* → *influenza* → *virus*

What is the Relationship between Common Cold and Immune (Immunity)? Investigators used two terms to describe the body's protective mechanism. One was the word, immune, and the other was the word, immunity. A search using common cold linked with immune retrieved one article with one sentence. The search using the term, immunity, resulted in a single article with one sentence. Table 14 shows the ideas involving the central term, common cold.

Table 14. Ideas Involving Common Cold
from the Search – Common Cold and
Immune (Immunity).

disease	outcome
influenza	evidence
immune	recovery
fever	
immunity	**environment**
infection	system
symptom	
disease	**treatment**
well-being	Vitamin C
	diet

Table 14 shows the ideas linking common cold and immune (immunity). Common cold is paired with influenza, immune, fever, infection, well-being, Vitamin C, recovery, and diet. In addition, there are some general terms, such as disease, evidence, and system. In a simplistic sense, this table brings together important informative terms in describing the relationship between Vitamin C and measures of health and disease, with particular reference to the common cold and disease sequellae.

From one perspective, Table 14 might satisfy a detailed description of the topic described in the message. The disease elements were included together with elements representing treatment and outcome. The environmental effects were weak. Perhaps, a better description could be developed by combining all of the results from the individual searches. These results are shown in Table 15.

Table 15. Ideas Involving Common Cold – Combined Analyses.

disease	metabolic	treatment
acute	antioxidant	antibiotic
damage	burst	antihistamine
deficiency	inhibition	antitussive
disease	integrity	beta-carotene
fever	oxidative	diet
illness	oxygen	dose
immune	reactive	drug
immunity	redox	nonsteroidal
infection	replication	placebo
inflammatory		prevention
influenza	**site**	prophylaxis
pathology	airway	protection
sinusitis	lung	suppression
symptom	olfactory	treatment
tonsillitis	tract	Vitamin C
URTI		Vitamin E
well-being	**environment**	zinc
	artic	
outcome	bacteria	
duration	cell	**behaviors**
evidence	cellular	consumption
failure	community	leisure
		physical
incidence	neutrophil	activity
prevention	people	work
recovery	population	
response	probiotic	
risk	species	
	system	
	viral	
	virus	

Table 15 shows the combined search results organized in categories. The combined set of terms presents a tabular version of the idea swarm. Each of the terms was related to common cold and that phrase represents the central node in this conceptual structure. The categories are: disease, outcome, metabolic, site, environmental, treatment and behavioral factors. While the disease category contained the essential descriptors representing common cold and related illnesses, other categories were more responsive in satisfying the professor's request for a detailed description. For example, the treatment category included a range of treatments dealing with prevention as well as management of acute illness. The metabolic category showed terms that formed a more complete conceptual structure describing the body's actions in management of the disease. The environmental factors included the infectious agents, climate and social measures. Outcome factors dealt with disease control and prevention.

In this example, that idea was -- common cold → orange juice. The phrase, common cold, was obviously important because that represented the topic of interest. The phrase, orange juice, was a fortuitous choice. Indeed, if that message had not included orange juice, only one of the searches – common cold → immune – would have identified this agent. As such, the apparent important role played by orange juice in the message may not have been supported by the independent searches.

If those searches began with relationships between common cold and respiratory, the search path might have pursued the idea, common cold → influenza and those results would have no link to Vitamin C. If the search had involved the idea – antioxidant → vitamin E – an article published in 2006 [Lunet 2006] would have presented the link between antioxidant, vitamin E and vitamin C. A report published in 1992 [Hemila 1992] brought the combination – antioxidant, Vitamin C and common cold – together, and even in the same sentence. That sentence was –

> The **common cold** studies indicate that the amounts of **vitamin C** which safely protect from scurvy may still be too low to provide an efficient rate for other reactions, possibly **antioxidant** in nature, in infected people.

Once Vitamin C was introduced, the results would have been the same as shown in the example used in this chapter. Accordingly, starting points might be different depending on the clues provided in the first message.

The premise tested was that the authors provide the direction and guidance required to develop a comprehensive and accurate description of the topic. The search and retrieval procedural rules that must be followed are:

1. Identify a starting idea and use that combination in the first search statement.
2. Identify all of the ideas from sentences containing the search idea.
3. Choose a subsequent idea from this set to use as a next search statement.
4. Repeat the identification, extraction and selection process until:
    a. You eliminate new ideas, given date of publication criteria.
    b. You accumulate enough data to build a sufficient description of the topic.

Summary

This chapter considered the techniques involved in summarizing existing knowledge and in building new descriptions of this information. Information is defined as the text, numeric expressions, or images that provide some insight when considering a topic. In formalizing the analysis of text, certain types of words take on more importance. The ones described in this chapter were nouns, namely, the words assigned to identify persons, places or things. By identifying the nouns in a sentence, even without specific understanding of the meaning of each, important and useful applications are possible. This chapter showed two such applications of scientific documents. One described postmodernism and the second radiation, light, and energy. A third approach involved author-guided, idea-driven search and retrieval called One-Stop Learning. That approach involved identification and retrieval of documents satisfying specific search statements. Within each of the retrieved documents, one or more sentences contained the idea used in the search statement. Those sentences were extracted and the ideas included were organized for subsequent searches and syntheses.

Cognitive Tasks: When the informative terms have been identified and the appropriate ideas extracted and stored in a database, the real intellectual pursuits can begin. Those involve the cognitive tasks of synthesis, comparison, evaluation, judgment, and application. Examples of these tasks were illustrated using the ideas from the two scientific documents and from the idea-driven search and retrieval.

Filtering: One of the important operations involved in building new syntheses requires the removal of less relevant ideas. This is called filtering and each idea (i.e., central and related terms) must be evaluated. Removal of non-pertinent nouns is clearly an individual task. The author selects those terms that s/he feels best describes the informational elements and ideas to be transmitted.

Categorization: Categorization has been illustrated using different approaches. In the postmodernism situation, the category labels were chosen using author terms, where possible, and then additional ones defined by the analyst. In that situation, all of the ideas were identified because of their links with a single central term, i.e., postmodernism. In that scenario, the attributes representing characteristics of the central term were further organized into arbitrarily chosen categories used to highlight and describe the meaning and/or functions associated with the central term.

In the Einstein situation, the ideas were not restricted to a single central term. Instead, they were related to one of more than 10 central terms. In that scenario, the author explored and described the links between these terms. Each category is, in essence, a swarm of ideas and in contrast to the post-modernism example, the category labels were chosen by Dr. Einstein. These swarms, when combined, form a network of informative terms and author-defined relationships among them. This array of ideas is operationally defined to be a conceptual structure. By building such structures, you can develop a gestalt view of the topic with potential to recognize gaps in the existing body of knowledge.

This chapter also considered the idea-driven search process. This situation involved a message dealing with the common cold. Orange juice, as a "medicine" in preventing or minimizing the disease related effects, was seen to contain an essential agent, Vitamin C or ascorbic acid. The searches conducted were:

1. Orange Juice and Common Cold.
2. Vitamin C and Common Cold.
3. Common Cold and Respiratory.
4. Vitamin C and Respiratory.
5. Antioxidant and Common Cold.
6. Influenza and Vitamin C.
7. Common Cold and Immune.
8. Common Cold and Immunity.

The second search idea represented a translation of orange juice into the active agent, Vitamin C. The third search explored the association between the disease affecting the upper respiratory tract and the effect on the lungs. The fourth search followed up on the active agent question by exploring the role of Vitamin C in lung conditions associated with the common cold. The fifth search was targeted to determine possible mechanisms by focusing on the antioxidant question, while the sixth expanded the fourth by introducing a specific lung disease. Finally, the last two searches explored further the possible defensive actions taken by the body in fighting off the effects of the common cold.

It could be argued that each of these searches was a logical extension of questions that could be raised in the exploration of this condition. While correct, note that the assumption invoked at the outset was that the student was not familiar with the topic. Accordingly, without prior knowledge of relevant concerns, the development of the set of logical questions must be based on expert guidance. In the idea-driven search and retrieval process, the subject specialist-authors served as the mentors guiding the student.

Appendix − Sentences and References for Ideas in the Idea Driven Search Strategy

Idea − Orange Juice → Common Cold

*A controlled **study** was made of the effects of **natural orange juice, synthetic orange juice,** and **placebo** in the **prevention** of the **common cold**; both **natural** and **synthetic** orange juices contained 80 mg of **ascorbic acid** daily.*
Baird IM, Hughes RE, Wilson HK, Davies JE, Howard AN. The effects of ascorbic acid and flavonoids on the occurrence of symptoms normally associated with the common cold. Am J Clin Nutr. 1979 Aug;32(8):1686-90.

Idea − Vitamin C → Common Cold

*Intensive promotion of the advantages of **vitamin C** as the compound that augments **immunity** to all sorts of **infections**, accelerates **recovery**, eliminates the symptoms of **common cold** and flu-like diseases, and contributes to general **well-being**, is of great importance to its intake in quantities far exceeding the recommended **dietary** allowance.*
*Moreover, the subjects who simultaneously take several anti-**common cold drugs** are not aware of the fact that almost each of them contains **ascorbic acid**.*
Wroblewski K. [Can the administration of large doses of vitamin C have a harmful effect?] Pol Merkuriusz Lek. 2005 Oct;19(112):600-3.

*These trials document that adequate intakes of **vitamin C** and **zinc** ameliorate symptoms and shorten the duration of **respiratory** tract **infections** including the **common cold**.*
Wintergerst ES, Maggini S, Hornig DH. Immune-enhancing role of vitamin C and zinc and effect on clinical conditions. Ann Nutr Metab. 2006;50(2):85-94.

***Vitamin C** may have a small role in preventing the **common cold**, with possibly a greater role in high-intensity **physical activity** and sub-**arctic** conditions.*
Arroll B. Non-antibiotic treatments for upper-respiratory tract infections (common cold). Respir Med. 2005 Dec;99(12):1477-84.

*To investigate the relationship between the **common cold** and **vitamin C** supplementation.*
*A randomized, controlled 5-year trial suggests that **vitamin C** supplementation significantly reduces the frequency of the **common cold** but had no apparent effect on the **duration** or **severity** of the common cold.*
Sasazuki S, Sasaki S, Tsubono Y, Okubo S, Hayashi M, Tsugane S. Effect of vitamin C on common cold: randomized controlled trial. Eur J Clin Nutr. 2006 Jan;60(1):9-17.

*Five small trials found a statistically significant 45 to 91% reduction in **common cold incidence** in the **vitamin C** group.*
Hemila H. Vitamin C supplementation and respiratory infections: a systematic review. Mil Med. 2004 Nov;169(11):920-5.

*The role of oral **vitamin C** (ascorbic acid) in the **prevention** and **treatment** of the **common cold** has been a subject of controversy for at least sixty years.*
*To discover whether oral **vitamin C** in **doses** of 200 mg or more daily, reduces the **incidence, duration** or **severity** of the **common cold** when used either as continuous **prophylaxis** or after the onset of **cold symptoms**.*
*Seven trial comparisons that involved 3,294 **respiratory** episodes contributed to the meta-analysis of **cold duration** during therapy with **vitamin C** that was initiated after the onset of **cold symptoms**, and no significant difference from **placebo** was seen.*
*The **failure** of **vitamin C** supplementation to reduce the **incidence** of **colds** in the normal **population** indicates that routine mega-**dose prophylaxis** is not rationally justified for **community** use.*
*The trials in which **vitamin C** was introduced at the **onset** of **colds** as **therapy** did not show any benefit in **doses** up to 4 grams daily, but one large trial reported equivocal benefit from an 8 gram therapeutic dose at onset of **symptoms**.*
Douglas RM, Hemila H, D'Souza R, Chalker EB, Treacy B. Vitamin C for preventing and treating the common cold. Cochrane Database Syst Rev. 2004 Oct 18;(4):CD000980.

Idea – Common Cold → Respiratory

*To investigate the effect of long-term **consumption** of **probiotic bacteria** on **viral respiratory tract infections** (**common cold, influenza**), a randomized, double blind, controlled intervention study was performed during two winter/spring periods (3 and 5 month).*
de Vrese M, Winkler P, Rautenberg P, Harder T, Noah C, Laue C, Ott S, Hampe J, Schreiber S, Heller K, Schrezenmeir J. Probiotic bacteria reduced duration and severity but not the incidence of common cold episodes in a double blind, randomized, controlled trial. Vaccine. 2006 Jun 6

*Although **acute upper respiratory diseases** (**AURDs**) such as **common cold** and **influenza** are common, few interventions have been proven to be effective in their **prevention** and **treatment**.*
Nobata K, Fujimura M, Ishiura Y, Myou S, Nakao S. Ambroxol for the prevention of acute upper respiratory disease. Clin Exp Med. 2006 Jun;6(2):79-83.

*To compare the effects of a complex homeopathic preparation (Engystol; Heel GmbH, Baden-Baden, Germany) with those of conventional therapies with **antihistamines, antitussives,** and **nonsteroidal antiinflammatory drugs** on upper **respiratory symptoms** of the **common cold** in a setting closely related to everyday clinical practice.*
Schmiedel V, Klein P. A complex homeopathic preparation for the symptomatic treatment of upper respiratory infections associated with the common cold: An observational study. Explore (NY). 2006 Mar;2(2):109-14.

*Post**viral olfactory** disorders usually occur after an **upper respiratory tract infection** (**URTI**) associated with a **common cold** or **influenza**.*
Welge-Lussen A, Wolfensberger M. Olfactory disorders following upper respiratory tract infections. Adv Otorhinolaryngol. 2006;63:125-32.

*This work was aimed at understanding how a **viral infection** mostly affecting the **upper respiratory tract**, such as the **common cold**, can repeatedly promote opportunistic **infections** in the lower **airways**, a site where **viral replication** is limited.*

Passariello C, Schippa S, Conti C, Russo P, Poggiali F, Garaci E, Palamara AT. Rhinoviruses promote internalisation of Staphylococcus aureus into non-fully permissive cultured pneumocytes. Microbes Infect. 2006 Mar;8(3):758-66.

*Antibiotic prescribing rates for **URTIs** have not declined between 1987 and 2001, but the volumes for **common cold, sinusitis** and **tonsillitis** have fallen down mainly attributable to declined **incidences**, which have probably been caused by a reduced inclination of patients to present **respiratory illness** to their GP.*

Kuyvenhoven M, van Essen G, Schellevis F, Verheij T. Management of upper respiratory tract infections in Dutch general practice; antibiotic prescribing rates and incidences in 1987 and 2001. Fam Pract. 2006 Apr;23(2):175-9.

Idea – Vitamin C → Respiratory

***Suppression** of the **respiratory burst** as well as **inhibition** of the uptake of the **antioxidant vitamin C** may disturb the balance between **oxidative damage** of invading particles and antioxidant **protection** in activated **neutrophils**.*

Laggner H, Phillipp K, Goldenberg H. Free zinc inhibits transport of vitamin C in differentiated HL-60 cells during respiratory burst. Free Radic Biol Med. 2006 Feb 1;40(3):436-43.

***Vitamin C** contributes to maintaining the **redox integrity** of **cells** and thereby protects them against **reactive oxygen species** generated during the **respiratory burst** and in the **inflammatory response**.*
*These trials document that adequate intakes of **vitamin C** and **zinc** ameliorate **symptoms** and shorten the **duration** of **respiratory tract infections** including the **common cold**.*

Wintergerst ES, Maggini S, Hornig DH. Immune-enhancing role of vitamin C and zinc and effect on clinical conditions. Ann Nutr Metab. 2006;50(2):85-94.

Idea – Antioxidant → Common Cold

*We evaluated whether **physical activity** at **work**, or at **leisure**, is associated with the **risk** of the **common cold**, and whether the **antioxidants vitamin E** and **beta-carotene** affect common cold risk in physically active **people**.*

Hemila H, Virtamo J, Albanes D, Kaprio J. Physical activity and the common cold in men administered vitamin E and beta-carotene. Med Sci Sports Exerc. 2003 Nov;35(11):1815-20

Idea – Influenza → Vitamin C

*This study was designed to determine the effects of **vitamin C deficiency** on the **immune response** to **infection** with **influenza virus**.*

*There were no differences in **lung influenza virus** titers between **vitamin** C-adequate and - deficient mice; however, **lung pathology** in the vitamin C-deficient mice was greater at 1 and 3 d after **infection** but less at d 7 compared with vitamin C-adequate mice.*
*These data suggest that **vitamin C** is required for an adequate **immune response** in limiting **lung pathology** after **influenza virus infection**.*
Li W, Maeda N, Beck MA. Vitamin C deficiency increases the lung pathology of influenza virus-infected gulo-/- mice. J Nutr. 2006 Oct;136(10):2611-6.

Idea -- Common Cold → Immune

*There is also no **evidence** that these medicines prolong the course of **colds** and **flu** by any effect on the **immune system** or by reducing **fever**.*
Eccles R. Efficacy and safety of over-the-counter analgesics in the treatment of common cold and flu. J Clin Pharm Ther. 2006 Aug;31(4):309-19.

Idea -- Common Cold → Immunity

*Intensive promotion of the advantages of **vitamin C** as the compound that augments **immunity** to all sorts of **infections**, accelerates **recovery**, eliminates the **symptoms** of **common cold** and **flu**-like **diseases**, and contributes to general **well-being**, is of great importance to its intake in quantities far exceeding the recommended **dietary** allowance.*
Wroblewski K. [Can the administration of large doses of vitamin C have a harmful effect?] Pol Merkuriusz Lek. 2005 Oct;19(112):600-3.

Chapter Eight – Drafting New Text

Introduction

This chapter shows that a credible first draft can be prepared in essentially minutes. Using original authors' words is perfectly acceptable *if* properly referenced and for drafting purposes. The focus used in drafting is the ideas. They are used to develop an outline of the proposed text. They are used to develop the first draft. There are two interpretations of the pair of informative terms within a sentence (i.e., an idea). One is the contextual meaning intended by the author. The second is the declaration that the author provided the idea. The latter agrees with the use of software in processing text. Software can report that the author of a specific sentence included a designated pair of terms in a specific body of words. The importance or pertinence of the idea is not an issue with software. Importance is in the perception of the analyst. The software simply provides the *fact* that a *specific idea* was present in a *designated sentence* contained within an *identified document*. This factual, accurate reporting is a critical feature in text mining.

The distinction between the author's intended context when using an idea and the identification and extraction of that idea for use in any other number of ways is an important distinction when considering *plagiarism*. The definition implies that any use of another's ideas, concepts, or statements, without proper referencing, is a violation. In the methods described in this chapter, the use of the ideas is properly referenced whether or not the context associated with the idea agrees with previous works or is a fresh perspective. The extraction of ideas by software with subsequent building of idea resources also eliminates the possibility of plagiarism by referencing each specific idea with the document and sentence involved. More importantly, however, is the fact that ideas are dimension-free and can be used in any way deemed appropriate by the individual building the new text. The new organization of ideas becomes the property of that individual. However, each idea used can be properly referenced back to the original authors. This referencing, however, should not be a blanket, arbitrary behavior. The context in which the idea was used plays a part in deciding referencing. A new use of the idea does not require referencing back to other uses, simply because that author included the idea in a sentence.

The strength of this approach is in the ability to carefully and deliberately assess the degree of ownership associated with an idea. When the ties to previous authors are strong, the referencing can be accomplished easily because of the document and sentence data. When the ties are weak or absent, the idea can be presented without referencing. A caveat is appropriate. When using an idea believed to be new, it is prudent to perform a search using the idea as a search statement to determine the other situations in which the idea was used. Typically, an idea new to a subject may be well established in another. As seen, in drafting, each of the sentences begins with clear indication that the authors were the owners. Once the draft is developed, the intent is to edit, rewrite, and to create a new original description of the topic. At that time, referencing of the use of the ideas depends on the contextual circumstances.

With plagiarism considered, a major reason for the inclination to commit the offense is because of the significant barrier associated with the 'blank page' phenomenon in developing new text. The first draft does not come easy. However, once the text is written, editing, revising, redrafting are easier to accomplish and faster to complete.

Suppose an outline consisted of the ideas used in the idea-driven search. That set of ideas from Chapter 6 was:

Orange Juice and Common Cold.

1. Vitamin C and Common Cold.
2. Common Cold and Respiratory.
3. Vitamin C and Respiratory.
4. Antioxidant and Common Cold.
5. Influenza and Vitamin C.
6. Common Cold and Immunity.

Further suppose that the first draft text consisted of those sentences containing the search ideas provided by the authors. Adopting a standard format for describing these sentences involves identifying the lead author in the first sentence together with a statement based on the title of the article. Subsequent sentences would include the sentence(s) retrieved. Minimal editing would be performed. The intent is to portray the authors' ideas with proper referencing and to present the specialists' views in an organized fashion. That product represents the perspective offered by the author-specialists rather than the student. As such, third party reviewers and mentors can explore the cited material with full knowledge of ownership. The student's contribution at this point is simply the organization of the authors' work in some way.

This drafting technique offers a starting point and facilitates development of a strategy for enhancement of the text. Decisions can be made regarding expansion with additional data from the articles. Decisions also can be made regarding elimination of any references. Importantly, decisions can be made regarding expansion of any of the ideas by more in-depth search and retrieval.

This process, involving stages of analysis and description, offers more effective text produced faster. It facilitates development of a method that enables learning and teaching. Each task will be shorter and more directed. The final result should be more comprehensive and accurate. A major benefit is in quality control. By performing each task, following the steps described, an audit trail of activities is developed.

The following outline and sentences illustrate the drafting process. The ideas and sentences have been organized using a well recognized format. This format is both acceptable and desirable *as a first draft,* although somewhat boring because of the repetition. However, it is superior to other formats in assigning authorship and the authors' interpretation of the embedded ideas. The major editing changes are italicized. Referencing uses the APA [American Psychological Association Referencing Style, 2003] format. This style is helpful in drafting because the lead author's name, for each reference used, is directly linked to the statements provided. The referencing style also shows the year of publication. This facilitates review of the text without flipping between text and reference section. The draft sentences follow.

Orange Juice and Common Cold

Baird [Baird et al 1979] described the effects of ascorbic acid and flavonoids on occurrence of symptoms associated with the common cold. *These authors* described a controlled study involving natural orange juice, synthetic orange juice, and placebo in the prevention of the common cold. *They indicated* that the concentration, daily, of both natural and synthetic orange juices was 80 mg of ascorbic acid.

Vitamin C and Common Cold

Wroblewski [Wroblewski 2005] studied large doses of vitamin C in order to determine if those doses had harmful effects. *This author* summarized the advantages of vitamin C. *Those included:* augmentation of immunity to all sorts of infections; acceleration of recovery, elimination of the symptoms of common cold and flu-like diseases, and contribution to general well-being. *However, Wroblewski indicated* that these advantages required intake of Vitamin C far exceeding the recommended dietary allowance. *This author* also expressed concerns that patients taking several anti-common cold drugs simultaneously might not be aware of the fact that almost each of them contained ascorbic acid.

Wintergerst [Wintergerst et al 2006] studied the immune-enhancing role of vitamin C and zinc and their effects on clinical conditions. *These authors* reported that clinical trials documented that adequate intakes of vitamin C and zinc ameliorated symptoms and shortened the duration of respiratory tract infections including the common cold.

Arroll [Arroll 2006] reported findings on non-antibiotic treatments for upper-respiratory tract infections (common cold). *This author* indicating that vitamin C might have a small role in preventing the common cold. *They suggested* that this vitamin might possibly have a greater role in high-intensity physical activity and sub-arctic conditions.

Sasazuki [Sasazuki et al 2006] reported the results of a randomized controlled trial evaluating the effect of Vitamin C on the common cold. *These authors investigated* the relationship between the common cold and vitamin C supplementation. *They conducted* a randomized, controlled 5-year trial and reported that vitamin C supplementation significantly reduced the frequency of the common cold but had no apparent effect on the duration or severity of the common cold.

Hemila [Hemila 2004] provided a review article describing the `relationship between Vitamin C and common cold. *That author indicated* that five small trials had been reported. *Those studies found* a statistically significant 45 to 91% reduction in common cold incidence in the vitamin C group.

Douglas [Douglas et al 2004] reported findings of a meta-analysis of studies dealing with the relationship between Vitamin C and common cold. *These authors indicated* that the role of oral vitamin C (ascorbic acid), in preventing and treating the common cold, had been a subject of controversy for at least sixty years. *They executed* a study to discover whether oral vitamin C in doses of 200 mg or more daily, reduced the incidence, duration or severity of the common cold when used either as continuous prophylaxis or after the onset of cold symptoms. *They stated* that seven trial comparisons that involved 3,294 respiratory episodes contributed to the meta-analysis of cold duration during therapy with vitamin C that was initiated after the onset of cold symptoms, and no significant difference from placebo was seen. *These authors reported* that the failure of vitamin C supplementation to reduce the incidence of colds in the normal population indicated that routine mega-dose prophylaxis was not rationally justified for community use. *They concluded that* the trials studying vitamin C at the onset of colds as therapy did not show any benefit in doses up to 4 grams daily. *They suggested that* one large trial reported equivocal benefit from an 8 gram therapeutic dose at onset of symptoms.

Common Cold and Respiratory

de Vrese [de Vrese et al 2006] studied probiotic bacteria in reducing duration and severity but not the incidence of common cold episodes in a double blind, randomized, controlled trial. *These authors investigated* the effect of long-term consumption of probiotic bacteria on viral respiratory tract infections (common cold, influenza). *They initiated* a randomized, double blind, controlled intervention study during two winter/spring periods (3 and 5 month).

Nobata [Nobata et al 2006] studied ambroxol for the prevention of acute upper respiratory disease. *They indicated that* acute upper respiratory diseases (AURDs) such as common cold and influenza were common. *These authors concluded* that few interventions had proven to be effective in their prevention and treatment.

Schmiedel and Klein [Schmiedel et al 2006] reported the results of an observational study dealing symptomatic treatment of upper respiratory infections associated with the common cold. *These authors compared* the effects of a complex homeopathic preparation (Engystol; Heel GmbH, Baden-Baden, Germany) with those of conventional therapies with antihistamines, antitussives, and nonsteroidal antiinflammatory drugs on upper respiratory symptoms of the common cold in a setting closely related to everyday clinical practice.

Welge-Lussen [Welge-Lussen and Wolfensburger 2006] studied olfactory disorders following upper respiratory tract infections. These authors indicated that postviral olfactory disorders usually occurred after an upper respiratory tract infection (URTI) associated with a common cold or influenza.

Passariello [Passariello et al 2006] studied the effects of rhinoviruses on Staphylococcus aureus and pneumocytes. *These authors indicated* that their study was aimed at understanding how a viral infection mostly affecting the upper respiratory tract, such as the common cold, can repeatedly promote opportunistic infections in the lower airways, a site where viral replication is limited.

Kuyvenhoven [Kuyvenhoven et al 2006] reported antibiotic prescribing rates and incidences in 1987 and 2001 in managing upper respiratory tract infections. *These authors indicated* that antibiotic prescribing rates for URTIs have not declined between 1987 and 2001, but the volumes for common cold, sinusitis and tonsillitis have fallen down mainly attributable to declined incidences, which have probably been caused by a reduced inclination of patients to present respiratory illness to their health care providers.

Vitamin C and Respiratory

Laggner [Laggner et al 2006] studied the relationship between Vitamin C, zinc and HL-60 cells. *These authors suggested* that suppression of the respiratory burst as well as inhibition of the uptake of the antioxidant vitamin C may disturb the balance between oxidative damage of invading particles and antioxidant protection in activated neutrophils.

Wintergerst [Wintergerst et al 2006] indicated that Vitamin C contributed to maintaining the redox integrity of cells and thereby protects them against reactive oxygen species generated during the respiratory burst and in the inflammatory response. *These authors suggested* that the trials documented that adequate intake of vitamin C and zinc ameliorated symptoms and shortened the duration of respiratory tract infections including the common cold.

Antioxidant and Common Cold

Hemila [Hemila et al 2003] studied physical activity and the common cold in men given antioxidants. *The authors evaluated* physical activity at work, or at leisure, and the risk of the common cold. *They studied* the association between antioxidants, vitamin E and beta-carotene, and common cold risk in physically active people.

Influenza and Vitamin C

Li [Li et al 2006] studied the relationship between Vitamin C and influenza. *These authors studied* the effects of vitamin C deficiency on the immune response to infection with influenza virus. *They indicated* that there were no differences in lung influenza virus titers between vitamin C-adequate and -deficient mice; however, lung pathology in the vitamin C-deficient mice was greater at 1 and 3 d after infection but less at d 7 compared with vitamin C-adequate mice. *They suggested* that vitamin C was required for an adequate immune response in limiting lung pathology after influenza virus infection.

Common Cold and Immunity

Eccles [Eccles 2006] studied the effects of over-the-counter analgesics in treating common colds. *This author reported* that there was no evidence that these medicines prolonged the course of colds and flu by any effect on the immune system or by reducing fever.

Wroblewski [Wroblewski 2005] studied the effects of large doses of Vitamin C. *This author suggested* that the advantages of mega-doses of vitamin C might be of great importance. *The advantages* of Vitamin C included augmentation of immunity to all sorts of infections, acceleration of recovery, elimination of the symptoms of common cold and flu-like diseases, and contribution to general well-being. *The author raised* the question of the possible harmful effects of Vitamin C when administered in doses exceeding the recommended dietary allowance.

Adding Graphics to the First Draft: Graphs showing idea swarms are helpful in assisting the student in understanding the conceptual structures involved. By preparing idea swarms using software such as Inspiration [Inspiration 2011], the meaning and/or function of the involved ideas can be explored. By developing categories and organizing the ideas in this way, the importance of specific ideas can be evaluated. Graphs or tables showing these conceptual structures should be used as communication aids. The desirability of developing conceptual structure descriptions in the form of graphics is an established tool in learning, with claims of superiority over other forms of note-taking. The graphics shown were intended to illustrate organization of the data in newer ways. Lastly, the combination of text, tables and/or graphs representing the final version should clearly reflect the individual's efforts and originality.

Figure 1. Disease Factor Ideas Linked with Common Cold.

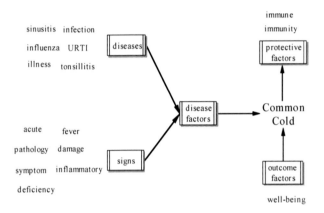

Figure 1 shows the idea swarm involving common cold with disease factors. The disease factors were subdivided into sub-categories – diseases, protective factors, outcome factors and signs. While each term could be considered a descriptor of disease, the subcategories in Figure 1 show a finer separation of meaning and/or function. For example, infection could be classified as a disease entity while inflammatory, as a sign of disease. The protective and outcome factors illustrate, still further, nuances of disease factors in common cold. The link between well-being and common cold shows a resolution of the disease. The links between common cold and immunity offer a glimpse into mechanisms that might operate to protect and enhance well-being.

Figure 2 shows the treatment factors linked with common cold. These factors have been further classified into subcategories – drug factors, antioxidants, treatment effects and nutritional factors. The treatment effect category could have been labeled as outcome factors. However, the label selected offers a clearer description of the role each term played in explaining or describing common cold management.

114

Figure 2. Treatment Factor Ideas Linked with Common Cold.

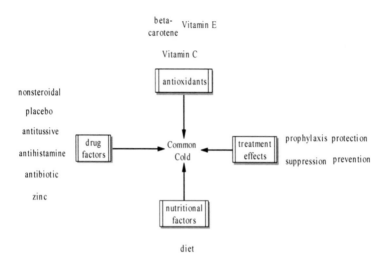

Scholar's WorkStation, Plagiarism and Beyond: The distinction between the author's intended context when using an idea and the identification and extraction of that idea for use in any other number of ways is an important distinction when considering plagiarism.   The definition implies that any use of another's ideas, concepts, or statements, without proper referencing, is a violation.   In the example above involving the development of a new draft, the suggestion was the *deliberate use* of the authors' sentences.   The format suggested involved beginning the sentence by identifying the author.   In addition, each subsequent sentence began with appropriate reference to the original author.   This referencing strategy eliminates the possibility of plagiarism.

The extraction of ideas and inclusion in the Scholar's WorkStation eliminates the possibility of plagiarism by referencing each specific idea with the document and sentence involved.   More importantly, however, is the fact that ideas are dimension-free and can be used in any way deemed appropriate by the individual building the new text.   The new organization of ideas becomes the property of that individual.   However, each idea used can be properly referenced back to the original authors.   A new use of the idea does not require referencing back to other uses, simply because that author included the idea in a sentence.

The strength of the Scholar's WorkStation approach is in the ability to carefully and deliberately assess the degree of ownership associated with an idea. When using an idea believed to be new, it is prudent to perform a search using the idea as a search statement to determine the other situations in which the idea was used. Typically, an idea new to a subject may be well established in another.

Ideas as Building Blocks: Exhibit 1 shows a sentence containing eight highlighted informative terms. These authors used the sentence in document *PubMed Identification number 17945451*, to describe a path of relationships in women screened for breast cancer to explore cardiovascular risk associated with calcifications. The term – breast – was repeated in this sentence. Software would use the first occurrence in constructing ideas.

Exhibit 1. Sentence 1 from Article 17945451 Showing Use of Informative Terms to Form Ideas.

> To assess whether breast arterial calcifications (BAC) are associated with altered serum markers of cardiovascular risk, mammograms and records from 1759 women (age range: 45-65 years) screened for breast cancer were revised. [Pidal D,   Sánchez Vidal MT, Rodríguez JC, Corte MD, Pravia P, Guinea O, Pidal I, Bongera M, Escribano D, González LO, Diez MC, Venta   R, Vizoso FJ. Relationship between arterial vascular calcifications seen on screening mammograms and biochemical markers of endothelial injury. Eur J Radiol. 2009 Jan;69(1):87-92.]

This sentence also shows the distinction between informative and general terms. The term – arterial – is an adjective that does not provide specific information relevant to breast cancer. Similarly, the term -- serum -- is general in interpretation. In contrast, the term – cardiovascular – is an adjective that modifies the noun – risk – to provide specific insight with respect to complications of breast cancer. These classifications may vary from person to person as each individual interprets the original author's intent in including the term. When common agreement regarding the classification of the term is reached, the criterion of specificity will be found among those used.

These informative terms could be formed into pairs describing the ideas presented. These pairs would be:

Calcification with respectively, markers, cardiovascular, risk, mammograms, women, breast, cancer

Markers with respectively, calcification, cardiovascular, risk, mammograms, women, breast, cancer

Cardiovascular with respectively, calcification, markers, risk, mammograms, women, breast, cancer

116

Risk with respectively, calcification, markers, cardiovascular, mammograms, women, breast, cancer

Mammograms with respectively, calcification, markers, cardiovascular, risk, women, breast, cancer

Women with respectively, calcification, markers, cardiovascular, risk, mammograms, breast, cancer

Breast with respectively, calcification, markers, cardiovascular, risk, mammograms, women, cancer

Cancer with respectively, calcification, markers, cardiovascular, risk, mammograms, women, breast

The authors used the following sequential pairs in providing thoughts in their sentence:

Calcification with markers

Markers with cardiovascular

Cardiovascular with risk

Risk with mammograms

Mammograms with women

Women with breast

Breast with cancer

In addition to the pairs above, however, the transitive law from mathematics suggests that the terms within the sentence are all interrelated. The transitive law is – if A equals B and B equals C, then A equals C. In a similar fashion, the highlighted terms could form complex arrangements. One such is shown in the sentence. The author constructed a complex idea involving eight terms. An alternative interpretation is that the authors constructed a concept based on the integration of a number of ideas, each composed of two terms. The number of such pairs would be –

$$n! \ / \ r! \ (n-r)! = 8x7x6x5x4x3x2x1 \ / \ (2x1)(6x5x4x3x2x1) = 8 \ x \ 7 \ / \ 2 = 28.$$

The symbol, *n*, is the total number of terms and *r* is the number of terms considered as a unit. From the 28 available pairs, the authors chose the ones shown to include in the sentence. In addition, the order of selection conformed to their intent to describe a particular situation. Another author could use the same ideas in a different arrangement.

Retrieving and Working with Subsets of Idea Records: With the ideas contained in a digital resource, software could be used to select and analyze specific subsets. Each record satisfies the definition of an idea – a primary and related term – contained within a specific sentence. Exhibit 2 shows an example of the idea records built by the text analysis software – Idea Analysis[tm]. The variables included in the record are – primary term, related term, year, identification number, sentence number. These are separated by pound signs (#). Records are stored in idea files. These idea files are labeled – ID101A.ext, ID102A.ext, etc.

As an example of the recall process, the Scholar's WorkStation contains 3 recall programs. The *primary* program identifies the ideas involving a specific term found in the first location within each record. The programs -- *related* and *triads* -- produce more complex set of ideas. The *related* program is used to identify a term in the second position for each record. This term was linked by authors to the common primary term. The identification numbers for documents containing the desired couplet are retrieved. The data records generated by the *triads* programs contain the central idea plus a third term from the same sentence.

Exhibit 2. Idea Records Representing Breast Disease

abdominal#adiposity#2009#19863467 # 3
abdominal#data#2009#19863467 # 3
abdominal#health#2009#19863467 # 3
abdominal#hormone#2009#19863467 # 3
abdominal#incidence#2009#19863467 # 3
abdominal#menopausal#2009#19863467 # 3
abdominal#metabolic#2009#19863467 # 3
abdominal#osteoporosis#2009#19863467 # 3
abdominal#placebo#2009#19863467 # 3
abdominal#women#2009#19863467 # 3
ablation#breast#2009#19913265 # 1
ablation#breast#2009#19913265 # 2
ablation#radiofrequency#2009#19913265 # 1
ablation#radiofrequency#2009#19913265 # 2
ablation#sonograph#2009#19913265 # 2
acid#breast#2009#20008677 # 1
acid#cancer#2009#20008677 # 1
acid#consumption#2009#19886512 # 6
acid#estrogen#2009#20008677 # 1
acid#lactation#2009#19886512 # 6
acid#nuclear#2009#20008677 # 1
acid#peroxisome#2009#20008677 # 1
acid#progression#2009#20008677 # 1
acid#receptor#2009#20008677 # 1
acid#women#2009#19886512 # 6
adenopathy#arthritis#2009#19847590 # 4
                    etc.

There are security systems that block the function of programs such as the above three. In that case, the idea files can be entered into excel and using the pound sign (#) separate the items into columns. The data can be sorted and then, searched using the FIND function to identify the records containing the designated primary term. Those can be color coded. The file can then be sorted using IDENT, SENTENCE, AND RELATED columns. This will bring all of the records from the same sentence together. Browsing through the file, the other record members of the sentence containing a color coded primary record can be color coded. The file can then be FILTERED and sorted by color. That function brings all of the color coded records to the top of the file. Those records can be copied and placed in a new excel file. That subset contains all of the records that would be obtained using the primary, related, and triads program. That subset of records can be processed to answer other questions.

Idea File Examples: Table 1 shows some of the ideas involving the primary term – breast. Related terms showed the range of vocabulary terms linked with the primary. One of those related terms is – cancer. The idea records are arranged by sentence for each identification number. This organization shows the ideas considered by each author. The related terms now shows the vocabulary linked by the authors to this central term.

Table 1. Terms Linked with Breast in the 2009 Literature – From Excel File.

Breast	Related	Year	Ident	Sentence
breast	ablation	2009	19913265	1
breast	ablation	2009	19913265	2
breast	acid	2009	20008677	1
breast	adenopathy	2009	19830102	8
breast	adriamycin	2009	19851170	2
breast	african	2009	19859902	1
breast	african	2009	19865486	1
breast	age	2009	19999267	10
breast	alcohol	2009	20104980	3
breast	allele	2009	19927780	3
breast	allelic	2009	19927780	3
breast	anthracycline	2009	19851170	2
breast	anthracycline	2009	20004966	10
	:	:	:	
breast	cancer	2009	19964909	1
breast	cancer	2009	20104976	1
breast	cancer	2009	20104976	2
breast	cancer	2009	20104976	10
breast	cancer	2009	20104976	11
breast	capsular	2009	19830102	5
breast	carcinogen	2009	19930591	1
breast	carcinoma	2009	19999267	6
breast	carcinoma	2009	19805950	1
breast	carcinoma	2009	19805950	2
	etc.		etc.	

Exhibit 3. Sentence 1 from Article 18392696 Showing Use of Informative Terms to Form Triadic Ideas with the Central Idea – Breast Cancer.

> Obesity is a risk factor for postmenopausal breast cancer, particularly for development of estrogen-receptor (ER)-positive tumors. [Nkhata KJ, Ray A, Dogan S, Grande JP, Cleary MP. Mammary tumor development from T47-D human breast cancer cells in obese ovariectomized mice with and without estradiol supplements. Breast Cancer Res Treat. 2009 Mar;114(1):71-83.]

Exhibit 3 shows another sentence. This sentence can be used to demonstrate a triadic idea. That form approximates the beginning of concepts. A concept is defined as a construction of multiple ideas to form a description of a phenomenon. The triadic idea is operationally defined as a combination of a central idea plus a third term, all within the same sentence. Assume that the central idea is – breast cancer. The triadic ideas in this sentence would be –

> *Breast cancer with obesity,*
> *Breast cancer with risk,*
> *Breast cancer with menopausal,*
> *Breast cancer with estrogen,*
> *Breast cancer with receptor, and*
> *Breast cancer with tumor*

Table 2 shows an excerpt of these triadic ideas based on the central idea – breast & cancer.

Table 2. Excerpt from Breast Cancer Triadic Ideas – 2009 – Excel File.

Breast	Cancer	Related	Year	Ident	Sentence
breast	cancer		2009	19956155	6
breast	cancer	colon	2009	19956155	6
breast	cancer	death	2009	19956155	6
breast	cancer	lung	2009	19956155	6
breast	cancer	prostate	2009	19956155	6
breast	cancer		2009	19956155	7
breast	cancer	kidney	2009	19956155	7
breast	cancer	lung	2009	19956155	7
breast	cancer	prostate	2009	19956155	7
breast	cancer	stomach	2009	19956155	7
breast	cancer		2009	19996622	1
breast	cancer	ethnic	2009	19996622	1
breast	cancer	women	2009	19996622	1
breast	cancer		2009	19996622	5
breast	cancer		2009	19996622	10
breast	cancer	detect	2009	19996622	10
	etc		etc		

Vocabulary of Informative Terms: Table 3 shows the terms in the vocabulary arranged by number of times each was linked with the central idea – breast cancer – for 2006-2009. The terms are ranked using the frequencies in 2009. This display facilitates comparison of use of ideas across time. High frequency ideas represent a type of consensus among the specialists. Those ideas depict current understanding of the topic. Low frequency ideas may represent those that are increasing or decreasing in popularity. They reflect the change in assignment of importance.

Table 3. Excerpt from Breast Cancer Triadic Idea Vocabulary – Excel File.

Breast Cancer Related Terms	2006	2007	2008	2009
risk	1347	2261	1765	1585
women	1291	2224	1651	1574
gene	845	1345	1073	1433
tumor	886	1227	1147	1158
expression	840	1390	1160	1135
receptor	522	851	815	800
data	468	618	664	617
estrogen	493	769	734	608
inhibit	402	638	594	599
metastatic	368	593	590	577
protein	433	583	587	545
survival	372	616	480	496
growth	348	534	530	467
stage	323	673	469	465
detect	330	521	475	423
primary	361	556	496	421
invasive	323	587	466	417
chemotherapy	344	612	472	411
screening	306	438	421	391
menopausal	302	563	410	369
node	339	473	427	363

Displaying the Ideas: Table 3 shows that the frequency of breast cancer related triadic ideas varies from 4 digit values to lower three digit ones. While different terms were linked with the central idea, in different concentrations, the number of times each term was linked with the central idea – breast cancer – was comparable for the years 2006-2009.

Figure 3 shows these higher frequency terms classified into groupings based on generic dimensions. These dimensions are:

1. Personal factors – variables describing attributes representing the individuals studied.
2. Disease factors – variables describing attributes of the disease. These were further classified into subgroups called concepts. These subgroups satisfy the definition of a

concept -- *an idea of something formed by combining all its characteristics or particulars.*

3. Treatment factors – variables describing the intervention used in treatment of the disease.
4. Outcome factors – variables representing results of the interactions between treatment and the disease factors and the interactions between disease and methods factors.
5. Method factors – methods and measures representing procedures used in determining characteristics and attributes in the other dimensions.

Figure 3. Higher Frequency Terms Linked with the Central Idea – Breast Cancer.

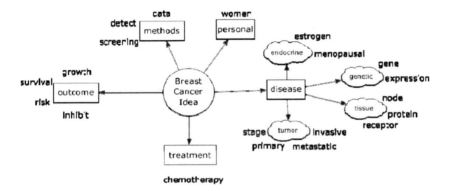

Describing the Topic using Ideas: A path could be developed based on the organization of the dimensions. That would be – personal factors → disease factors → treatment factors → outcome factors. The methods factors could be linked with any of the others. Examples would be:

women → breast cancer → stage → chemotherapy → survival.

That path would be appropriate in describing the effects of treatment with respect to outcome in women defined with specific stages of breast cancer.

Another path describing the triadic ideas from document 18392696 is shown in Table 4. This display shows an alphabetic arrangement of the terms related to the central idea.

122

Table 4. Terms Linked with Central Idea – Breast Cancer – from Document 18392696.

Breast	Cancer	Related	Year	Ident	Sentence
breast	cancer	estrogen	2009	18392696	1
breast	cancer	menopausal	2009	18392696	1
breast	cancer	obesity	2009	18392696	1
breast	cancer	receptor	2009	18392696	1
breast	cancer	risk	2009	18392696	1
breast	cancer	tumor	2009	18392696	1

This path is comparable to the one used in article 18392696.

women → breast cancer → menopausal → estrogen → receptor → risk.

The personal factor is now augmented with a disease factor from the endocrine concept giving – menopausal women. The disease factors from endocrine and tissue concepts (i.e., estrogen and receptor, respectively) led to a term from the outcome factors (risk).

Building Conceptual Structures: In addition to the enhanced efficiency in retrieval of individual abstracts, the Scholar's WorkStation offers advantages in building new descriptions of a topic. In this setting, the focus is not on retrieval but, instead, on building conceptual structures.

Ideas are building blocks and are dimension free. By considering these ideas and the way they can be combined, conceptual structures can be built. That process is the cognitive function of synthesis. The resulting structures can be compared using established criteria for assessment of the information potential associated with each. Criteria can be developed to select the conceptual structure that best fits new intentions. Criteria can be developed together with a plan to translate the conceptual structure into a new information capture and knowledge generating exercise.

The benefit of this creation process is the diversity that can result. There is no 'right' synthesis that will provide the ultimate information. The synthesis that is chosen is frequently the one that provides economic feasibility, study capability, and knowledge enhancement to some degree. Since these criteria are arbitrary and must be tailored to fit the needs of the investigator, any number of syntheses could be declared to be the 'best'.

When the syntheses, comparisons, evaluations, and judgments have been performed, specific data will be needed to construct the application of interest. At this stage in knowledge organization, the data contained in specific documents will be essential. Those documents are the ones that must be retrieved and carefully studied. Typically, that set constitutes less than 10% of the total number initially retrieved. With the Scholar WorkStation approach, the documents to retrieve are known. That simplifies the development considerably.

Backward Analysis Using Idea Tracking: When the subject area is new and essentially foreign, it is difficult to decide relevance of ideas. One useful approach is to develop an analysis of a subject specialist's text. Two sources are useful. One is RePort (Research Portfolio Online Reporting Tools) [http://report.nih.gov/] and the other is abstracts from PubMed. The RePort database reports the abstracts for research proposals that have been submitted to various governmental agencies. Each of these proposals would be scrutinized by a committee of peers. Those approved would be funded and the research initiated. The PubMed abstract represents another version of peer review and approval. A manuscript is submitted to a journal. An editorial and reviewer assessment of the manuscript is performed and the document assigned a priority for publication.

Assessment Criteria: In both situations, the proposed text is assessed by subject specialists and evaluated using a number of different criteria. The more frequent criteria involve timeliness, authority of the authors or organization, and clarity of presentation. These criteria focus on the characteristics of the presenter rather than those of the presentation. Criteria involving the content would include:

1. *Selection of primary issue.* The primary knowledge issue described in the text would be identified and judged. Is it innovative? Is it important? What are the ramifications associated with better understanding of the issue?
2. *Selection of knowledge generation procedures.* The methods used in identifying, organizing and utilizing the informational elements would be assessed. Is the new description accurate? Is it comprehensive? Does the description identify gaps and/or inconsistencies in the described issues?
3. *Alteration of the wisdom base.* The role of the subject expert includes development of wisdom by prioritizing and organizing existing knowledge. A document considered to be innovative and important would be expected to change established wisdom by supplying new information and insights.

These and related criteria are based on the assumption that the individual has sufficient knowledge to make accurate assessments. The focus on author ideas, however, provides the necessary information to make such evaluations. Comparing the consensus of world's ideas in a topic with those of a particular document provides evidence of the credibility of the document. The author, the organization represented, or the time of preparation take a backseat to the accuracy and completeness of the ideas presented.

In addition to learning and applying criteria in evaluating new text, the backward analysis aids in showing the novice how the expert built the particular innovative strategy approved by peer review. This form of second guessing is helpful in identifying the conceptual structure of ideas employed by the subject specialist.

Prostate Cancer and Genetic Epidemiology: To illustrate this, consider the abstract from RePort[Stanford JL. Genetic Epidemiology of Prostate Cancer, 5R01CA080122-08, from 2006 RePort database]. This abstract represented a request for continuation of a previously funded program. As such, many of the ideas involved in the conceptual structure will be established. The search, then, is directed toward those ideas that represent new or newer contributions to the knowledge generation exercise. To accomplish this feat requires awareness and organization of previous work as well as procedure to recognize established versus new entries. The author's abstract follows:

*This proposal is a competitive renewal for the grant entitled, "**Genetic Epidemiology of Prostate Cancer**" The project involves a multidisciplinary group of researchers working on The **Prostate Cancer Genetic** Research Study (PROGRESS), an investigation of high-risk prostate cancer families aimed at **mapping loci** for the **hereditary** form of this disease. In addition, the study aims to further knowledge of the **genetic epidemiology** and **molecular biology** of **prostate cancer**. During the grant period covered by this continuation, we will utilize baseline and follow-up **survey data**, medical records, **genotyping data**, and **DNA samples** from members of PROGRESS **families** to address the following primary aims: 1) To complete **linkage** analyses of 421 **genome**-wide **markers** in 255 **hereditary prostate cancer** (HPC) **families** stratified by the presence of other primary **cancers** in the family; 2) To complete **linkage** and regression analyses of 421 **genome**-wide **markers** in 255 PROGRESS **families**, incorporating clinical **data** to search for **loci** associated with more aggressive **phenotypes**; 3) To **genotype** selected PROGRESS **families** for **mutations** in the **BRCA2 gene** to determine the role of such **mutations** in HPC; and, 4) To continue follow-up of members of 271 HPC **families**, with expansion of **pedigrees** and **data** collection as men newly diagnosed with **prostate cancer** are identified. In addition to the primary aims, we will address the following secondary aims: 5) To continue recruitment of **African American families** with **prostate cancer**; and, 6) To evaluate knowledge of and interest in **genetic** testing among affected and unaffected men. **Genomic scan data**, family **cancer** history **data**, and clinical **data** on **prostate** cases will be available. These **data** will be used to stratify **families** into more homogeneous subgroups for **linkage** analyses and to incorporate such **data** into regression models as quantitative traits. These approaches may lead to identification of new **loci** for HPC, including those linked to more aggressive disease. PROGRESS is a unique resource for addressing these aims and represents one of the largest collections of HPC **families** in the world. Finding such **linkages** and associated **genes** may provide novel and important insights into the underlying **genetic epidemiology** of **prostate cancer**, including the **hereditary** and sporadic forms of this common and complex disease.*

The informative terms are highlighted. These form the vocabulary that will be compared with the one used in the epidemiology research Scholar WorkStation.

Identifying Triads: Triads of informative terms can be identified from sentences containing a designated idea. In the sentences retrieved, the central idea was – *prostate* & *cancer*. Triads involving this idea help to develop a conceptual structure that is more specific than one based exclusively on pairs. In the triadic structure, the central node is composed of an idea. The terms related to this idea form a type of idea swarm more comparable to those presented by subject specialists. The words that occur with greatest frequency with an idea are called core terms. These represent a more precise description of the topic.

By identifying the terms forming triads with the designated idea, the subject specialist's organization of ideas can be better understood. As such, developing a path from the ideas to the triads to the conceptual structure developed by the expert is made more feasible.

Comparing Expert and Scholar WorkStation Vocabularies: The Scholar WorkStation vocabulary in epidemiologic research consists of approximately 1300 terms. In selecting terms for the vocabulary, the potential word must appear in an idea. In addition, the word must convey specific information about the topic. In this situation, the topic is epidemiologic research and while specific terms may have meaning, the question to be answered is, "Does the word have meaning in the specific topic of interest?"

Table 4 shows the terms chosen by the subject specialist in describing the funded epidemiologic study of prostate cancer entered in RePort. A total of 33 terms was used by the author. Of those, 7 terms did not match with the Scholar WorkStation vocabulary and 26 terms did match (82% agreement). The Scholar WorkStation vocabulary is used to identify ideas in new text. The terms not matching the Scholar WorkStation vocabulary were: BRCA2, Gleason [score], loci, mapping, PSA, scan, stage. Of these terms, some would be relevant and frequently used in diagnostic and management topics. Their application in epidemiologic research apparently was relatively rare. BRCA2 and PSA are examples of terms that could and should have been frequently employed in epidemiologic research.

Table 4. Terms from Expert Text.

Absent Terms	Matching Terms	Matching Terms
BRCA	biologic	linkage
Gleason	chromosome	marker
loci	data	molecular
mapping	DNA	mutation
PSA	epidemiology	pedigree
scan	families	phenotype
stage	gene	sample
MatchingTerms	genetic	screening
age	genome	survey
risk	genomic	susceptibility
african	genotype	
american	hereditary	

Is a 80% Match Between Vocabularies Satisfactory? The computer software can identify every noun and incorporate those words in the Scholar WorkStation vocabulary. Would that be an efficient approach? Nouns have been divided into two groups. The first consists of words that describe some attribute of the topic. The second consists of words that are non-specific. Since the number of ideas stored in the Scholar WorkStation is a function of the number of informative terms in each sentence, there is a trade-off between having a sufficient number of ideas that aid in describing the topic versus a larger number of ideas including many that provide general or irrelevant information. By invoking rules based on frequency of occurrence of new terms in update, the resulting vocabulary tends to consist of 80% of the terms used by specialists in their descriptions of the topic.

Sequential Ideas in Expert Text: As previously discussed, one idea extraction procedure involved sequential identification of ideas in each sentence. This approach was applied to the expert's text. The ideas from that text have been extracted and organized and are shown in Table 5. The sequential analysis approach yielded a subset of ideas.

Table 5A shows the nodes involving central terms: cancer, data, epidemiology, and families. Associated with each nodal term are terms forming ideas. These ideas expand the basic idea – prostate & cancer. Table 5B shows the other nodal terms with their related terms.   The distinction between Tables 5A and B are in terms of number of ideas associated with each node.
Two columns in Table 5 describe weightings. The weighting values represent the number of times each of the terms was linked with the prostate & cancer idea in the sentences retrieved from the epidemiology research Scholar WorkStation. These weightings show the collective emphasis by the specialists in epidemiologic research and prostate cancer. If a term was frequently included in a sentence with the primary idea, the term can be assumed to be important. If the term was included rarely, an assumption of lesser importance may be reasonable. Used in this way, the weightings help identify a rationale for the expert's proposal. In a comparable fashion, these weightings may aid in discerning the reason that the review committee approved the proposal.

Table 5A. Sequential Ideas Linked with Prostate Cancer
from Expert Text. More Links.

Weight	Nodal Term	Related Term	Weight
		families	47
3853	cancer	genetic	87
		hereditary	41
		prostate	3478
		DNA	25
199	data	genotyping	99
		medical	29
		survey	16
		genetic	87
70	epidemiology	molecular	34
		prostate	3478
		cancer	3853
47	families	mapping	3
		samples	41

127

Table 5B. Sequential Ideas Linked with Prostate Cancer from Expert Text. Fewer Links.

Weight	Nodal Term	Related Term	Weight
		gene	97
87	genetic	epidemiology	70
		research	36
6	genome	analyses	139
		markers	60
24	linkages	analyses	139
		gene	97
1012	risk	prostate	3478
		research	36

Analysis of the Ideas in the Conceptual Structure: The swarms in Table 5 form a conceptual structure depicting the expert's perceptions of the topic. The nodes form the following structure– *cancer* → *data* → *epidemiology* → *families* → *genetic* → *genome* → *linkages* → *risk*. The order of the nodal terms is dictated by the frequency of related terms. The first idea swarms associated with the prostate cancer idea had nodal terms, cancer and data. Four terms were linked, by the expert, to each primary. The third, fourth and fifth swarms involved primary terms -- epidemiology, families, and genetic with three terms related to each primary. The last swarms were genome, linkages and risk. Each was associated with two terms. These swarms make up the expert's set of ideas, as perceived using the *sequential idea identification* method.

Central Idea Identification: An alternative approach in idea analysis involves identification of all terms linked to a central term. In this situation, the central node is the idea – prostate & cancer.

Table 6 shows the terms from the expert's sentences linked with the idea – prostate & cancer. Each half of the table consists of three columns. The first column describes the number of times each term was linked to the central idea. For example, the term – families – was linked with the idea 8 times in research proposal sentences [Stanford 2006]. The second column describes the terms serving as nodes in that text. The third shows the frequency of each term in sentences containing the idea – prostate & cancer. The highlighted terms represent those with low frequencies in the involved sentences. When terms in Tables 5 and 6 are compared, the terms added in Table 6 were -- mutation, African, American, and biology.

The terms with the lowest weightings were: mapping (3), biology (4), phenotype (4), genome (6), and loci (9). Those indicate that the world's literature dealing with the epidemiologic research and the idea -- prostate & cancer, prior to the development of the expert's text [Stanford 2006], did not include sufficient exploration of the involved ideas. Those ideas, while not missing from the epidemiologic literature dealing with prostate cancer, may have suggested to the expert and the review committee that additional study of these ideas would be notable.

Table 6. Terms Linked to Central Idea – Prostate & Cancer.

Frequency	Terms	Weight	Frequency	Terms	Weight
8	families	47	1	African	70
4	genetic	87	1	American	70
5	hereditary	41	1	**biology**	4
3	data	199	1	BRCA2	27
3	linkage	24	1	DNA	25
2	gene	97	1	**mapping**	3
2	**genome**	6	1	**pedigree**	6
2	genotype	99	1	**phenotype**	4
2	**loci**	9	1	risk	1012
2	marker	60	1	samples	41
2	mutation	42	1	survey	16

This chapter showed a process that allows the student to *duplicate the results of the expert's method instead of the procedure that the expert might have employed.* The backward analysis is designed to take the specialist's result and show a reproducible path leading to that result. Accordingly, this approach is more useful in learning a subject and related decision criteria.

Decision Paths in Funding Research Proposals: This example of prostate cancer and genetic epidemiology illustrated one of the three conceptual structure development paths resulting in favorable funding of research proposals. Those paths involve the following conditions:

1. *The ideas considered have not been employed in the topic.* This is the most frequently used path to new knowledge generation, although, manual identification of a missing idea could represent an extraordinary amount of work. This is the procedure most frequently employed in the forward analysis. This is the one that Scholar WorkStations were designed to address.

2. *The ideas considered have been studied previously with conflicting results.* This is the situation where studies report statistically significant findings and others report non-significance. As such, the ideas are clearly enunciated but the methods previously used could be flawed. This also is the one where study conditions may have been inadequate. This path can be objectively explored by identifying the frequency of statistically significant, non-significant and non-tested results expressed in the sentences of the encyclopedia. Scholar WorkStation repositories transform this task from a manually intensive effort to one that uses cognitive functions effectively.

3. *The ideas have been infrequently considered previously.* In this decision process, the available information is insufficient and additional studies would be required. The ideas of interest have been previously considered, but, in the opinion of the investigator and reviewers, additional data are required. An objective approach to this path would begin with a backward analysis and

129

weightings from an encyclopedia of sentences containing specific ideas. The prostate cancer – genetic epidemiology scenario illustrated this decision path.

Forward Analysis: The forward analysis approach relies on an organization of the total set of ideas and a subsequent reduction in ideas until a feasible concept structure is developed. Table 7 shows the informative terms linked with the idea – prostate & cancer, from two repositories. The first contains ideas dealing with prostate & cancer. The second is the genetic & cancer resource. The column entitled, Ca-P, shows the frequencies for terms linked with the idea – prostate & cancer. In the first half of the table, the terms are arranged in descending order of occurrence in those sentences. The column entitled, Gen-1, shows the frequencies linked with the two ideas – prostate & cancer and genetic & epidemiologic from the prostate & cancer. The column, labeled Gen-2, shows the same terms now identified in sentences from the genetic & cancer resource. The terms are organized based on descending order of occurrence.

Table 7. Informative Terms Linked with Designated Ideas.

Term	Ca-P	Gen-1	Term	Ca-P	Gen-2
genetic	942	13	cancer	106	14
epidemiologic	829	12	genetic	942	13
risk	153	3	prostate	13	13
molecular	124	4	epidemiologic	829	12
data	123	3	molecular	124	4
cancer	106	14	hereditary	14	4
population	105	2	risk	153	3
genes	71	3	data	123	3
marker	44	3	genes	71	3
genes	35	2	marker	44	3
genotype	35	0	population	105	2
DNA	26	0	gene	35	2
sample	25	0	linkage	20	1
families	21	0	lung	15	1
linkage	20	1	breast	12	1
lung	15	1	case-control	9	1
hereditary	14	4	genotype	35	0
mutation	14	0	DNA	26	0
prostate	13	13	sample	25	0
breast	12	1	families	21	0
case-control	9	1	mutation	14	0

The Gen-2 column in Table 7 approximates the conceptual structure seen in the funded research proposal. The more frequent terms were *cancer → prostate → genetic → epidemiology*. The lesser frequent terms were: molecular, hereditary, risk, data, genes, marker, population, linkage, lung, breast, and case-control. The terms -- genotype, DNA, sample, families, and mutation –

were observed 0 times in these sentences. These missing ideas create a situation comparable to the first decision path discussed above. Missing ideas are the easiest to justify as contributing new information to the existing knowledge. Of the terms shown, lung, breast, and case-control were not included in the funded research proposal.

History of Hereditary Prostate Cancer and Genetic Assessment: The earliest publication in PubMed dealing with prostate cancer and familial aggregation of cases was in 1984. [Flanders 1984] Links between epidemiologic investigation using genetic characteristics and familial aggregation of prostate cancer was discussed in a paper published in 1992. [Sandberg, 1992] Exploration of genetic characteristics in men with family history of cancer was expanded to include Caucasians, African Americans and Asians in 1995. [Whittemore 1995] The author of the funded research proposal [Stanford JL, 2006] participated in 7 articles published between 2000 and 2006. The association between prostate cancer, familial aggregation of cases, and genetic measures was published in 2000. [Goode, 2000]

The relationship between family history of prostate cancer and the presentation of new cases was studied in multiracial groups. [Cotter 2002] In addition, a study was approved exploring hereditary prostate cancer in African American families.[Cooney, 1999] Also in 1999, Stanford and colleagues submitted their subsequently funded proposal to study genetic polymorphisms and risk of prostate cancer.[Stanford 1999] That proposal linked genetic characteristics with family history of cancer. The phrase – hereditary prostate cancer – was not included in that proposal.

Hereditary prostate cancer as an important concept has appeared in 56 scientific publications between 1995 and 2006 and genetic characteristics were featured in a paper published in 1997. [Gronberg, 1997]

However, the link between hereditary prostate cancer and genetic epidemiology was described in general terms. This relation was further clarified by two articles identified from the Scholar WorkStation sentences containing the combined ideas. Those abstracts were:

> *OBJECTIVES: To conduct **genetic linkage** analysis in order to localize predisposition **genes** for **hereditary prostate cancer** (CaP), as various **epidemiologica**l studies have demonstrated a family aggregation in 15 to 25% of cases, and the development of **hereditary** forms in 5 to 10% of cases of CaP. MATERIAL AND METHODS: A **genetic** study on 47 French and German **families** included 122 patients and 72 subjects considered to be healthy after **PSA** assay. This study was conducted by **linkage** analysis of 364 microsatellite **markers** distributed throughout the **genome** (on average every 10 cM). RESULTS: Parametric and nonparametric **linkage** analysis identified a locus on **chromosome** 1q 42.2-43, which could be with a **gene** predisposing to CaP (called PCaP). The primary site was confirmed by several **markers**, using 3 different **genetic** models. The maximum LOD score (probability of **linkage** between the locus and the disease) on two-point analysis was 2.7 for the D1S2785 **marker**. Parametric and nonparametric multipoint analysis provided an HLOD score and an NPL score of 2.2 and 3.1, respectively (with P = 0.001). Heterogeneity analysis with calculations of LOD scores by multipoint analysis estimated that up to 50% of **hereditary** CaPs were related*

to this locus, with a heterogeneity probability of 157/1. Analysis of a subgroup of 9/47 **families** *characterized by early onset CaP (before the age of 60 years) confirmed the very high probability of localization of a predisposition* **gene** *at locus 1q42.2-43 for these* **families** *(multipoint LOD score and NPL score of 3.31 and 3.32, respectively; with P = 0.001). CONCLUSION: The identification of predisposition* **genes** *will eventually allow identification within certain* **families** *of those subjects who have inherited the* **genetic** *abnormality and who therefore present a high risk of CaP. It will then be possible to perform targeted* **screening** *of CaP in order to diagnose CaP as early as possible. PMID: 10555221* [Valeri 1999]

PURPOSE: We review the current *epidemiologica*l and *genetic* knowledge regarding *hereditary prostate cancer*, and outline its clinical implications. MATERIALS AND METHODS: Published articles on *hereditary prostate cancer* were identified using the MEDLINE data base. RESULTS: A risk of *prostate cancer*, particularly early onset disease, is strongly affected by *families* history (number of relatives with *prostate cancer* and their *age* at diagnosis). A *families* history of *prostate cancer* increases the positive predictive value of *PSA* testing and, hence, *hereditary* should always be assessed when deciding whether to perform biopsies in a man with a *PSA* level of 3 to 10 ng./ml. *Epidemiologica*l studies indicate that dominantly inherited susceptibility *genes* with high penetrance cause 5% to 10% of all *prostate cancer* cases, and as much as 30% to 40% of early onset disease. More than a half dozen *chromosome loci* that may comprise such *genes* have been mapped, but as of May 2002 no *prostate cancer* susceptibility *gene* of major importance had been cloned. Most likely, environmental factors and comparatively common variants of several other *genes* affect *prostate cancer* risk in *families* with or without multiple cases of the disease. On average, *hereditary prostate cancer* is diagnosed 6 to 7 years earlier than sporadic *prostate cancer*, but does not otherwise differ clinically from the sporadic form. As a consequence of the earlier onset, a greater proportion of *men* with *hereditary prostate cancer* die of the disease than those with non*hereditary prostate cancer*. At present, the only clinically applicable measure to reduce *prostate cancer* mortality in *families* with *hereditary* disease is *screening*, with the aim of diagnosing the disease when it is still in a curable stage. CONCLUSIONS: *Hereditary* susceptibility is now considered the strongest risk factor for *prostate cancer* and has profound clinical importance. The *genetic* mechanism behind such susceptibility has turned out to be more complex than initially thought, and will probably not be completely understood for many years to come. PMID: 12187189 [Bratt, 2002.]

These two articles, one from France and one from Sweden, emphasize the importance of studying the genetic characteristics of individuals and families with hereditary prostate cancer. It is possible that these articles providing the specific connections were considered relevant by Stanford and colleagues [Stanford 2006] as they crafted their renewal proposal funded in 2006.

Summary

In this example, both backward and forward analyses led to the conclusion that the ideas proposed in the funded research application were not new. Instead, the analyses showed that additional data were needed to clarify the conceptual structure. The investigators of the funded proposal proposed to do just that.

The investigation began with a backward analysis designed to trace the final product of the investigators' intellectual efforts back to the origins of those ideas in the literature. Once those ideas were identified, the frequency of each was determined in the literature. Those occurring infrequently would be of value to pursue in order to clarify existing knowledge. Those occurring more frequently could be used to form the systemic structure representing the topic. In the example, four terms represented this structure – prostate → cancer → genetic → epidemiologic. The rarer terms formed the basis of the proposed research. Those were focused on assessing genes and related issues in families with history of prostate cancer. This emphasis on hereditary prostate cancer was, undoubtedly, a strong point in the proposed research.

The identification of the desired concept structure was approached using the forward analysis. In that method, the total set of ideas from the epidemiologic research Scholar WorkStation was used to determine the ideas of interest. The first exploration involved retrieval of the sentences containing the idea – prostate & cancer. These sentences were used in supporting the backward analysis. The second exploration involved retrieval of sentences containing the idea – genetic & epidemiologic. These sentences were further reduced by selecting those sentences containing both ideas – prostate & cancer and genetic & epidemiologic. This exploration was designed to identify terms linked to the two ideas in sentences. These terms form the basis for developing a knowledge generation strategy. The terms involved were shown in Table 7.

In addition to determining a developmental path that yields the same result as the investigator's intellectual efforts, there are other advantages to these objective approaches. An important result is that the guidance of the experts (in terms of their ideas) can be relied upon when building a credible conceptual structure representing the topic.

Another result is that the time involved in matching the expert's results is significantly shorter. The organization of the pertinent vocabulary, as ideas provided by the specialists, helps speed up the analytic process. One reduction is due to the elimination of the mechanical tasks in extracting and organizing the data. That has been accomplished using the computer software. Once the ideas have been stripped from the article, the need to go back for new information is based on specific requirements – methods or data results.

A third advantage is the availability of the knowledge resource in a personalized format – the Scholar's WorkStation. By having continuing free access to the resource, the user can pick his/her time from any location.

A fourth advantage is the ability to document each step in the analysis, thus leaving an audit trail. This quality control device is an essential part of a credible research process. Having the ability to trace each step in the evolution of a new research strategy or a new description of a topic means a significant reduction in frustration. Some of the audit products are produced by the software. Others are prepared by the analyst.

Chapter Nine – Developing Research Strategies

Introduction

The methodology involving ideas as building blocks has been found to be effective in developing new descriptions of topics and in developing new research strategies. This success is not surprising since it follows the '*natural*' investigative process:
1. Determine the existence of a problem (*Discovery of an Idea*).
2. Develop a detailed description of that problem (**Problem Description**).
3. Develop an appropriate intervention to correct or eliminate the problem (**Interventions**).
4. Conduct a detailed, quality-controlled process to bring the intervention and the problem together (**Protocol Development**).
5. Capture the findings of this interaction (**Study Conduct**).
6. Analyze the findings against the original description of the problem (**Analyses**).
7. Develop and disseminate the results of the process with emphasis on the modifications necessary to existing knowledge (**Report Preparation**).
8. Ensure that others can benefit by making the development process transparent (**Data Curation**).

The research design system is illustrated. Seven phases of activities comprise the components of the research design. While there are different basic designs to deal with generation of specific knowledge, the phases described are essential to proper conduct. In each design, data collection, data management, staff and participant orientation, quality assurance, analytic exercises, generation of reports and study closing are important in ensuring that the investigation accomplishes its objectives. The tasks in these phases address the specific behaviors required of the investigative group and the participants. This interaction between the investigators and the participants, following the rules of research procedure, offers the best chance of generating credible information.

A research study is a complex process designed to answer specific questions and to generate information leading to new investigations. The process is the primary information generating approach and, when conducted as intended, is the most formalized set of behaviors used in acquiring new knowledge. There are different sets of procedures, each intended to address a specific type of question. By following the rules of development and conduct, investigators assure each other that careful attention has been paid to the quality of the information gathered. In addition, the fact that teams of investigators may be involved, each representing a unique specialty and perspective, requires that the design be clearly and completely understood and followed. The design ensures the quality of participant recruitment, compliance, data collection, data processing (entry, editing, storage, retrieval), analytic procedures employed and, ultimately, the quality of reports of the results with potential contributions to the body of knowledge.

To validate that the research study is properly developed and executed, the processes are divided into phases of activity.

Phase I - Design of data collection instruments.

Data collection instruments form the essence of a study. The measures and/or observations to be used are displayed. The process involved is as follows:

1. **Data forms and Sections:** Identify the questions making up a section of a form. A data form is operationally defined as a series of sections where each section consists of questions related to a specific characteristic. The data form is a circumscribed set of characteristics, all interrelated, in describing some aspect of the study.

   Examples of sections within a data form would be:

   a. *Identifying data* – name, address, phone, social security number, GIS (geographic information system) data. These items would be managed in a particularly secure fashion in order to protect confidentiality of the respondents while allowing designated persons access to the information as necessary. These encrypted data would be managed as a separate, independent component and access to this information would be carefully restricted. The only link between the remaining data and this set should be an arbitrarily generated identification number.

   b. *Past medical history* – diseases experienced by the respondent. Depending on the study, highlights of each disease course and pertinent measures would be recorded.

   c. *Hobbies* – recreational behaviors experienced by the respondent.

   d. *Occupational history* – work-related behaviors experienced by the respondent.

   e. *Exposure history* – substances and diet experienced by the respondent. The different environments experienced by the individual could be of value.

   f. *Laboratory measures* of various body tissues and/or fluids.

   g. *Collection and transmittal* of laboratory specimens by research institutions to designated research laboratories.

   h. *Outcome experience* –beneficial and adverse events associated with the purpose of the study.

2. **Numeric Responses:** Draft the questions within a section and assign the appropriate response set to each. While the data can be made secure using modern techniques, the most effective security measure continues to be seemingly random numeric entries. The entries may be one of the following:

136

a. Scaled Values. The size of the data field is described during the design of the form and the numbers of digits preceding and following the decimal point are specified.

b. Date entries using the format -- month, day and year. The full four characters of the year are used.

c. Coded entries using numbers to depict various types of text descriptors. If a single choice, the number assigned to each choice could be scaled. An example of this option would be a Likert scale with, say, 1 representing minimal and 7 representing maximal. Values between 1 and 7 would represent degrees of agreement between the extremes.

d. Check box entries consisting of codes 1 and 2. Code 2 is typically used to represent the presence of the attribute. Code 1 represents the absence of the attribute.

3. **Review and Evaluation:** This evaluation process, using expert reviewers, is the first step in the preparation of a form. The second step is to pilot the form to determine if the questions are appropriately worded and the responses represent the attributes considered. The pilot data are extracted and a report generated for evaluation by the investigator group. Items that appear suspect can be modified.

4. **Choice of a Database System:** When forms have evolved sufficiently, the final version should be constructed depending on the database system selected. The selected system is intended to perform the data management programming required to conduct the study. The critical entries in accomplishing this task are the question, the statistical label assigned to the variable, edit rules, and the type of response anticipated (scaled entries, coded entries, dates, or check boxes). With this information, data entry can be readily accomplished using the selected database tools.

5. **Final version:** With the construction of the data management process, final pilot data can be collected and evaluated. Modifications to the data form(s) can be reviewed by the investigator group and the accepted version(s) used in the study.

Phase II - Development of Manual of Procedures.

The Manual of Procedures consists of two types of documents. The first type is a description of the data collection process including a display of the questions, statistical labels, and type of responses. This document is often described as a codebook. Each data collection instrument is described in detail.

The second type describes the study procedures. This document consists of a series of modules, each depicting a part of the study process. The modules can be reviewed for clarity and accuracy by the investigative group. Pertinent information can be presented in ways acceptable to professional staff. A current version of the manual of procedures would be available for use.

These documents are updated as changes are made in the study. The codebooks are updated as the data collection forms are changed. The instructional modules are updated as changes are instituted. An important advantage is the ability to keep this description of the study timely, accurate and available to the participants, staff and/or institutions participating.

Phase III - Preparation of Supplemental Information for Respondents.

Each respondent is required to sign an informed consent describing the study and its rationale. To supplement that, orientation modules can be prepared. The modules illustrate and re-enforce the important procedures in the study and provide rationales for these actions.

This instructional approach should provide sufficient information to the respondents so that they will better appreciate the study's intent and procedures. All respondents can receive orientation during attendance at the research locations, via private discussions with staff, or via computer-assisted instruction. As new information is acquired from the scientific literature or from the study findings, appropriate additional modules can be prepared and provided to respondents.

Phase IV - Data Quality Monitoring.

Once design of the study is completed and ready for execution, the program begins with recruitment of participants and associated collection of data. An important requirement from the outset is the establishment of data assurance monitoring procedures to ensure that the data being collected are timely, accurate and complete.

There are three types of data quality to be considered in a study of this type. The first is the *accuracy of reported data* and that can be assessed by inclusion of comparable questions within questionnaires to capture 'equal' responses at the time of interview and by prompt re-interview of randomly selected respondents to determine the consistency of their responses after some elapsed time.

A second form of data quality monitoring involves *extraction of selected data* for routine evaluation of performance associated with study conduct. These extractions are performed regularly to ensure adherence to the study protocol in terms of accrual of participants, adherence to the data collection schedule, acceptability of data, given defined ranges, consistency of findings within participant and within family as appropriate, and reliability of data in terms of correlated responses. These quality control measures are reported to the investigative group for evaluation and modification of the study as needed.

Reports can be developed for different users. These reports represent the ultimate reason for the study and should be subjected to the most rigorous quality control. New important findings can be translated into instructional modules for use by the research staff, participant group and other professionals.

Reports can include:

1. Participant Accrual.
2. Completeness of Baseline Questionnaire Data.
3. Accuracy of Selected Baseline Indicator Items.
4. Consistency of Paired Baseline Indicator Items.
5. Adherence to Laboratory Collection and Transmittal Procedures.
6. Completeness of Pre-Exposure Data.
7. Consistency of Pre-Exposure Data Over Time.
8. Completeness of Post-Exposure Data.
9. Consistency of Post-Exposure Data Over Time.
10. Outcome events.
11. Reporting Accuracy.

Progress Reports: In addition, progress reports can be generated according to a defined schedule summarizing important study landmarks. These include:

1. Accrual.
2. Description of the Baseline Questionnaire Data.
3. Description of Institutional Performance in Managing Laboratory Specimens.
4. Description of the Baseline Laboratory Data.
5. Temporal Patterns of Pre-Exposure Data.
6. Event Occurrence.
7. Temporal Patterns of Post-Exposure Data.
8. Specific Reports as Needed.

Phase V -Data Extractions for Interim Analyses.

The data are collected from each participant and entered into the data management system. These data can be used to determine the quality of the study in terms of adherence to the protocol as well as the correctness of the data entries.

Data extractions can be prepared to conform with study protocol requirements and special requests. These analytic files are developed to deal with specific scientific questions. The extractions enable answering of questions relevant in factors with respect to identified outcomes. In addition, extractions to consider patterns of change within individuals could be prepared for analysis. Similarly, multiple records associated with temporal assessment of identified families could be generated for analysis. If required, multiple records within defined subgroups could be selected for analysis.

Reports address the primary data extraction and analysis issues. These are:

1. Analysis using Baseline Questionnaire and Laboratory Data and Event Occurrence Data. These single records link to yield a composite record containing baseline and outcome data. This is the simplest form of data extraction.
2. Temporal Patterns within Single Individuals and/or Families. Using more complex selection and orientation procedures, any individual or family can be evaluated with respect to temporal charts of selected data. This analysis is frequently used in evaluating clinical progress by charting the multiple time series relevant to the question.
3. Temporal Patterns within defined subgroups. Using more advanced procedures, temporal subgroup statistics (e.g., means, medians, variances, ranges) can be computed and displayed.

Phase VI - Data Extractions for Definitive Analyses.

Data extractions can be prepared, as required, to provide analytic files directed toward answering specific scientific questions. These analytic files may explore risk factors associated with baseline characteristics and defined outcomes. In addition, multiple record files could be generated to explore temporal questions. These extractions undoubtedly could differ from the interim ones in terms of the data reduction requirements. The final analysis files could include records portraying the variables describing the baseline or change process together with the appropriate event variables.

Phase VII – End of the Study

The end of the study is an important phase and could involve additional time for maintenance of the database. Preservation of the data involves extraction of general analytic files. This extraction process yields the simplest approach to continued use of the data for exploration. In addition, the database would continue to be duplicated in the designated off-site locations together with the system programs required to manage the database. This replication of the host system ensures that any final analyses can be performed in a smooth and efficient fashion. This more elaborate approach ensures that complex questions can be addressed using the power of the systems developed for the study. While the majority of the study questions should be addressed during the study period, occurrence of rare events may require added time before analyses can be considered. By maintaining the data and the systems, these interesting questions can be considered by the investigative group.

Developing Research Strategies: Developing research strategies is tedious and time-consuming. While the computer can play a useful role, it cannot replace the individual. Or can it? Assume that innovative research satisfies one of two conditions:

1. The research is designed to supply the missing information.

2.   The research is designed to clarify conflicting results.

The computer can identify missing information by comparing findings in different topics. That process is essential in satisfying the first scenario. In meeting the requirements of the second scenario, the computer can present findings describing the conflict. That process is possible by searching for terms that have been used to assign importance to results. An example of that would be the search for statistically significant and non-significant results dealing with the same phenomenon.

These important tasks performed by computer software are still more mechanical than intellectual. In each situation, the software is instructed to compare patterns. That function can be performed with nearly 100% accuracy. Indeed, the strength of computer activity is in the transformation of the mechanical actions to potentially usable informational elements. Software can identify patterns by comparing them with established ones. Other programs can rapidly sort patterns. Software can process these patterns, according to defined rules, facilitating storage and retrieval. Computers can perform assigned functions repeatedly and tirelessly. Error rates, with respect to mechanical failures, are remarkably small. These capabilities mean that software can be constructed to accurately and rapidly identify, extract, organize, store and retrieve. The ingredients used can be numbers, terms, ideas (pairs of terms), sentences containing these ideas, and associated bibliographic data.

The proposed research could be feasible from a methodologic view. That is, the sample size could be adequate. The measurements could be correct in depicting the attributes of interest. The analytic approach could be effective in finding the secrets in the data. The proposed interpretations of findings could be accurate. While those are critical elements in the research, they don't describe the intangible required for innovation. The definition of the term focuses on something that is new. However, innovative research must be new and important or new and imaginative. Computer software can identify a new term, idea, sentence or reference. It can't recognize the importance of the finding and it certainly can't determine the degree of imagination involved. That judgment requires a decision performed by a trained individual. The ability to determine the importance of a phenomenon, in the context of a scientific topic, is a high priority in graduate and continuing post-graduate education.

Discovery Support Systems: The following analysis illustrates what has been described as a *discovery support system*.[Gordon 1996] The ultimate objective in this approach would be to use data mining techniques on existing literature to generate new hypotheses. This approach evolved from efforts by Weiner [Weiner 1979, 1983, 2004, 2005, 2009], Chen [Chen 1988], Hoffman [Hoffman 1980], [Smalheiser 1998], Srinvasan [Srinvasan 2004] and Weeber [Weeber 2003]. The first three authors introduced the concept that ideas were critical in understanding existing literature and in building new descriptions. The approach described by Smalheiser and Swanson involved a computer system termed *Arrowsmith*. That program was suggested to be effective in linking concepts across documents. However, this system relied on experts in recognizing relations between terms. Other systems attempted to generate hypotheses based on analysis of text in Medline abstracts.[Srinvasan 2004] or reports.[Weeber 2003] In addition, there are systems that build new descriptions of a document set by creating clusters of documents with statistically derived labels. (ClusterMed, RefViz, and Latent Semantic Indexing [e.g., Dumais 1996, Landauer 1994, Hearst 2003, Yu 2002]) Other document content systems include swarm intelligence [Eberhart 2001] and frame analyses [Gildea 2002]

Phases of Discovery: In contrast with other *discovery support systems*, the Idea Analysis method [Weiner 1979] is designed to build new descriptions of topics either using graphics, tables or draft text. The first phase involved identification, extraction and organization (as knowledge bases) of pertinent data from the text. These tasks are appropriately performed by software because of the tedious nature and mechanical operations involved. Using manual methods leads to significant error, although the hundreds of years of experience in doing these tasks have led to a perception suggesting that such acts are part of the intellectual process.

The second phase involves construction of descriptions of existing idea structures. The simplest of these descriptions is a table or map depicting important terms (i.e., nodes) and the connections between these nodes. These have been described as networks and depict representations of terms and their interrelationships. The network describes the conceptual issues inherent in the topic. Building these descriptions of existing knowledge is a technical procedure and can be performed by following defined algorithms.

The third phase involves real intellectual functions consisting of synthesis, comparison, evaluation, judgment and application. These activities are the province of the subject specialist and acquiring skills in using them is a challenge. By having the products and results from the first two phases available, the cognitive functions can be initiated earlier and can be accomplished more effectively and efficiently. This is evident simply by the elimination of the enormous amount of replication involved in identifying, extracting and organizing data items from literature.

However, there is a more compelling reason. That is, the contrast between document management and information utilization. In document management, the intent is to provide a label enabling retrieval. Once documents are retrieved, subsequent analysis of the text is performed manually. In information utilization, the pertinent data from the document are stripped and organized to develop new descriptions. The intent is to build new rather than simply retrieve. The document source is less important than the informational elements contained in it. If the approach was completely successful, retrieval of documents would be obsolete. Instead, retrieval of pertinent data would be the standard.

Using the Authors' Combinations of Informative Terms: Informative terms have been described. The author combines informative terms in sentences. These informative terms, when considered as pairs, are defined operationally as ideas. The simple sentence is composed on three terms – a subject, a verb, and an object. The idea would be the pair – subject & object. As seen in previous examples, sentences consist of more than one idea. The typical sentence in a scientific report will include a median of 10 ideas.

Table 1A. Higher Frequency Ideas Involving *Epidemiologic* **– Disease Factors – 1996 - 2000.**

Term	1996	1997	1998	1999	2000
biologic	0	0	0	0	0
breast	34	34	21	17	52
cancer	183	221	132	78	274
cardiovascular	38	46	28	30	68
chronic	0	0	0	0	0
coronary	32	33	26	15	42
depression	14	19	8	5	15
disease	0	0	0	0	0
genetic	83	80	57	59	140
health	0	22	13	49	129
infection	151	182	86	92	256
molecular	70	71	38	46	106
pathogen	0	57	24	25	89
transmission	33	40	39	33	67
tuberculosis	28	43	28	19	45
vascular	43	45	34	35	78

As a consequence, the major question is what data should be considered as pertinent? Pertinence depends on perception and each user brings different perceptions to the process. The cognitive phase can reflect the multitude of attitudes considered relevant by the users. While this diversity exists and is desirable, the existence of a comprehensive and accurate repository containing pertinent data makes it easier to express the diversity of emphasis and to leave an audit trail in the process. The Idea Analysis system extracts informative terms (i.e., nouns or adjectives and verbs behaving as nouns), couplets of these terms within sentences, links to associated sentences and bibliographic data for each document. These data are stored in resources called Scholar's WorkStations. These repositories are freely available [learning@tutorghost.com]. With the ideas as the basic informational elements, the user can pick and choose the ideas of interest.

Ideas in the Epidemiologic Scholar WorkStation: The Scholar WorkStation has a number of uses. If the subject matter is new to the student, an overview can be developed by selecting an important term and then, the ideas containing that term. This display of ideas has been called an idea swarm. The ideas, individually, contain the selected primary term. As an example, consider the word – *epidemiologic* -- as the primary term in the idea swarm. With this as the primary, an understanding of the issues involved in describing that term can be developed. In organizing the content of the idea swarm, it is convenient to classify the terms in the swarm into categories. The categories representing basic components of a topic are:

1. Environmental Factors.
2. Personal Factors.
3. Disease Factors.
4. Intervention or Treatment Factors.
5. Outcome Factors.

Table 1B. Higher Frequency Ideas Involving *Epidemiologic* – Disease Factors – 2001-2005.

Term	2001	2002	2003	2004	2005
biologic	24	58	81	9	18
breast	41	54	60	17	16
cancer	193	225	260	60	161
cardiovascular	72	59	80	8	41
chronic	35	37	71	8	26
coronary	51	27	34	2	12
depression	19	24	26	7	46
disease	121	307	363	28	184
genetic	119	105	127	5	55
health	122	145	157	16	80
infection	84	122	85	18	83
molecular	82	76	96	17	62
pathogen	30	47	45	6	33
transmission	34	49	32	6	27
tuberculosis	42	61	59	2	15
vascular	81	78	91	10	55

In the following example, the ideas comprising the disease category are shown. That is, terms with meaning and/or function depicting various attributes associated with disease. Table 1A showed the terms in this category linked with the term – *epidemiologic* – and occurring with relatively higher frequency in a selected time period. Table 1A showed that during 1996 through 2000, cancer and infection were most frequently linked with the primary term. The temporal occurrence of ideas can be classified into three groups. These were low, moderate and high frequencies. For 2001 through 2005 (see Table 1B), the moderate frequency ideas involved –

genetic and molecular. The high frequency ideas involved – cancer and infection. The remaining terms were in the low frequency group.

A Formalized Procedure for Discovery: The delays in achieving investigative independence and the reductions in funding of investigator-initiated grants are consistent with the difficulties in identifying relevant and new research strategies. The analysis illustrated in the following begins with a large volume of vocabulary and ideas extracted from the epidemiologic research literature. The ideas can be organized in a number of ways. The approach suggested involves:

1. Determining the present/absence of terms and ideas in the knowledge base.
2. Developing categories for the terms representing different attributes of the topic.
3. Assigning terms and ideas to these categories based on meaning and/or function.
4. Using the consensus experience of the authors of scientific reports to identify relevant ideas.

Ideas Associated with Genetic Factors in Cancer: Table 1 showed that two ideas occurred with high frequency throughout the time period considered. Those were – epidemiologic & cancer and epidemiologic & genetics. To illustrate the author-guided, idea approach, consider the application of genetics and cancer in epidemiology. The analysis focuses on ideas linking genetics terms with different cancers. The analysis of discovery began by identifying ideas present and missing in the 1996 literature. Then, year by year, the use of these ideas by authors was identified. As they appeared, they were entered into the knowledge base.

Table 2 shows the year of first occurrence for terms describing genetic factors in breast, ovarian and laryngeal cancers. These results describe epidemiologic studies. As seen, one term was involved with missing genetic ideas in breast cancer. Three terms were involved in missing genetic ideas in ovarian cancer. Thirteen terms were involved with missing genetic ideas in laryngeal cancer.

Occurrence of Genetic Ideas in Breast Cancer: Each term describing a genetic characteristic was assessed by year first observed in the knowledge bases. *Allele, biomarker, DNA, genetic, genotype, missense, mutation, phenotype, polymerase, polymorphism, proband* and *receptor,* respectively, were linked with breast cancer in the 1996 knowledge base. This year was arbitrarily chosen as the first year in the analysis. Most of the genetics terms were already in use in the epidemiologic literature. *Apoptosis, chromosome* and *gene,* respectively, were first linked with breast cancer in 1997. *Chromatid* and *genome* were first linked with breast cancer in 2001. The only term not linked with breast cancer was *microsatellite.*

Table 2. Missing Ideas Involving Genetic Factors in Different Cancers.

Term	Breast Cancer	Ovarian Cancer	Laryngeal Cancer
Allele	1996	1999	2000
Apoptosis	1997	2000	0
Biomarker	1996	2002	0
Chromatid	2001	0	0
Chromosome	1997	2005	0
DNA	1996	1996	1998
Gene	1997	1998	0
Genetic	1996	1996	1999
Genome	2001	2002	0
Genotype	1996	1996	1998
Microsatellite	0	0	0
Missense	1996	1996	0
Mutation	1996	1996	0
Phenotype	1996	1996	0
Polymerase	1996	2002	0
Polymorphism	1996	1996	2000
Proband	1996	1997	0
Receptor	1996	1996	0

Ovarian Cancer and Genetics Ideas: Table 2 also showed the occurrence of each of the genetic ideas in ovarian cancer by year first observed in the knowledge base. *DNA, genetic, genotype, missense, mutation, phenotype,* and *polymorphism*, respectively, were first linked with ovarian cancer in 1996. *Proband* was first linked with this cancer in 1997. *Gene* and ovarian cancer was introduced in 1998. *Allele* and ovarian cancer entered the knowledge base in 1999. *Apoptosis* with ovarian cancer was first linked in 2000. *Biomarker, genome,* and *polymerase*, respectively, were linked with ovarian cancer in 2002. *Chromatid* and *chromosome* respectively, with ovarian cancer were missing from the knowledge bases throughout the period studied. Ovarian cancer and *microsatellite* was reported in the literature in the 2005 knowledge base.

Laryngeal Cancer and Genetics Ideas: Finally, Table 2 showed the ideas present and missing when genetic factors and laryngeal cancer were considered. *DNA* and *genotype*, respectively, were first linked with laryngeal cancer in 1998. *Allele* and *polymorphism*, respectively were linked with laryngeal cancer in 2000. *Genetic* and laryngeal cancer were linked in 2001. As of the time of the analysis, the rest of the genetic terms had not been linked with this cancer.

Table 3 shows the frequency of missing ideas dealing with the terms in the genetics set linked with each of these cancers. As seen. breast cancer and colorectal cancer, respectively, had only 1 missing genetic idea. In contrast, laryngeal, nasopharyngeal and uterine had large numbers of missing genetic factor ideas.

Table 3. Frequency of Missing Ideas Associated with Genetic Factors by Specific Cancer.

Cancer	No.Missing Ideas
Breast	1
Colorectal	1
Gastric	3
Laryngeal	13
Nasopharyngeal	16
Ovarian	3
Pancreatic	5
Prostate	1
Uterine	17

Missing Ideas and New Research: Identifying missing ideas using manual methods is a Herculean task requiring considerable time and effort. However, it can and is done by subject specialists throughout the world. The process involves reading, identifying, extracting, and organizing data. The typical repository is the human brain. The surge in scientific publication following the Second World War and the race to conquer space led to attempts to develop mechanisms to augment human capabilities. These newer approaches included computer support and led to literally thousands of computerized bibliographic repositories such as Medline and PubMed. These resources were intended to provide instantaneous access to the desired information. By selecting specific terms, singly or in combination, the intent was to identify and retrieve documents satisfying the search parameters and, importantly, providing the user with the required information.

While this access is a critical component of information processing, an important disconnect between information technology and information utilization has occurred. The technologic improvements provide the capabilities to effectively and rapidly manage text. Over the years, search and retrieval mechanisms have dominated information management. The success and popularity of search systems illustrate the importance of finding information. These systems use microscopic amounts of time in finding potential information sources. However, the results of such searches force the individual to perform the real text processing and expend large amounts of time.

That process, performed using manual and private methods, must necessarily begin with the mechanical extraction and organization of data. Those tasks consume approximately 90% of the time and energy involved in a new scientific creative process. Following that effort, the individual can begin the higher level cognitive tasks involving building new constructs, comparing these, and selecting one for application. Those tasks require approximately 10% of the total effort using traditional manual methods. Imagine a change in the energy expenditures with 10% involved in mechanical tasks and 90% in higher level cognitive tasks. Further, imagine the improvements in research productivity if the individual could begin with the synthesis task without the fatigue of the preceding recall and analytic effort. Finally, imagine the satisfaction realized by eliminating the time and effort associated with manual processing, using appropriate computer and technical algorithms.

To accomplish this transformation, a number of conditions must be considered. These are:

1. **Text is structured by the subject specialists.** The majority of text mining approaches assume terms can be considered as random events. This assumption, in essence, negates the expertise of the authors, the peer reviewers, and the editors of scientific journals. In contrast, Idea Analysis[tm] assumes that the authors' choice of terms and the organization of those terms are integral to the understanding of the topic.

2. **The sentence is the universal domain used to communicate thoughts.** Authors express thoughts by combining informative terms within the domain of the sentence. This contrasts with the usual linking that seeks to combine selected terms irrespective of their location.

3. **Thoughts, operationally, can be defined as couplets of informative terms, called ideas.** Ideas can be considered as the building blocks used to develop concepts, issues, and topics. The term – idea – however, is used to describe words, phrases, and issues. Some of this labeling may be due to the need for shortcuts in manual processing. That is, instead of describing an idea swarm it is easier to assign the central term label to the entire swarm. With time, the related terms in the swarm become masked. The primary term becomes the entire swarm, i.e., the idea. In contrast, the Idea Analysis[tm] method identifies the idea as a pair of informative terms provided by the author and placed in a sentence. This definition facilitates identification and subsequent processing by software.

4. **Informative terms are defined to be nouns or adjectives and verbs behaving like nouns.** The software can identify the terms of interest using various criteria. One such compares new terms against a list of terms presumed to be informative in the topic. The best way to determine informative terms is to see how the authors use the term in their ideas.

5. **The computer can identify, extract and organize ideas, associated sentences and bibliographic data. These are stored in the knowledge bases.** The computer's

accuracy in performing these mechanical tasks exceeds 99%. In addition, this accuracy can be observed 24 hours per day and 7 days per week. There is no fatigue factor.

6. ***Ideas can be organized in new ways independent of their original use.*** Ideas are dimension free and independent of their original context. They can be combined to form new descriptions.

7. ***Such organizations indicate important aspects of the topic and its issues.*** The important fact in these organizations is the shift in human energy and effort from the mechanical to the higher level cognitive. By using computer support in building new organizations of ideas, the individual can accelerate the transition from student to professional.

<u>**Summary**</u>

Analysis of the literature describing a subject is simplified and enhanced by identification and organization of ideas provided by the authors. The process employs software to read the text, identify vocabulary and ideas. These data are extracted together with associated sentences and bibliographic data. The vocabulary is arranged alphabetically and all of the ideas involving each term are appropriately linked and displayed. For each idea, the sentences can be displayed and, if relevant to the user's needs, the associated document can be retrieved from PubMed.

This organization differs in important ways from the typical search and retrieval system. Of primary interest is the fact that the vocabulary is readily available to the user. In other systems, the user is presented with a blank box and must guess at the terms to use in attempting to match those actually used by the authors. This peculiar search strategy is a common one in current systems and quite curious. In order to perform a search of the language actually used by the author, the computer must read the text. Given that has occurred, the software could provide a display showing the terms actually used by the authors. Indeed, modern search engines and text mining systems do that.

The intent of Idea Analysis[tm] is to organize clusters of ideas (i.e., idea swarms) rather than clusters of documents. The method yields a high degree of accuracy in retrieving precisely the documents of interest and of greater importance is the reduced need to retrieve documents in order to extract needed information.

Inherent in this organizational capability is the identification of ideas presented in the literature by degree of frequency. This is relevant information. In learning a new topic, the higher frequency ideas represent those ideas considered most important by the authors. Alternatively, individuals seeking to develop new research might seek low frequency ideas, particularly those recently entered into the literature. Such ideas could represent new issues of interest. Finally, individuals seeking to develop new research could focus on the ideas that were missing from the literature. The identification of those ideas is not difficult or taxing. Indeed, when the information is properly organized, missing links are obvious. Given that set of ideas, the challenge facing the investigator is one that is exclusively private and important. Namely, the challenge is one of identifying the most important of those missing ideas for inclusion in new research.

Chapter Ten – Models and Simulation in Higher Cognitive Functions

Introduction

The application of the higher cognitive functions – synthesis, comparison, evaluation, judgment, and application – requires practice. One way of developing these skills is to use an algorithm that provides a step-by-step construction of the desired product. The process involves:

1. Laying the groundwork by choosing one of the four templates for investigative study. These are:
   a. A new idea must be studied to determine the possible relationships it has with established ones.
   b. A new idea is found worthy of further study and relationships must be fleshed out.
   c. A new idea has been demonstrated to be interesting and the question is whether this idea is 'better' than existing ones.
   d. A new idea has been demonstrated to be useful in describing the phenomenon of interest and attention changes to short term and long term implications of substituting the new idea for previous ones.
2. Based on the review of existing literature, develop a matrix composed on individual records as rows and variables of interest as columns. Add a final column representing the variable denoting the situation under study, i.e., a binomial variable if the question is a difference between groups, or a scaled variable if the question is a relationship among the variables. This latter possibility may include increasing values across the range of the multiple groups considered.
3. Populate the matrix with random numbers each depicting the range of values considered appropriate in representing the variable. This step is based on the *null hypothesis* concept, namely, that there is no relationship among the different variables and none with the group designator.
4. Perform an analysis involving the distribution of each variable within the designated groups and determining the degree of apparent relationship between each variable with the group designator. This analysis will provide insights into what truly random, no relationship data can look like and demonstrate the principles associated with statistical testing. In that situation, a relatively small number of the possible outcomes will appear to be non-random. This is called – *statistical testing* – and the probability of such an outcome is determined by its frequency of occurrence in multiple samplings and analyses.

5.   Develop a schedule of planned alterations to the random values. Those changes would depend on data from literature or from possible outcomes believed to be of interest. Examples might be changing values to higher or lower ones to create more of a relationship. Perform an analysis after each scheduled change to determine the result of the alterations. These represent possible outcomes and their probability of occurrence might be of interest. An important result is the imposition of a structure on the original randomness and the effect of a form of intervention which changes the null hypothesis into an alternative one.

6.   Confirm a potentially interesting outcome by performing repeated random sampling and modification to represent multiple studies of a particular model. Compare that model's results with those of comparable sized studies using the data representing the null hypothesis. Track the number of times the modified model differs from its null counterpart. With those data, report the probability of a *real change* associated with the modified model.

These steps represent syntheses that are modified based on the schedule of changes. With each modification, the analyses will provide measures useful in comparing the outcomes. These measures can be assessed using evaluation criteria and based on the findings, the next modification may proceed or be changed. With each replication, the cognitive functions are brought to bear on the operation and decisions are made. The benefits are two-fold. The first is the practice and insights obtained from the simulation process. The second is development of skill in data-driven thinking about the possibilities which exist within every problem. Since much of the investigative process dealing with complex problems is costly and time consuming, the application of modeling and simulation offers an effective and economically feasible way to consider the different possible outcomes before investing real dollars, personal, equipment, and time in scenarios which appear to be interesting but without data support.

Comparison of Two Methods: This example deals with comparison of a process called critical thinking and a second one called information literacy.[AASL 1998, ALA 1989,ACRL 2000] Critical thinking [Allen 2004] is described using Bloom's taxonomy of learning functions – recall, analysis, synthesis, comparison, evaluation, judgment, and application. [Bloom 1956, Bloom 1984] These functions are employed in developing a better awareness of a specific subject. The use of this process would result in an enhanced understanding and functioning in the subject. Information literacy is a set of skills leading to the same results – enhanced access, management, and utilization of information in order to learn more effectively and to make better decisions in work and in life. There is an emphasis of lifelong learning. [Obama 2009, Scharwzennegger 2009]

Suppose that an investigator is interested in developing measures, criteria, and decision-structures leading to effective differentiation of the two similar yet possibly distinct procedures.

The literature review suggested that there were specific indicators or measures that could be used to denote the different functions in Bloom's taxonomy. Those measures would be terms representing attributes of each of the functions. Consider the following structure: Let the specific function be represented by terms in different ranges. Those would be:

1. Recall – 1
2. Analysis – 2
3. Synthesis – 3
4. Comparison – 4
5. Evaluation – 5
6. Judgment – 6
7. Application – 7

In addition, consider the types of words contained in sentences dealing with the two methods:

1. Informative nouns – 1
2. Non-informative nouns – 2
3. Informative adjectives – 3
4. Non-informative adjectives – 4
5. Gerunds– 5
6. Non-informative verbs – 6
7. Remaining terms – 7

In the evolving scheme, the words forming ideas would represent variables related to the functions. As such, a sentence would be the domain to be analyzed and would be displayed as rows in the matrix. Each sentence would contain 10 terms. The columns would display the words (range from 1 to 7) used in the sentence together with the designator variable representing Bloom's functions (range 1 to 7). An example of this might be –

Sentence 1 = 3, 1, 6, 7, 5, 2, 4, 7, 5, 2, 3, 1

This sentence would contain --

Informative Terms	Non-Informative Terms
3	6
1	7
5	2
5	4
	7
	2

with a cognitive function term suggesting synthesis (3).

The ideas in this sentence would be:
3, respectively with, 1, 5, 5, 3

153

1, respectively with, 3, 1, 5, 3
5, respectively with, 3, 1, 5, 3
5, respectively with, 3, 1, 5, 3
3, respectively with, 3, 1, 5, 5

With this structure imposed on random numbers, the specific samples could reveal relationships between the ideas and the cognitive functions. A final variable would represent the two methods – critical thinking (1) and information literacy (2). Now the ideas linked with cognitive functions could be explored within the critical thinking set and within the information literacy one.

The sentences would have a range of ideas numbering from 0 to 55 (11 x 10 / 2 = 55) and would represent typical academic sentences. The website [random generation 2011] would be used to select random numbers. That site allows selection of random numbers of designated size. Each column of 100 numbers would be copied and pasted into an excel file representing the matrix of values.

The random numbers represent the different types of words. In addition, codes denote Bloom's functions. The words would be paired as ideas and linked with Bloom's functional code within each sentence. Those ideas would be summarized and displayed using different graphics. The ideas linked with each of the Bloom's functions would be compared between the two procedure sets. Given that the data are random with no apparent relationship with either Bloom's functions or with the procedural designators, the display for each group should be quite similar.

These graphs should provide the clearest view of the null hypothesis possible using random numbers. With that algorithm established, the findings for the actual analysis of the critical thinking and information literature literatures will be added. This summary graph would show the degree of approximation between the simulation and the actual. The building of the random model is illustrated below.

The first step was - *Laying the groundwork by choosing one of the four templates for investigative study.* The one selected for this example was - *A new idea is found worthy of further study and relationships must be fleshed out.* In this example, the idea involves a comparison of critical thinking and information literacy. The study design is a form of survey involving retrieval of articles dealing with each of the subjects. The sentences for each report are separated and the ideas in each are extracted and organized. The ideas are linked with Bloom's taxonomy of learning functions and the frequency of these ideas within each function is determined. The null hypothesis is that there would be equal frequencies of ideas associated with the cognitive functions. That is, no differences would be observed between the two methods.

In preparation for this comparison, a simulation model was developed depicting the frequency of ideas composed of random numbers. With this model, true lack of relationship between the ideas and the cognitive functions should be observed and would provide the basis for interpreting the actual findings. If the model results closely approximate the actual ones, the null hypothesis would have some credibility and the two methods could be considered to be similar. If, however, the model differs from the actual data, there would be evidence that an alternative hypothesis suggesting that critical thinking methodology differs from that in information literacy.

Table 1. Comparison of Percentages of Randomly Generated and Actual Ideas by Bloom's Cognitive Functions.

Bloom's Functions	Random CT %	Actual CT %	Random IL %	Actual IL %
Recall	13.4	4.6	16.5	6.6
Analysis	15.2	23.1	6.2	37
Synthesis	11.6	20.1	26.3	17.2
Comparison	9.8	1.1	**9.4**	4.2
Evaluation	16.5	11.4	21	8.1
Judgment	17.9	10.1	13.3	5.1
Application	15.2	29.6	7.1	21.8

Table 1 shows the percentages of randomly generated "informative ideas" (i.e., pairs of informative nouns, adjectives, and gerunds) in the null hypothesis simulation model compared with the percentages of actual ideas. The latter were determined by the analysis of reports dealing with Critical Thinking and Information Literacy. The study included the 8745 articles dealing with critical thinking and 8201 reports dealing with information literacy entered into ERIC or PubMed from 2000-2009. In the randomly generated ideas groups, the Recall and Comparison function ideas were comparable in frequency. The Analysis function decreased from 15% in the random Critical Thinking group to 6% in the random Information Literacy group. The Synthesis function showed increases in the random ideas from 12% to 26%. The Application function showed a decrease in the random ideas from 15% to 7%.

In the actual data sets, the percent of ideas dealing with Analysis increased from 23% in the Critical Thinking group to 37% in the Information Literacy group. The Judgment ideas decreased from 10% to 5%. The remainder of the ideas was similar between the two methods.

The graphs in Figure 1 provide information related to two important questions – the difference between randomly generated ideas and the actual data and the potential differences between the two methods – Critical Thinking and Information Literacy. The Comparison function had the

155

lowest frequencies for both random and actual data. In addition, the random values were essentially the same, while the actual value ideas showed an increase from 1% to 4%. The synthesis function was next with an increase from random ideas representing Critical Thinking to those for Information Literacy. The actual ideas showed a higher value for the Critical Thinking group. The Recall function showed lower concentrations of actual ideas with comparable differences between the two methods. The Analysis function showed a decrease in the random ideas and an increase in the actual. The ideas representing Critical Thinking were 23% while the Information Literacy ideas were 37%. The Application function showed comparable patterns between the random and actual data. Evaluation and Judgment functions were comparable.

Figure 1.   Comparison of Terms Linked with Critical Thinking and/or Information Literacy. Percent of Random Ideas in each of Bloom's Cognitive Categories vs. the Percent of Informative Ideas from Analysis of the Scientific Reports in ERIC and PubMed – 2000 to 2009.

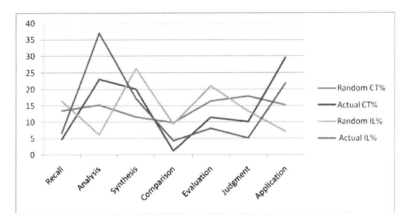

Figure 1 shows the relatively stable pattern across the cognitive functions for the randomly generated ideas. The actual ideas show larger fluctuations with more pronounced cycles. The graphs also indicate the simularities in frequency occurrence between the Critical Thinking and Information Literacy. The largest difference was observed with the Analysis function. The actual ideas representing Information Literacy exceeded those from the Critical Thinking group. These preliminary data show potential deviations from the null hypothesis with respect to differences between the two methods – Critical Thinking and Information Literacy. However, the observed differences in the actual data suggest that the two methods are comparable

Meaning of the Cognitive Functions: Figure 2 provides another way of comparing the two methods – Critical Thinking and Information Literacy by examining the terms linked with either of the methods. These terms form triadic ideas. Bloom's cognitive functions were depicted by clouds. A triadic idea consists of a central idea coupled with a related term. An example would be – information literacy & access. The central idea is – information & literacy. The related term is – access. That idea is in the recall function in Figure 2. These triadic ideas provide an enhanced description of each cognitive function.

Figure 2. Terms Linked with Either Critical Thinking, Information Literacy, or Both to form Triadic Ideas.

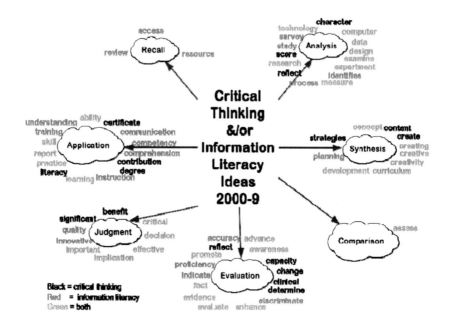

The ideas representing both critical thinking and information literacy were seen in the -- analysis, synthesis, comparison, evaluation, judgment, and application functions. The only Bloom function represented by information literacy alone was recall.

Analysis is defined as -- *the separating of any material or abstract entity into its constituent elements*. In terms of the ideas, *analysis* could be described as involving *computer technology* together with *experimental designs* intended to perform *research* and to *examine* the resulting *measures* and *data*. This description suggests a process employing specific tasks and expertise with an emphasis on objective procedures. Disciplines such as Statistics provide the tools associated with performing these analytic tasks with numeric data. Tools, such as copying and sorting, provide comparable functions in managing text.

The ideas expanding the meaning of *synthesis* emphasize the important mental processes involved in *concept development* and *creativity*. There is a methodological aspect as well involving *curriculum*. The latter suggests that a set of tasks involving synthesis can be determined and taught to students enabling them to accomplish the conceptual and creative outcomes.

The term, comparison, was defined -- as *the function used to indicate degrees of superiority or inferiority in quality, quantity, or intensity*.[dictionary.com] There was one idea identified in the comparison category. The term – assess – was linked with both creative thinking and information literacy. The definition of that term was -- *to estimate or judge the value or character*.[dictionary.com] The implication suggested is the development of measures, criteria, and procedures designed to accomplish the recognition and ranking of the attributes compared.

The evaluation function involved seven terms linked with both critical thinking and information literacy. The meaning of *evaluation* suggested by these ideas would be – an *awareness* of the *facts* and *evidence* intended to *advance, enhance*, or *promote* decisions associated with the characteristics being compared.

The meaning of the term – *judgment* – could be expanded to – an *effective* and *important implication* leading to a *critical decision*.

The ideas in the *application* function suggest that the meaning is – an *ability* or *skill* determined by *practice* and *learning* leading to a *report*.

Cognitive Functions and Ideas: The connection between usual cognitive tasks and the idea-based approach can be illustrated by considering the ideas identified. This array is like a thesaurus, where each is linked, by one or more authors, to a central term. That array augments the meaning of the central one. It provides a formal representation of a set of concepts within a domain based on the relationships among the contributing terms. This result matches the definition of ontology as used in computer and information science.

Usually, developing an ontology requires the efforts of experts. As an example, Allen et al [Allen 2004] suggested an instructional program involving 17 dimensions to provide nursing students with the skills and tools associated with critical thinking. Those dimensions were developed using a group of experts and the Delphi decision process. [Scheffer 2000] Comparing the descriptors in these dimensions with those from the Idea Analysis[tm] showed that 86% of the terms matched. The terms not matched were – inquisitive, truth, result, intuition, logical, open-mindedness, and perseverance. Inquisitive is defined as *given to inquiry, research, or asking questions; eager for knowledge; intellectually curious.* Of those explanatory terms, research, question, knowledge, and intellectual matched with the terms from the Idea Analysis[tm]. The term – intuition – is defined *as direct perception of truth, fact, independent of any reasoning process.* Of those defining terms – fact, reasoning, and process – were included in the ideas from the literature analysis. The term, logic, was defined as *the science that investigates the principles governing correct or reliable inference.* The term, correct, was the only one not included in the ideas. The definition of the word, truth, contained terms matching with the ideas. Those were fact and reality.

Using experts, to develop knowledge and wisdom, is a key component of Idea Analysis[tm], although the procedure is different. The ideas, presented by the authors in their sentences, are the data involved in the analysis. Those authors chose the terms and placed them within the constrained region defined by the sentence. This proximity is a key element in ensuring the contextual meaning of the relationships.[Carretti 2007] In contrast to manual analyses or keyword focus, the software attempts to identify, extract, and organize all of the ideas presented in the sentences. This results in a larger-than-usual array of ideas. Some will be considered important based on the criterion -- frequency of use. Others will be considered dated because they were popular at one time and less so currently. A third group, preliminarily identified by low frequency of use, may represent ideas in their ascendancy. [Salton 1988, Sparck Jones 1972]

The analysis showed that critical thinking and information literacy involved all but one of Bloom's taxonomy of learning functions. Recall was considered only in information literacy related ideas. In comparing the ideas dealing with critical thinking and information literacy, the finding that both phrases could be described using the same related terms suggests an application of the transitive law in mathematics. That law states that if A is equal to B and B is equal to C, then A is equal to C. Similarly, terms linked with critical thinking, and the same terms linked with information literacy, suggests that the two phrases described the same phenomenon.[Britannica 2009]

Enhancing acquisition of information is a significant component in many instructional programs presented by academic libraries. Mission statements emphasize collection maintenance, accessing information, and assistance in acquiring information literacy. Online tutorials and classroom presentations have been prepared in enhancing identification and access to data from bibliographic databases. Bibliographic databases can be searched by developing one or more terms that the analyst thinks are relevant in identifying the topics of interest. The search statement can be constructed using the most general terms believed pertinent.

Differences Between Methods: Given the similarities in meaning between the two phrases, an essential difference may result from the focus employed. Critical thinking may represent a subject-specific, often individualized approach. It may appear to be subject-specific despite the fact that a large number of disciplines separately and individually embrace it. Each discipline develops attitudes, procedures, and perceptions necessary in dealing with information in that subject. In contrast, information literacy may represent a general any-information-set, formalized, quality-controlled process. It may be perceived as being focused on the general approach to effective identification, access, processing and utilization of information. The methodology would be available to everyone, irrespective of initial background. The emphasis would be on methods and procedures that would be appropriate and effective for any subject rather than those targeted in a subject.

There were articles with sentences including the two phrases, thus providing possible insights as to the emphasis and importance of each in instructing students. One such article dealt with problem-based learning in nursing. Jauhiainen and Pulkkinen [Jauhiainen 2009] described the curriculum development and introduction of problem-based learning pedagogy (PBL) in undergraduate nursing education. The authors stated that "*PBL pedagogy developed information literacy skills, critical thinking, and evidence-based nursing skills, communication, co-operation and team working skills, problem solving and self-assessment skills.*" The implication being that problem based learning offered opportunities to develop both critical thinking and information literacy. The emphasis in this learning approach is process-coupled-with-topic. The intent and desired results would be a better understanding of the topic. This would be an example of a critical thinking approach.

A second example of this critical thinking application is an article by Near [Near 2007]. The topic was psychoactive drugs. The authors indicated that they included lecture, short homework papers, small-group discussions, and whole class discussions. They indicated that their instruction methods were inquiry based and interactive. Their intent was to accomplish the following: "*1) to foster the development of an organized knowledge base about psychoactive drugs that will have practical applicability in the daily lives of the students; 2) to promote the rational application of this knowledge in thinking about current medical, social, legal, and ethical issues involving psychoactive drugs; and 3) to cultivate science literacy, critical thinking, and communication skills among students.*"

These examples agree with the definitions of critical thinking and information literacy. In addition, the focus in each example was to convey knowledge and effective management of information in a specific field, rather than emphasizing methods in processing and using information in any field. These examples also differ in interpretation from a perspective proved by Scirven [Scriven 1987]. That author suggested that the phrase should be considered as a separate discipline involving content and process. That approach would be comparable to a course in research methodology that includes the content from a variety of disciplines coupled with the procedures effective in developing, conducting, analyzing, interpreting, and reporting results. This suggestion remains untested.

A current theme in academia is the elimination of boundaries between disciplines so that the student may effectively move from topic to topic. A number of support groups have been introduced. These efforts included orientation programs to assist students in adjusting to campus life. Learning communities were introduced to assist students in adjusting to the rigors of higher education instruction. Writing centers were provided to assist students in preparing the diversity of written reports required by courses in all disciplines. Tutorial services were expanded as were programs of individual mentoring. Libraries introduced learning commons designed to supplement classroom learning as well as to provide self-learning opportunities by making general support services available (e.g., information availability services, report preparation, and media development assistance) . These were intended to assist and supplement the faculty's efforts in providing students with critical thinking capabilities. At the same time, the distinction between critical thinking and information literacy may be diminished, resulting in a merging of the two. Faculty may build information literacy (e.g., information management methods) into the course curriculum and use the subject specific data as an example in using an information processing method.

Librarians may build aspects of critical thinking into their interactions with clients. Instead of stopping with information access and retrieval, they may actively interact with their clients in assessing and organizing the information, in assisting in the development of new descriptions and in the preparation of reports from these efforts. These actions are incorporated in the newer learning, information, scholar, or knowledge commons that are an integral part of academic libraries.[Weiner 2009] While the name may change depending on the institution, the addition of this resource was in response to the awareness that students were under-prepared to meet the challenges of a global society and failed to possess competencies in information literacy.

Information literacy, as a discipline in dealing with text, may be analogous to the situation faced by Statistics in dealing with numeric data. That branch of mathematical science has been applied to a myriad of different disciplines all using numerical data. The processing of such data from its initial capture to the final report of findings is subject to a set of defined algorithms employing computer, technical and intellectual tasks. This methodological approach has demonstrated its effectiveness in supporting and enhancing the critical thinking associated with numeric data. However, it was recognized that more than calculations were required in conceiving, conducting, and completing new research studies. As such, courses dealing with research methodology were introduced to augment the concepts and procedures in Statistics.

161

Text processing is approaching a similar situation. At the present time, formalized methods have emphasized search and retrieval. However, computer-supported text mining is in the offing. Idea Analysis[tm] is one such attempt to affect a change in the management of text. By focusing on the ideas presented in each sentence, a data repository comparable to the numeric database can be constructed. That resource is the Scholar's WorkStation and contains the ideas provided by the authors. The resulting information can be analyzed using algorithms. As a result, a new course of instruction may be considered. That one, comparable to research methodology, may incorporate the tools, techniques, and concepts from information literacy with the specifics needed for effective management of content. That course would incorporate computer, technical, and intellectual functions and provide a protocol-driven approach to knowledge utilization. In a fashion comparable to the use of numeric data, intellectual prowess would be evidenced by innovation and creativity. The advantages would be similar to numeric analysis in that text management would require less time and effort on mechanical tasks and more time devoted to higher level cognitive tasks considered by Bloom as relevant in learning.

With that similarity, the distinction between critical thinking and information literacy might be explained by focus and origin rather than by meaning or intent. Critical thinking was subject-specific even though a number of different disciplines had "invented" the process. This focus on effective processing of information *within* a subject is different from a focus on effective processing *irrespective* of the information set.

This distinction is comparable to the employment of Statistics in dealing with numeric data. A large number of sciences employ the technology in solving their specific problems. The emphasis is on the challenges associated with the subject rather than those dealing with statistical methodology. Similarly, information literacy could focus on the tools and techniques required to effectively process and use any body of information. Merging the two – critical thinking and information literacy -- may result in a new, formalized course of instruction, comparable in intent, to those in research methodology. The development of a curriculum of this type would clarify the role of information processing in specific subjects as well as provide effective and efficient procedures useful in providing the needed answers and insights in a rapid and accurate way.

Summary

This chapter dealt with the development of models with simulation of the data. This approach offers a significant advantage by considering different possibilities. The example showed the comparison of the null hypothesis versus the actual data. An analysis of the education and health science literature dealing with critical thinking and/or information literacy was performed in order to determine the expanded meaning of each phrase. In considering the definitions of the two phrases, there was an obvious similarity. This comparability was even more striking when the ideas describing each phrase were examined. The vocabularies matched and both could be conveniently organized using the functions from Bloom's Taxonomy of Learning.

With that similarity, the distinction between critical thinking and information literacy might be explained by focus and origin rather than by meaning or intent. Critical thinking was subject-specific even though a number of different disciplines had "invented" the process. This focus on effective processing of information *within* a subject is different from a focus on effective processing *irrespective* of the information set.

This distinction is comparable to the employment of Statistics in dealing with numeric data. A large number of sciences employ the technology in solving their specific problems. The emphasis is on the challenges associated with the subject rather than those dealing with statistical methodology. Similarly, information literacy could focus on the tools and techniques required to effectively process and use any body of information. Merging the two – critical thinking and information literacy -- may result in a new, formalized course of instruction, comparable in intent, to those in research methodology. The development of a curriculum of this type would clarify the role of information processing in specific subjects as well as provide effective and efficient procedures useful in providing the needed answers and insights in a rapid and accurate way.

Chapter Eleven – Cognitive Functions

Introduction

In this chapter, the idea serves as the construction element and ways to display them are illustrated. The idea building blocks are comparable to bricks. Bricks can be used to build houses, schools, churches, and/or office buildings. Each of these final constructions is unique and represents the architect's intellectual contributions. In a similar fashion, the ideas can be used by different individuals to form a variety of different descriptions of existing knowledge as well as in developing strategies for acquiring new knowledge.

The benefits associated with a formalized process using ideas are:

1. The *time* required to process (identify, extract, and organize) the information contained in a 250 word abstract is 0.2 minute per abstract. This contrasts with the manual time of 0.5 minute for triaging and 1 to 3 minutes for processing. This difference results in a savings in time ranging from 14 to 34 times that associated with manual processing. As such, the larger volumes associated with scientific topics can be more effectively and efficiently managed. A significant savings in time results from the fact that specific text is processed only once instead of the thousands of times associated with manual analysis. The fact that each analyst may be interested in a different subset of the ideas is addressed by capturing all of them and placing them in an accessible repository.

2. There is a *shift in task* from the clerical/mechanical ones associated with manual processing of text to the higher cognitive functions associated with creativity and innovation. By having the authors' ideas properly organized and available, the analyst can begin with the synthesis function as illustrated by the construction of graphs depicting the ideas as well as new simple and then academic sentences. This new text can be compared using measures and criteria. The results can be judged and if found satisfactory, can be presented as a new representation.

3. In contrast to the paper-oriented, manual processing methods, the emphasis based on idea resources delays and *reduces the need for full documents*. As such, the major effort can be focused on various arrangements and translations of the ideas. When a satisfactory result has been developed, the articles contributing data can be retrieved in order to enhance the new description. This retrieval strategy would use all of the articles dealing with a subject once. The idea resource would replace the need for repeated search and retrieval of articles and replace that mechanical function with retrieval of selected small sets of documents, with known content, for specific purposes. The need to triage documents based on flawed search strategies would be eliminated. The need to repeatedly access

bibliographic databases and to repeatedly identify, extract, and organize ideas would be eliminated.

Health Finance Literature – 2009: Six thousand five hundred and sixteen articles dealing with health finance were entered into PubMed during 2009. These articles presumably would describe the role of these business and related procedures in the health industry. To investigate this possibility, these reports were analyzed using the Idea Analysis[tm] system to identify the ideas presented by the authors in their sentences. This approach differs from other text mining systems by focusing on the authors' relationships among the informative terms making up the authors' vocabulary. The results should provide sufficient understanding of the informational structure describing this body of knowledge.

**Table 1. Number of Ideas Associated
with Each of the Terms – from Health Literature – 2009.**

Term	Freq
health	5971
finance	2915
system	2679
work	1914
public	1837
age	1520
data	1185
insurance	1058
private	1058
financial	1012
hospital	982
social	965
cost	936
quality	915
economic	906
measure	763
policy	749
government	722
department	702
population	678
etc.	etc.

The analytic system identified 61,027 relationships or ideas expressed in the authors' sentences. The ideas considered by the authors to be important are denoted by the frequency of use in the sentences. Those ideas, representing either evolving concepts or declining ones, are denoted by lower frequencies. In order to develop a current description of the topic, the higher frequency ideas are of value and represent a type of consensus among the author-specialists. Table 1 shows the terms and the number of ideas associated with each from the 2009 Health Literature.

Health Ideas: Figure 1 shows the higher frequency ideas involving the central term – health. The inner tier shows the four highest frequency ideas involving health. These ideas could be arranged by frequency as follows: *health (5971)* → *system (495)* → *finance (386)* → *public (320)* → *insurance (211).* A sentence involving these ideas might be –
The health finance system involves public insurance.

The second tier expands on the preliminary sentence by adding ideas including access to health facilities, age of participants, quality of the work, and social policy. The outer tier includes the population involved, and economic measures.

Figure 1. Terms Linked with the Central Term – Health.

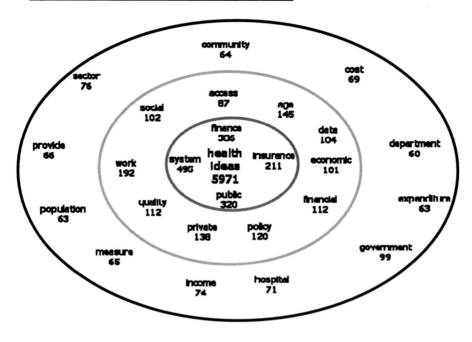

Finance Ideas: Figure 2 shows the idea-pairs using the central term – finance – and the terms associated with it. Only those higher frequency ideas are shown in this graph. The inner tier shows the possibilities associated with building more complex ideas. The pair – finance & health – contributed 386 ideas or 13% of the total associated with the central term.

Figure 2. Terms Linked with the Central Term – Finance.

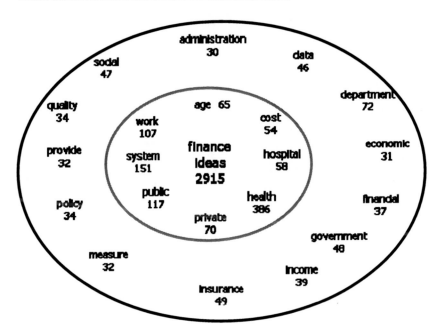

The inner tier provides the possible terms used to build a description of the topic. For example, arranging the terms with respect to frequency of linking with finance would yield – *finance (2915)* → *health (386)* → *system (151)* → *public (117)* → *work (107)* → *private (70)* → *age (65)* → *hospital (58)* → *cost (54)*. Sentences could be built using these terms. An example might be:

> **The finance health system represents public and private work designed to defray hospital costs for targeted age groups.**

Exhibit 1 contains two example sentences showing how authors used the ideas. These sentences show the power of the idea. The authors can take these building blocks and use them in various ways to convey their facts, opinions, and interpretations. This is possible because the idea is dimension-free and represents a specific thought. Beginning with the pair in a simple sentence, the ideas can be combined to form complex concepts. Operationally, an idea is a thought, while a concept is a grouping of thoughts describing a specific attribute or characteristic making up a part of the total topic.

Exhibit 1.   Representative Sentences containing Some of the Ideas Involving Health, Finance, Public, and System.

The effects of the economic crisis emerge in 4 areas: deterioration in **health** *status, as poverty contributed to higher disease rates; reductions in the government's ability to maintain* **public** *health and medical services; increased reliance on foreign aid to finance the health* **system;** *and growing national debate over the role of the state in health care.* [Morgan LM. [J Public Health Policy. 1987 Spring;8(1):86-105. Health without wealth? Costa Rica's health system under economic crisis.] PMID: 292787

This diagnosis led to three major planks for reform: (1) enactment of national **health** *insurance legislation granting a basic package of care to each citizen and hence bringing most of the* **system's finance** *under* **public** *auspices; (2) divesting the Government from the organization, management and provision of care; hence integrating the management of preventive and psychiatric services provided by the government with the primary and other services provided by sick funds, and granting financial and operational independence to at least government hospitals; and (3) restructuring the Ministry of Health.* [Chernichovsky D, Chinitz D. **The political economy of healthy system reform in Israel.** Health Econ. **1995 Mar-Apr;4(2):127-41.**] **PMID:** 3108317

Health & Finance & System as a Triadic Idea: Table 2 shows an excerpt from the file composed of terms linked with the central triadic idea – health & finance & system. The ideas from a specific article are denoted by the common identification number assigned by PubMed. One advantage associated with the idea emphasis is the accurate retrieval of articles containing text of interest to the analyst. As an example, the abstract associated with the first record in Table 2 was retrieved from PubMed and shown as the first sentence in Exhibit 1.

Table 2. Terms Linked with the Central Triadic Idea – Health & Finance & System – from the Health Finance Literature – 2009.

Health	Finance	System	Quadruplets	Year	Ident
health	finance	system	evaluation	2009	292787
health	finance	system	measure	2009	1573358
health	finance	system	communication	2009	2335342
health	finance	system	work	2009	2335342
health	finance	system	economic	2009	3108317
health	finance	system	poverty	2009	3108317
health	finance	system	public	2009	3108317
health	finance	system	reliance	2009	3108317
health	finance	system	profit	2009	3557773
health	finance	system	fiscal	2009	3935717
health	finance	system	integrity	2009	3935717
health	finance	system	medicare	2009	3935717
health	finance	system	analysis	2009	3961548
health	finance	system	demand	2009	3961548
health	finance	system	data	2009	6422557
health	finance	system	evidence	2009	6422557
health	finance	system	payment	2009	6422557
health	finance	system	provide	2009	6422557
health	finance	system	rating	2009	6422557
health	finance	system	age	2009	7613597
health	finance	system	government	2009	7613597
health	finance	system	insurance	2009	7613597
health	finance	system	public	2009	7613597
health	finance	system	rating	2009	7613597

Building New Text: Figure 3 shows the higher frequency ideas making up the information structure representing the central triad – health & finance & system. Building a new description of this triadic idea begins with considering the ideas making up each of the tiers. Starting with the simple pairs, the inner tier contains the following ideas:

Health finance system with:
> public (14)
> age (7)
> financial (7)
> insurance (7)
> work (6)
> cost (5)
> data (5)
> evidence (5)
> measure (5)

Figure 3. Terms Linked with the Central Triad – Health & Finance & System.

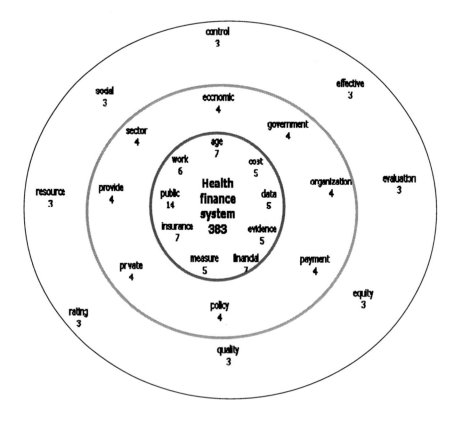

Possible sentences would be:

Health finance system is **public.**
Health finance system focuses on **age** groups.
Health finance system concerns the **financial** aspects.
Health finance system involves **insurance.**
Health finance system is associated with **work**.
Health finance system is related to **costs.**
Health finance system generates **data.**
Health finance system provides **evidence.**
Health finance system generates **measures.**

The quadrupletic idea (*health & finance & system & related term*) in each sentence is bolded and the verb chosen to link the subject with the object is shown in red. These verbs are arbitrary and represent one author's construction. However, irrespective of the verbs chosen, the fact remains that one or more authors combined the central triadic idea with an additional term to form the quadruplet shown in each sentence. The verbs chosen above were intended to be generic and to simply serve as a bridge. In real applications, the verbs would be more 'interesting' as the authors present their statements of fact, opinion, or interpretation.

The academic sentence is one consisting of two or more simple sentences joined to form a more complex thought or the beginnings of a concept. Possible academic sentences, with the informative terms bolded and the verbs in red, might be:

Health finance system is designed to provide the **public,** consisting of different **age** groups, with **insurance.** This **health finance system** provides the **data** and **evidence** associated with meeting the **financial costs** of **health** care. The benefits of the **health finance system** can be determined using **cost measures**.

The second tier provides ideas describing the involvement of the private and governmental sectors in meeting the burden of payment. The outer tier includes ideas involving quality, equity, and control of the health finance system.

Power of the Idea: This example demonstrated the power of the idea in developing a description of financial issues in the delivery of health care. Certain observations are suggestive.

1. A rapid and effective description of a previously unknown topic can be accomplished by considering the authors' ideas. These subject specialists provide a special form of guidance via their ideas and the frequency of using them. This frequency measure is a form of consensus agreement across geographic boundaries.

2. This description can be quality-controlled and monitored by using the intermediate files, created as part of the cognitive tasks, involved in synthesis,

comparison, evaluation, judgment, and application. The majority of these intermediate files consist of syntheses of the ideas in the form of graphs, subset excel files, and draft text. Comparison can be demonstrated by the notes and drafts developed by the analyst. Evaluation can be determined by considering the criteria used. Judgment can be seen using the final drafts of the desired report. Finally, the application is represented by the finished product.

3.   This transparent process is an important deviation from the manual approach. In that setting, the bulk of the work is performed with little or no   recorded   data. With the use of the software to build the idea repository and the subsequent software (Excel, Word, Inspiration, Notepad), the cognitive functions representing the intellectual approach can be moved to the foreground. The advantage is more than supervision. By carefully tracking the process leading to a new description of a topic, the student can more rapidly develop an understanding of the topic. In addition, the student can better understand the process involved in the transformation from student to professional. As a student, the individual is asked to learn pre-constructed text. As a professional, the individual is expected to develop accurate, informed descriptions of the subject. The latter act, using manual methods, is time-consuming and evasive. That act, using a focus on ideas and the supporting algorithms, is rapid and effective.

What Was Learned About Finance and Health? Figure 4 shows the information network consisting of the three nodal terms – health & finance & system – together with the terms linked with them.

This information network shows the higher frequency ideas associated with each of the nodes. The lines indicate the links between nodes and with the related terms. Health is linked with finance, system, public, and insurance, suggesting that a possible summary paragraph might be –

> The *health finance system is concerned* with the *public* and the availability of *insurance* although there *is* no higher frequency link between *public* and *insurance*. The *finance system provides cost* for *private hospitals* and specific *age* groups. The *system includes* both *private* and *government insurance designed to be economical* in *cost* and *provide quality* care. The *system includes measures* of *social data*.

Depending on the analyst, any number of arrangements could be developed by incorporating selected higher frequency ideas with lower frequency ones.

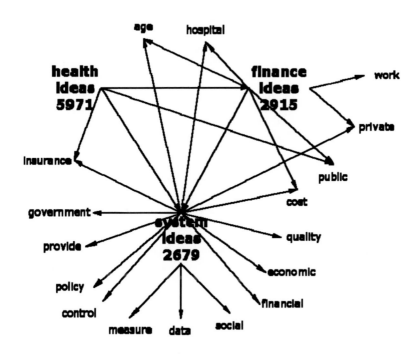

Can Ideas Really Be Extracted and Used without the Original Context? The underlying hypotheses considered in the Idea Analysis[tm] and Conceptual Architecture approaches are:

1.   The extractability of ideas.
2.   The combinability of ideas.

Traditionally, ideas would be considered within the context of previous study conditions and circumstances. As such, studies in breast cancer would focus on the ideas presented in previous breast cancer studies. While this approach has merit, there also is considerable experience in considering ideas across topics. In this regard, studies of head and neck cancer motivate bridges to studies of cervical cancer. Similarly, studies of breast cancer could motivate studies of prostate cancer. When these cross-topic experiences are considered, the primary question is first – "Does the idea found to be important in condition X, also apply when the conditions are changed to those in Y?" Posing such a question is tantamount to suggesting that ideas can be extracted from one set of conditions and tested within the context of another. If that observation is correct, then, Idea Analysis^{tm} – a formalized process of identifying and extracting ideas – can be used to generate the data used in developing conceptual structures independent of particular, restrictive conditions. That would suggest that having the ideas from each document is sufficient in building new structures.

Conceptual Structures are Skeletons: Investigators might have concerns in accepting a conceptual structure in some stand-alone fashion, and rightly so. An outline (i.e., conceptual structure) is a primary and succinct organization of information. Transformation of that into a viable description or new research process requires augmenting the skeleton with methods and data from previous studies. Previous studies of the same condition often are used to provide such detail. However, studies of other conditions may be and can be used to introduce additional methods and data, supporting the new research. The result of this means that specific articles, in the form of abstracts or full documents, would be required to build the final new document.

Critical Article Identification: The approach suggested is that only critical articles need to be studied in depth. The problem is the recognition of critical articles. A critical article could be one that brings method, design and results together to enhance understanding of the new research to be undertaken. A single article may not offer all of these informational elements in one convenient package, but selected elements should be available. As such, the retrieval and examination of a particular article can depend on the information needed. Given the category – statistical significance, data without statistical significance, opinion, or method – the article can be retrieved and the information identified.

Recognition of Gaps and/or Inconsistencies

Recognition of gaps requires confirmation that the missing information is really missing and not just a flaw in retrieval. Inconsistencies may be identified by conflicting results between studies purportedly describing the same situation. Both gaps and inconsistencies can be prioritized in terms of importance, feasibility of study, and institutional and investigator capabilities. Finding the subset of possible studies based on high scores of these attributes provides the new investigator with problems to study.

Idea Maps: An important requirement in determining missing ideas in a subject is a mechanism for visualizing ideas present in describing the topic. An established graphic device for visualizing these ideas is the idea map developed using computer software [Inspiration 2011]. There are several different formats used. The simplest of these is the idea swarm.

175

Figure 5. Format of the Idea Swarm.

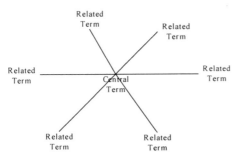

The graph (Figure 5) shows the term involved in all of the ideas. Each of these ideas consisted of the one *central term* coupled with another term labeled – *related term*.

The sentences providing these ideas would have the following format: Central term .... related term .... related term .... etc. The map shows only the ideas linked with the central and not all of the other ideas involving the pairs of related terms. Consider the following paragraph:

> *Hospital admission rates* for *childhood asthma* are influenced by the *prevalence* of asthma and the *quality* of asthma *care*. *Parents* were asked about their *childrens weight* and *height* using a **questionnaire** which included the *International Study* of *Asthma* and *Allergies* in *Childhood* (ISAAC) *core questions* on asthma. Primary *end-point* was the *development* of *atopic dermatitis*, *bronchial asthma* or *allergic rhinitis* during *childhood*.

All of the informative terms are highlighted. There were 28 [N(N-1)/2 = (8)(7)/2] ideas in the first sentence, 66 in the second sentence, and 36 in the third sentence. In the formula, the value, N, is the number of informative terms in the sentence. Of the 28 ideas in the first sentence, the ideas involving asthma were:

Asthma → hospital
Asthma → admission
Asthma → rates
Asthma → childhood
Asthma → prevalence
Asthma → quality
Asthma → care

**Figure 6. Idea Swarm Involving Asthma as \
Central Term – From Sentence 1.**

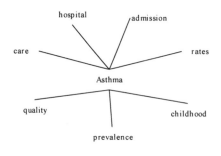

Comparing the informative terms in the first sentence with the list of ideas and the idea swarm in Figure 6, shows that the list and the map provide the same information. The map in Figure 6 shows only the ideas involving asthma as the central term, i.e., the term common to all of the identified ideas. When considering all possible ideas, any of the terms – hospital, admission, etc. – could be the central term. By identifying all of the ideas from each sentence, the ability to construct idea swarm maps describing any of the informative terms becomes a simple task.

One advantage to computerized processing of the informative terms in each sentence is this identification, extraction and organization of all possible ideas. That resource for selected topics is freely available for use in personalized resources called the Scholar's WorkStation. The capture of all of the ideas involved in a sentence implies that the author did not impose a prioritization of the ideas. Typically, the author will select the ideas s/he feels are pertinent in describing the topic. Those ideas are identified by the sequential arrangement of informative terms in the sentence. For the first sentence in the example paragraph -- *Hospital admission rates* for *childhood asthma* are influenced by the *prevalence* of *asthma* and the *quality* of *asthma care* – the sequential ideas would be:

1. hospital → admission
2. admission → rates
3. rates → childhood
4. childhood → asthma
5. asthma → prevalence
6. prevalence → asthma
7. asthma → quality
8. quality → asthma
9. asthma → care

177

Figure 7. Sequential Idea Map. Sentence 1.

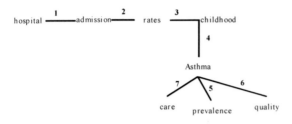

As seen in Figure 7, the sequence of ideas is indicated by the numbers. The first idea involved hospital with admission. Then admission was linked with rates. The author created a swarm within the sentence by repeatedly introducing the term – asthma -- so that childhood, prevalence, quality and care were all specifically linked with it. This repetition by the author of the term – asthma – is a clear example of the emphasis placed on it and its importance (to the author) in describing the topic.

Recognizing Gaps Using Idea Maps: The idea map is useful in depicting the ideas presented by the world's authors contributing to understanding of the topic. However, the map also shows the ideas that have not yet been studied. These presumably missing ideas require confirmation and the first task is to construct a search strategy dealing with this idea. Most of the search engines require statements such as – first term AND second term. The conjunction is capitalized in order to ensure that the search software realizes that the two terms are to be found in each document.

In contrast to the idea found in a sentence, search software will identify the required two terms wherever they occur. As a result, each retrieved article must be inspected to determine the existence of the idea (i.e., the pair of terms in a sentence) in contrast to the two distinct terms. Finding the idea means that the gap can be filled in the evolving idea map. After retrieval and inspection, if the idea is still missing, it could initiate a research strategy, if the idea was sufficiently important and feasible. This approach to building a specific knowledge resource dealing with a topic is efficient and effective in directing attention to the known and unknown components in a topic.

Recognizing Inconsistencies: Recognition of inconsistent findings is a more challenging effort. The relevant ideas must be identified and organized. For each idea, the findings from previous studies must be retrieved and arrayed so that inconsistency is apparent. Possible reasons for the inconsistency must be determined before a new strategy can be constructed. The intent of the new strategy is to optimize description of the idea(s) and accordingly, eliminate previous contradictory results. As such, an inconsistent result stimulates:

1. Query of participant selection and recruitment.
2. Measurement and observation procedures.

3. Accuracy and validity of measurements.
4. Study conduct procedures.
5. Data analysis methods.
6. Effectiveness of interpretation and explanation of the observed findings.

Development of Knowledge Generation Design: A third area of emphasis is the translation of the interesting and innovative research question into a feasible and efficient design yielding the data needed to answer the new question. A program of continued learning must be based on thorough awareness and utilization of existing knowledge coupled with mechanisms to introduce new and meaningful information. By developing a comprehensive idea map for the topic, the focus can shift to prioritizing ideas and then the strength of the important ideas in the different contributing studies. These observations and deliberations are essential precursors to the development of a design and a plan for a new study. The ideas important to the knowledge generation objective must be identified, as well as, the participant group suitable for study. The pertinent measurements and/or observations must be determined as well as the validity and accuracy associated with each. The statistical model to be employed in analyzing the data must be determined as well as the mechanisms necessary for the management of the data.

Critical Elements in Design: The design or plan is a detailed description of those elements and must clearly present the relevant knowledge, the missing or inconsistent issues, and how these will be addressed. In addition, the feasibility of capturing the data and the importance of the resulting findings must be presented. The critical elements include:

1. Organized description of the relevant background knowledge leading to a succinct statement of study intention.
2. Description and justification of the information elements making up the study. The measurements and observations to be made, the participants to be studied, and the management procedures to be employed.
3. Description and justification of the statistical analysis to be employed as well as demonstration of the study feasibility.
4. Discussion of the contributions expected from the study in terms of elucidating the previously existing knowledge and the effects of the new findings.

Figure 8. Design Schema.

179

Figure 8 shows a general schema for studies. In most studies, participants are defined using characteristics representing personal or environmental factors coupled with disease attributes. Personal factors include attributes such as – age, gender, height, weight, race, and/or ethnicity. Environmental factors include attributes such as – temperature, rainfall, flora, fauna, population, and social structure. Disease factors may be sub-classified into – laboratory, physical, and psychological attributes. Intervention factors deal with biologic, pharmacologic, psychologic, and physical forms of treatment as well as various forms of communication, personal and/or mass media. Outcome factors deal with disease control, survival, or quality of life issues. Depending on the research question to be considered, these groupings of factors may be emphasized or minimized.

Summary

Developing skill in performing the higher cognitive functions is challenging and particularly so when the student is first acquiring an understanding of the subject. To assist the student, this chapter focuses on ideas to assist in developing an gestalt perspective. With that, the process of developing the measures, criteria, and decision-structures needed in accomplishing each of the cognitive functions can be performed.

For example, synthesis is an important component in the intellectual process. The term is defined as -- *the combining of the constituent elements of separate material or abstract entities into a single or unified entity (opposed to analysis).* The process of 'putting together' implies a need for building blocks to use in construction. The idea serves as this building block by enabling the development of concepts composed of ideas describing attributes of a characteristic. The idea and associated concepts provide insights into the topic and the entire subject.

These constructions are examples of syntheses. With those in place, the individual can learn to develop measures helpful in performing comparisons. These measures and associated decision criteria provide evidence needed in evaluating the findings. The measures, criteria, and decision-structures used in evaluation will prioritize the findings so that a judgment can be made as to the best, or most effective, or most economical. Based on that decision, a new structure can be considered to report findings and/or to build a new knowledge-generating scheme.

Chapter Twelve – Case Studies

These studies illustrated the power of ideas in rapidly acquiring understanding of a new subject. In addition, the studies showed the feasibility of tracing an idea from a current, peer-reviewed, and approved research proposal, back to its origins. This process is effective in helping the student recognize the ways in which innovative actions, i.e., creativity is translated into a realistic program.

Case Study in Emergency Medicine

Development of Knowledge Base: There were 6,500 articles dealing with emergency medicine and entered in PubMed during the period 2000 through 2004. The computerized text mining procedure extracted over 180,000 ideas, linked each idea to its associated sentence and, in turn, linked each sentence to its original document. The time required was about 7 hours to prepare the web-based resource containing the information.

Analysis of Grant: Seventy-nine abstracts dealing with *emergency medicine* were retrieved from Report 2005 database.[RePORT 2011] Of these, approximately 10% were initially funded in 2005 and dealt with investigator-initiated proposals. The remaining were either educational programs or continuing grants.

The Report database describes research applications that were reviewed by peers, approved, and funded by various agencies of the United States government. An abstract from the 8 R01s was randomly selected. That application dealt with a new system for dispensing medication to elders. The sentences in the abstract were analyzed and the vocabulary and ideas extracted. Six ideas illustrated the primary theme described in the research proposal. These six ideas were:

1. *medication* with *monitoring*.
2. *monitoring* with *medication*
3. *medication* with *compliance*.
4. *compliance* with *medication*
5. *monitoring* with *compliance*.
6. *compliance* with *monitoring*.

Ideas involving these terms were retrieved from the Scholar's WorkStation dealing with *emergency medicine, 2000 - 2004*. The term, *medication*, was used in 759 ideas in these Reports during 2000 – 2004. *Compliance* was used in 229 ideas. *Monitoring* was used in 850 ideas.

Figure 1 shows the terms and ideas extracted from the REPORT summary of the grant application.[1R42AG021844-01] The terms were selected by the author. The black lines represent those ideas chosen by the author *and* present in the emergency medicine knowledge base for the period 2000 – 2004. The red lines represent those ideas that were not in that knowledge base.

Eleven terms were involved in ideas presented in that literature. *Safe* was linked with *health, monitoring* and *data*. *Health* was linked with *medicine* and *elderly*. *Response* was coupled with *emergency. Elderly* also was linked with *management* and *medication. Management* was coupled with *compliance* and *medication. Compliance* was linked with *caregiver* and *medicine.* The terms – *system, rate, web, cost, resource,* and *dispensing* – were involved with ideas provided *only* by the Report author. The author linked *system* with *medication, elderly, emergency, response* and *health. Rate* was linked with *medication. Web* was coupled with *medication* and *caregiver. Cost* and *resource* were combined, respectively, with *elderly. Dispensing* was linked with *medication.* The author-supplied ideas introduced the innovative concept of a web-based medication dispensing system for elders.

Figure 1. Terms and Ideas Extracted from a REPORT Application -- 1R42AG021844.

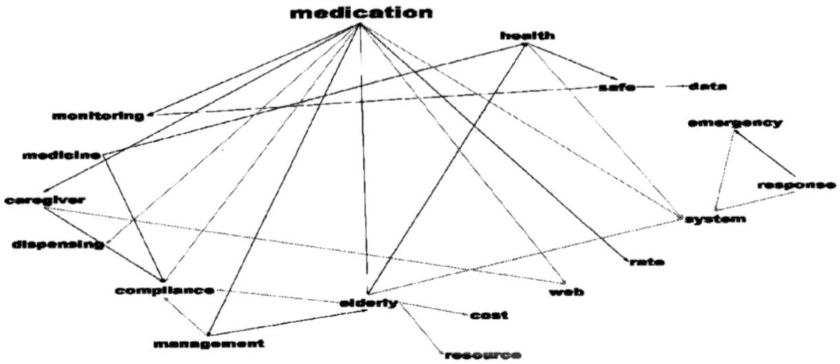

An investigator is not restricted to one literature topic. To illustrate the possibilities associated with integrating ideas across different topics, Figure 2 shows the ideas, identified by green lines, linking *medication* with the terms chosen by the author-investigator. The geriatrics Scholar's WorkStation contributed ideas involving *medication* with *health, response, data, cost* and *compliance.* The remaining ideas shown by green lines came from the epidemiology or internal medicine Scholar WorkStations The idea -- *medication* and *compliance* -- denotes an idea provided by the author *and* included in the other knowledge bases.

Missing Ideas: A search of the general medical literature for the period 2000 – 2004 dealing with *web-based medication dispensing systems* showed that only 8 articles tangentially dealt with that topic. Three described data collection systems and two dealt with ordering systems. There were 207 articles dealing with *medication* and *dispensing* and one article described the combination of *medication* and *worldwide web*. There were 167 dealing with the combination of *medication* and *internet*. These ideas were central to the author's research proposal and were represented in the general medical literature but not in the *emergency medicine* literature.

Figure 2. Terms and Ideas From Other Knowledge Bases.

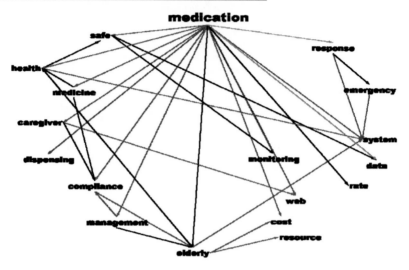

Figure 3. Ideas Linked with Medication.

Exploring the 'Black Box': The ideas involving *medication* shown in Figure 3 present an interesting story regarding the availability of information in the emergency medicine knowledge base. Two ideas – *medication* with, respectively, *rate* and *elderly* – were present in that resource. However, exploring the ideas available in related resources – epidemiology, geriatrics and internal medicine – provided most of the ideas required by the author. These were

183

medication with, respectively, *caregiver, medicine, safe, health, response, data, monitoring, cost, management,* and *compliance.* Three ideas, well represented in the general medical literature, were required. These were – *medication* with, respectively, *system, web,* and *dispensing.*

This creative action appears to be one of bringing ideas from other topics into the emergency medicine topic. However, the focus on a medication system for the elderly could have emerged from the geriatrics literature. While the search of Report identified the abstract as belonging in Emergency Medicine, the analysis using the geriatrics knowledge base suggested that the study could have been classified as belonging to that discipline. In that knowledge base, 12 of the 15 *medication* related ideas were present. The missing ideas were *medication* with, respectively, *system, rate,* and *dispensing.* Contrast that with the fact that in the emergency medicine knowledge base, only *medication* with *rate, medication* and *elderly* were identified ideas. In each analysis – *emergency medicine* or *geriatrics* – *medication* with *dispensing* and *medication* with *system* had to be supplied by the author. Further, articles related to *medication dispensing* were available in the general medical literature.

Erroneous Classification: The search of Report consisted of seeking those grants funded in 2005 dealing with emergency medicine. The abstract was included in the retrieved set. However, review of the thesaurus terms showed that *emergency* was used in the phrase – *emergency services* – and *medicine* came from the phrase – *geriatrics medicine.* The erroneous combination is an example of a frequent occurrence involving *a posteriori Boolean combinations.* In the Report search engine, terms involved in the search statement were forced into an *AND Boolean* operation and ignored the author's use of the terms. While the terms used in the search strategy were present, retrieval of the abstract would be considered a *false hit.* By focusing on the ideas involved and their sources in the various knowledge bases, the classification of an emergency medicine grant should be more appropriately changed to a member of the geriatrics grants. Confirmation of the accuracy of the reclassification can be seen by the participants in the research and the funding agency. All were from geriatrics. The principal investigator has an MD as well as a PhD in Biomedical Engineering and is in charge of a medical clinic dealing with management of geriatric patients.

Role of New Technology: This Report illustrated the advantages of using computerized text mining to build a web knowledge base containing a comprehensive array of the pertinent information needed to build new cognitive structures. One relevant finding was the likely misclassification of the Report document as belonging to Emergency Medicine when Geriatrics would have been a more accurate category. If the research proposal is considered as belonging to Emergency Medicine, three of the medication related ideas used by the author were present in that resource. However, the author is not restricted to one knowledge base and exploring the epidemiology, geriatrics, and internal medicine knowledge bases filled in a number of the ideas used by the author. When the proposal was considered as belonging to Geriatrics, 12 of the 15 ideas were present in that Scholar's WorkStation suggesting that the problem considered was one more familiar to geriatric specialists. The author's study proposal would still be considered innovative because the application of an innovative medication dispensing system for the elderly with an Internet record of medication-taking had not been studied in either discipline. The author's contribution appears to be one of bringing ideas from other topics into the topic of interest. This is a frequently employed approach in research and is made easier and faster by the knowledge bases presenting the ideas in each discipline.

In this proposal, the engineering concepts came from the investigator's experience and knowledge of Biomedical Engineering. The dispensing machine can be programmed to dispense up to 6 different medications daily, each delivered with instructions. As the patient complies, an entry is made to a web-based data record enabling ease of monitoring. The machine also is programmed to alert up to 4 caregivers if the patient fails to comply. The research proposal involved the development of a randomized study to determine the effectiveness of this device.[Sahai 2005]

Case Study in Gynecologic Oncology

Development of Knowledge Base: Gynecologic oncologists in academic medicine, as with other surgical disciplines, face significant challenges in performing the duties expected as physicians and academicians. In contrast to other disciplines, surgical specialists must spend large blocks of time in direct care of their patients. This hands-on approach to healthcare delivery leaves little protected time to engage in research planning or conduct. As such, it is not surprising to find that in the first 6 months of 2005, there was only 1 investigator-initiated grant application funded by the agencies of the federal government and reported in Report.[Report 2005]

The scientific Reports dealing with *uterine cancer* were retrieved from PubMed for the years 1994 through June 2005. There was an annual average of 500 articles dealing with uterine cancer entered in PubMed during the period 1994 through 2004 for a total of about 5,500 articles. The computerized text mining procedure extracted an estimated 300,000 ideas, linked each idea to its associated sentence and, in turn, linked each sentence to its original document.

Figure 4. Ideas in the Third Sentence.

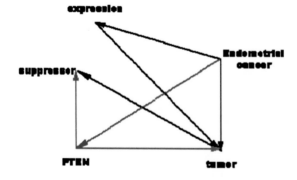

Analysis of Grant: Thirty-seven abstracts dealing with gynecologic cancer were retrieved from REPORT 2005 database.[RePORT 2011] An abstract for a grant initiated during 2005, dealt with the study of PTEN, a tumor suppressor, in endometrial cancer. The sentences in the abstract were analyzed and the vocabulary and ideas extracted.

Thirty-four terms were used by the author of the funded report grant. The ideas were explored using the Scholar WorkStations for 1994 through 2004. *Endometrial* with *cancer* was reported 4,168 times in the uterine cancer literature. *Estrogen* and *cancer* were reported 173 times. *Estrogen* and *receptor* was studied 366 times. Tumor and suppressor was previously reported 2 times.

The ideas in each sentence, from the Report abstract -- 1F31GM073349-01, were extracted and compared with those in the web-based *knowledge base*. Figure 4 shows the ideas for the third sentence. The author's contributions are the ideas linking *PTEN* with *tumor, suppressor* and *endometrial cancer*. These ideas were not previously included in the uterine cancer knowledge base and the idea linking *tumor* with *suppressor* was previously reported only 2 times. The author selected *PTEN* as the primary element in the study. Ideas previously reported in the literature were *endometrial cancer* with *expression* and *tumor*. In addition, *tumor* was previously linked with *suppressor*.

Figure 5 expands the ideas associated with PTEN. This display also shows the contribution of the author in selecting *PTEN* as the *tumor suppressor* and the hypothesized interactions with *estrogen* related *carcinogenesis*.

Figure 5. Ideas in the Fourth Sentence.

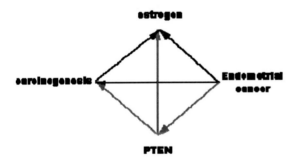

Figure 6 shows the ideas in the fifth sentence. The author's new ideas focused on linking, respectively, *PTEN* with *cell, epidermal growth factor (EGF), estrogen receptor (ER), gene* and *endometrial cancer*. As seen in this display, these new ideas complete the description. The ideas already present in the literature involved *endometrial cancer* with *cell, EGF, ER* and *gene*. In addition, ideas had been reported linking *cell* with *EGF, ER, gene* and *endometrial cancer*.

The approved study was designed to determine if *PTEN* affected the interaction between *EGF* and *ER*.

In testing the feasibility of the web-based resource to support this creative process, the terms and ideas from an approved Report grant were identified. The terms and ideas included in the Report author's abstract (i.e., sentences 3-5) were compared respectively with the vocabulary and ideas in the uterine cancer knowledge base. (See Figures 4-6)

Figure 6.   Ideas in Fifth Sentence.

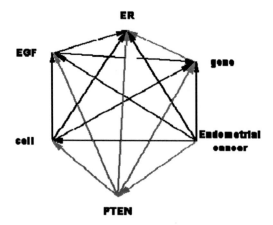

These idea representations of the author's sentences illustrate the cognitive process employed by the author. While the actual process employed is unknown, if the author had selected the terms associated with *endometrial cancer, estrogen* and *tumor suppression*, the web-based resource would have provided the ideas, sentences containing those, and the links to the original documents. The author could have selected PTEN as the tumor suppressor of interest in order to explore the relationships between epidermal growth factor (EGF) and estrogen receptor (ER) in carcinogenesis.

Value of Ideas: The ideas shown in the figures may or may not have been studied in the same context as the grant proposed, but as ideas, they were pertinent to the problem that the author wanted to study. Displaying the literature-provided ideas showed gaps in the description. The author supplied additional ideas completing the scenario associated with the links between estrogen, EGF, ER and endometrial carcinogenesis. By gleaning the full set of ideas in a topic and/or related topics, the author can construct an idea map that graphically details the intended research and, using the web-based knowledge bases, can do so in a short time. If the resource had been used by the author, the ideas representing the theme might have led to the display shown in The contribution associated with incorporating PTEN into the existing knowledge is evident. An

187

additional search employing PTEN, endometrial cancer and receptor yielded 12 articles. None of these explored the relations suggested in the research proposal. However, there were 201 articles published between 1994 and 2004 dealing with PTEN in other cancers. As such, as an idea, PTEN and cancer was well established.

A possible explanation for the author's selection of PTEN in endometrial cancer was the need to supply a missing piece of information regarding the function of this tumor suppressor. The unique contribution of the proposal was seen in the decision of the peer-review. While the reviewers' comments are unknown, their actions in approving the grant application suggest that the consensus opinion was clear. Namely, the proposed investigation offered new information relevant to the problem of understanding the carcinogenesis of endometrial cancer.

Case Study in Chronic Renal Failure

Development of Knowledge Base: There were over 14,500 articles dealing with chronic renal failure entered into PubMed during 2000 – 2004. A current concept in this array of ideas is *renoprotect* and there were 204 ideas involving this term in the 2000-2004 knowledge bases. The term first appeared in the 1998 literature. The *renoprotect* ideas were classified into five categories. The treatment factors linked with *renoprotect* included *losartan, transplant, ACE, angiotensin* and *irbesartan.* The disease factors included *hypertension, diabetes,* and *renal disease.* Renal factors included protein, filtration, calcium and uria conditions. A literature review in 2003 suggested that the angiotensin II blocker, Irbesartan, showed blood pressure reduction plus an important reduction in albuminuria suggesting that the angiotensin II blocker offered significant reduction in deterioration of the kidneys. [Lewis 2003]

Renoprotect and Complications? A funded grant application describing kidney failure from the Report database [RePORT 2011] suggested that there might be significant complications associated with the administration of the angiotensin II blockade. The principal adverse effects were hypothesized to be androgen deficiency leading to a drop in serum levels of testosterone together with diminution of erythropoietin production with resulting anemia.

Exploration of the Creative Act: This Report explores the paths possible in leading to this creative act. The sentences provided by the author of the grant were analyzed and the ideas presented were compared with those in the 2000-2004 knowledge base.

The missing ideas were – *androgen* with *kidney, androgen* with *depression,* and *anemia* with *depression.* The other ideas expressed by the author were present in the knowledge base.
The author linked *testosterone* with *renin, angiotensin, blockade, erythropoietin,* and *anemia.* These ideas were not included in the knowledge base for 2000 – 2004. Similarly, *renin* with *blockade, erythropoietin, testosterone, deficiency* and *anemia* were not in the knowledge base. These missing ideas illustrate the difference between the author's emphasis and that provided by the world's literature. The ideas in the knowledge base connect *renin* with *angiotensin, angiotensin* with *blockade, erythropoietin, deficiency,* and *anemia.* In contrast, the ideas in the knowledge base connect *testosterone* with *deficiency* and *anemia.* If the intent of new research is to identify and fill missing ideas, this study illustrates the contribution made by this author.

This author's contribution to the body of knowledge is associated with providing missing information. Those were *testosterone* with *erythropoietin, angiotensin* and *anemia*. There are ideas that would continue to be missing *after* completion of the author's research. *Renin* with, respectively, *testosterone, androgen,* and *anemia* would be missing. In addition, a direct connection between *angiotensin* and *androgen* would be missing.

The Role of Androgens: Recklehoff and Grainger [Recklehoff 1999] hypothesized that androgens increased arterial pressure by causing a hypertensive shift in the pressure-natriuresis relationship, either by having a direct effect by increasing proximal tubular reabsorption or by activation of the renin-angiotensin system. They also hypothesized that the enhanced proximal tubular reabsorption led to a tubuloglomerular feedback-mediated afferent vasodilation, which, in combination with the increase in arterial pressure, resulted in glomerular hypertension and renal injury. Gandolfo et al [Gandolfo 2004] suggested that androgens contributed to continuous loss of kidney cells though the stimulation of apoptotic pathways. They reported that *in vitro* studies indicated that androgens primed a Fas/FasL dependent apoptotic pathway in kidney tubule cells. They suggested that androgens had a role in promoting chronic renal injury in men.

The Role of Testosterone: Silbiger [Silbiger 2003] considered the hypothesis that testosterone explained a worse course of chronic renal disease in men than experienced by women. They indicated that the gender difference in renal disease existed in animals as well as humans. Lavoie et al [Lavoie 2004] evaluated the physiologic significance of a tissue renin-angiotensin system in the kidney tubule. These investigators produced mice that expressed human renin and human angiotensinogen. They reported that female mice with these transgenes showed an increase in mean arterial pressure when testosterone was administered. DeLong et al [DeLong 2005] reported that the renin-angiotensin system blockade was associated with lower levels of serum testosterone in men treated with hemodialysis. These investigators also reported that serum testosterone was negatively correlated with erythropoietin dose.

Angiotensin-Renin Blockade: Gronroos et al [Gronroos 1997] explored the effects of ramipril, an angiotensin-converting enzyme (ACE) inhibitor, on a series of hormones. They indicated that ramipril decreased free thyroxine. The other endocrinologic tests, including serum testosterone, were not affected by this ACE inhibitor. Chiurchiu et al [Chiurchiu 2005] reported that clinical studies showed a significant correlation between urinary protein excretion and rate of GFR decline in chronic renal disease. They indicated that randomized trials, in particular, the Ramipril Efficacy In Nephropathy (REIN) study, showed that treatments designed to reduce proteinuria were renoprotective and limited progression to ESRD. Meta-analyses of randomized clinical trials confirmed the predictive value of proteinuria and the renoprotective effect of proteinuria reduction by ACE inhibition therapy.

Creativity in Identifying Missing Ideas: The creative act suggested by the author of the grant involved supplying missing ideas. The author's hypothesis, when viewed in terms of ideas, could be considered as a simple completion process. Missing ideas were identified and the proposal offered to provide the information.

This example may represent a distinction between unimportant and not studied. The many clinical trials and meta-analyses dealing with the study of angiotensin-renin blockade did not emphasize the angiotensin-testosterone-anemia effects. This could be due to the lack of adverse effects or to lack of focus on hormonal relationships in chronic renal disease. The author's grant proposal and the article by DeLong [DeLong 2005] seek to provide missing information. The study group in the DeLong report involved patients receiving hemodialysis. Anemia is not an uncommon event in such patients and numerous causes can be identified. The triad involving *angiotensin-testosterone-anemia* is not the only one that may be operative in this patient group. However, the peer-review process recognized that the question dealing with renoprotective therapy and anemia was an important one. The analysis of the ideas involved showed that those provided by the author were missing both from the knowledge base considered (2000-2004) and from the general medical literature.

Investigator's Insights: The recognition of the missing ideas by the investigator and colleagues was somewhat *mystical* as none of the authors of the 2005 article [DeLong 2005] had a publication history linking *testosterone, androgen deficiency, renin-angiotensin blockade,* and *anemia*. While there were over 250 articles in PubMed linking *testosterone* with *renal function*, 13 articles dealt with the specific triad of *testosterone, renal function* and *angiotensin*. Of those, the DeLong et al article [DeLong 2005] was the only one suggesting an adverse effect of angiotensin. Accordingly, the decision to study *testosterone* and *renin-angiotensin blockade* isn't apparent on the basis of personal experience characterized by publication history or general publication knowledge dealing with the pertinent combination of variables. When queried regarding the possible path leading to the creative act, the investigator suggested that the result was the consequence of an extensive review of the literature. No further insights were offered.[Logan 2005]

Case Study in Substance Abuse

Approximately 8000 articles were retrieved from PubMed representing substance abuse research in 2003-2004. A knowledge base dealing with over 205,000 ideas was developed. About 2100 research proposals were entered into RePORT [RePORT 2011] for the first 8 months of 2005. These entries represent grants initially funded in 2005 as well as those receiving continuing funding. A grant abstract was randomly selected from the set that were initially funded in 2005.

The ideas in the abstract. [Report 2005--1R03DA017668] have been classified arbitrarily into categories. The assignment was based on meaning and/or function. All of the terms were linked to substance abuse in the knowledge base. One idea – *prevention* and *stress* -- was not in the knowledge base. Three of the missing ideas involved *coping*. These were, respectively, *coping* with *children, violence* and *family*. The last missing idea involved *trauma* and *community*.

Of interest, is the possibility that these missing ideas were not essential to the proposed study. That is, the new grant application described the development of a knowledge base involving apparently previously studied measures in a purposive sample of women. The study aims were to determine the prevalence of substance abuse, partner violence, comorbidity among women subjected to this violence. In addition, the study sought to describe the relationship between substance abuse and post-traumatic stress syndrome symptom severity. Based on these data, intervention models would be developed. The only idea that had not been previously studied was the link between *partner* and *severity*. This idea was not described as central to the rationale for the research.

Methodologic Issues? A new study designed to correct the methodologic problems observed in previous reports would be approved if the methods improved on those employed before. The new study proposed to study 200 women identified as having been the victims of partner violence as well as substance abuse. Total sample sizes from prior studies are shown in Figure 7. The median was approximately 800. The smallest sample size was 103 and the largest was 6,004. Eight of the 10 studies exceeded the 200 sample size proposed in the new study. None of the studies – new or existing – reported using random samples from defined populations. Instead, all used purposive samples based on arrest or medical records.

Figure 7. Total Sample Sizes of Prior Partner Violence Studies.

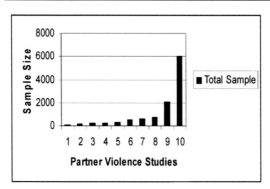

Figure 8 showed the number of women studied in previous studies. The median in the 8 prior studies was approximately 220, comparable to the proposed study. Four of the prior studies were less than the proposed 200 and the other four were 303, 400, 526, and 1025. As such, approval of the new application was not based on improving the study process by increasing the size of the sample.

Study Design: Reports from 2000 through 2004 showed a preponderance of purposive studies. One article, predating the current knowledge base, involved an intervention program dealing with safety behaviors. [McFarlane 2002] These authors reported results of a two-group randomized, controlled clinical trial involving 75 abused women who received six telephone intervention sessions. A control group of 75 women received standard care. The authors re-interviewed women in both groups at 3 months and 6 months. They found that significantly more women in the intervention group adopted safety behaviors at both the 3-month and 6-

month interviews. The new study did not improve on the design. Instead, the new study proposed a purposive design.

Figure 8. Sample Sizes of Prior Partner Violence Studies -- Women.

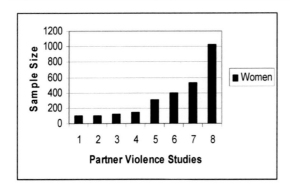

Other Factors Related to Partner Violence: Thirteen articles entered into PubMed during 2003 and 2004 contained the idea – *partner* and *violence*. Those were reviewed and summarized into four categories – Problem Drinking, Risk Factors, Patterns of Injury, and Therapy.

Partner Violence and Problem Drinking: White et al [White 2002] examined the role of problem drinking in intimate partner violence (IPV) perpetration and victimization for men and women in a longitudinal design. The authors performed regression analyses to determine if relationship dissatisfaction and partner drinking patterns mediated the effects of problem drinking on IPV after controlling for eight common risk factors. The authors reported that the relationship between problem drinking and IPV was not spurious. They indicated that heavier drinking by partners put women at greater risk for physical assault and, further, mediated the effects of their own problem drinking. Stuart [Stuart 2004] compared hazardous and nonhazardous drinking women on violence and victimization. They explored whether group differences in these variables were attributable to women's drinking, their general propensity for violence, their partners' drinking, or a combination of these factors. They reported that the hazardous drinking group scored higher on physical assault, psychological abuse, sexual abuse, and injuries. They used regression analyses and found that women's drinking, women's general violence, and partner drinking all contributed to some form of violence or victimization.

Partner Violence and Risk Factors: Parrott et al [Parrott 2003] examined the effects of substance dependence and posttraumatic stress disorder (PTSD) on perpetration of partner violence. These authors indicated that participants with comorbid cocaine dependence and PTSD reported the highest frequency of partner violence. Field and Caetano [Field 2003] examined ethnic-specific longitudinal predictors of male-to-female and female-to-male partner violence in white, black, and Hispanic couples in the U.S. general population. They indicated that they used the following risk factors: gender, history of childhood abuse, exposure to parental violence, impulsivity, alcohol problems, frequency of drinking five or more drinks per occasion, volume of alcohol consumed per week in average standard drinks, approval of marital aggression and partner violence. They used ethnic-specific multivariate logistic regression models. They reported that Black and Hispanic couples were at approximately two to three times greater risk of partner violence at follow-up in comparison to white couples even after controlling for socio-demographic characteristics, alcohol consumption, and psychosocial variables. Chase et al [Chase 2003] reported that women committed more violent acts overall and were more likely to commit severely violent acts than the men. They indicated that risk factors for partner violence were: less education, lower income, greater relationship problems, stronger beliefs in the link between relationship problems and the female patient's drinking, greater cocaine use by the perpetrator of violence and greater emotional distress of the men. El-Bassel et al [El-Bassel 2003] used two instruments -- Alcohol Use Disorders Identification Test (AUDIT) and Drug Abuse Severity Test (DAST). They reported higher scores among physically abused women. They indicated that a higher proportion of abused women reported a history of regular crack, cocaine, or heroin use and visiting shooting galleries or crack houses.

Patterns of Traumatic Injury: Crandall and colleagues [Crandall 2004] identified women aged 16 to 65 years discharged from acute care hospitals in a single year with a primary diagnosis of injury. The authors collected data from 14 states across the United States. The analysis featured multivariate logistic regression. They reported that women who suffered blunt intentional trauma exhibited very different injury patterns than those hospitalized for motor vehicle collisions or falls.

Partner Violence and Therapy: O'Farrell et al [O'Farrell 2004] examined partner violence before and after behavioral couples therapy for 303 married or cohabiting male alcoholic patients and used a demographically matched nonalcoholic comparison sample. They reported that structural equation modeling indicated that greater treatment involvement was related to lower violence after treatment and that this association was mediated by reduced problem drinking and enhanced relationship functioning.

Partner Violence – 2000-2002: A search of PubMed using – *partner violence* – during the period 2000 through 2002 identified an additional 323 articles. Only one of these described a randomized study.[McFarlane 2002] Another described the development of a national guideline for the recognition of abused women. Realizing that this guideline was not being followed, the author urged the initiation of randomized controlled studies.[Goodyear-Smith 2002] The remaining articles were results from purposive sample studies.

Gaps, Discrepancies or Inconsistencies: Important reasons for funding a grant application are recognition of gaps, inconsistencies and/or discrepancies in the existing knowledge. The new study revisits a previously studied relationship between partner violence and post-traumatic stress syndrome in the abused women.[e.g., Najavits 2004] Considering the ideas involved, it is clear that the impact of post-traumatic stress required further clarification. While the links between violence and trauma and morbidity were present, the links adding violence and stress as well as trauma, morbidity and stress were not present. The new study seeks to provide those data.

These new findings presumably will identify the links leading to new interventions in dealing with this complex problem. Presumably, the reviewers of this grant application concurred with the author by their decision to approve and recommend funding for this study.

Case Study of Endometriosis

There were 3,637 articles dealing with endometriosis entered into PubMed during the period 1990 through 2002. These articles were analyzed using Idea Analysis and the resulting data entered into a knowledge base. There were over 23,000 ideas identified.

This research proposal described a randomized study comparing *oral contraceptives* versus the combination of *leuprolide* and *norethindrone* following surgery to remove endometriosis adhesions. The informative terms are highlighted in the sentence. The terms – *efficacy, effective, operative, treatment and pelvic* – were not in the knowledge base vocabulary and that fact is denoted by the red highlighting. The predominant missing ideas were associated with *cost*. One of the objectives in the research proposal was the determination of costs associated with the two treatment regimens. However the primary objective was to compare the comparison of leuprolide and norethindrone versus oral contraceptives in a randomized study. The author stated that this would be the first such clinical trial.

Randomized Clinical Trials: Four articles were published during the period, 1987 – 2002, dealing with randomized clinical trials of post-operative treatments to control the recurrence of endometriosis and/or control of associated pelvic pain.

Danazol vs. Medroxyprogesterone: Telimaa et al [Telimaa 1987] evaluated the clinical efficacy and tolerance of danazol, a gonadotropin inhibitor, versus high-dose medroxy-progesterone acetate (a progestin) in the treatment of mild-moderate endometriosis. The authors indicated that total or partial resolution of peritoneal implants was observed in 60% of the patients receiving danazol and in 63% of the patients receiving medroxy-progesterone. They reported that danazol and medroxyprogesterone significantly alleviated endometriosis-associated pelvic pain, lower back pain and defecation pain, but they did not differ from each other in these actions.

Danazol vs. Buserelin: Dmowski et al [Dmowski 1989] compared the effectiveness of Buserelin (an agent that decreases production of testosterone) and danazol in inducing ovarian suppression for the management of endometriosis. They reported that they the two agents induced a similar degree of ovarian suppression resulting in a comparable clinical improvement and regression of endometriotic lesions.

Gonadotrophin-Releasing Hormone Analogue vs. Leuprolide: Busacca and colleagues [Busacca 2002] reported results of a study of 89 women randomized to receive monthly injections of gonadotrophin-releasing hormone analogue plus leuprolide (n = 44) or no additional treatment (n = 45). They indicated that there were no differences in pregnancy rate or pelvic pain occurrence.

Leuprolide Plus Four Randomized Regimens: Surrey et al [Surrey 2002] reported results of a randomized clinical trial. They indicated that all patients received monthly leuprolide and were randomized to one of four groups:
1.   Daily placebo;
2.   Daily norethindrone;
3.   Daily norethindrone and low dose conjugated equine estrogens; and
4.   Daily norethindrone and higher dose conjugated equine estrogens.
They indicated that symptom and pelvic examination scores remained significantly below baseline for at least 8 months after completion of therapy for all four groups. No differences between the treatment regimens were reported.

Frequency of Occurrence of Ideas: The frequency of occurrence of each idea is an indicator of stability in describing the topic. For example, progesterone linked with other terms occurred 61 times in the knowledge base. Oophorectomy ideas occurred 38 times. Danazol ideas occurred 93 times, estrogen ideas 104 times, and gonadotropin ideas 46 times. Infertility ideas occurred 475 times, pregnancy ideas 169, and menopausal ideas 54 times. The median number of ideas per term was 62 in the set of terms not used by the author. In contrast, the median number of ideas per term was 33 in the set of terms used by the author.

Authors tend to include less frequently occurring ideas in their research. While some of the terms included are used to anchor the new proposal to existing knowledge and thus occur frequently in writings, the new ideas will be more recent additions to the knowledge. This fact seems to contrast with the well established assumption from linguistics that the prevalent terms represent the language of the topic. The distinction between term frequency and idea frequency is an important one. The former is an indicator of language. The latter is an indicator of how the language is used. To understand creativity, it is necessary to determine usage.

New Randomized Study: The preceding studies set the stage for the proposal presented by the author of the approved Report grant application. With reported equivalence in pregnancy, pain control and recurrence associated with previous treatments, the author stated that the proposed study was designed to recognize the difference between the two randomized regimens (i.e., oral contraceptives vs. leuprolide plus norethindrone) using pain as the primary measure and cost as a secondary one.

Case Study in Epidemiology

The epidemiology Scholar's WorkStation contains scientific Reports from PubMed for the period 1996 to the present. There are over 68,000 ideas including the terms – *epidemiology* or *epidemiologic*. Report contained over 3700 funded grant applications. From those initiated in 2005, one was randomly selected for analysis. [Report 2005, 1K23AG026754]

Study Aims: Two ideas – *biomarker* , respectively, with *spouse* and *offspring* – were not included in the knowledge base. The term, *centenarian*, was not included in the vocabulary for the epidemiology knowledge base.

Building Blocks in Studying Creativity: Table 1 shows the word pairs forming ideas in these two sentences. The sentence containing the word pair is indicated by a number, 1 or 2. The numbers indicate the sentence(s) containing the ideas. These word pairs are used differently in this analysis. The focus here is to determine the building blocks used by the author in presenting concepts and issues underlying the creative act. In contrast, the usual application of word pairs is in forming labels describing documents. The labels are used to retrieve documents that, then, must be subjected to manual analysis. The Idea Analysis system seeks to minimize the manual effort involved by identifying, extracting and organizing the ideas (word pairs) from the authors' sentences. The investigator, using this system, can begin by forming new syntheses, comparisons, and the rest of the higher cognitive functions, without the drudgery associated with the initial mechanical operations.

Table 1. Word Pairs forming Ideas in First and Second Sentences.
:

	Off-sprg	Spouse	Heart	Hlth	Prevalence	Vasc	Bio-marker	Polymorphism	Gene
Offspring		1	1,2	1	1	1	1	2	2
Spouse			1	1	1	1	1		
Cardiovascular	1	1		1	1	1	1	2	2
Health	1	1	1		1	1	1		
Prevalence	1	1	1	1		1	1		
Vascular	1	1	1	1	1		1		
Bio-marker	1	1	1	1	1	1			
Polymorphism	2		2						2
Gene	2		2					2	

These data Table 1 demonstrate that the investigator did not identify missing ideas and use that information to construct the new grant application. In addition, there is no indication that these ideas led to inconsistencies or discrepancies requiring replication with improved methods.

Ideas From the Epidemiologic Knowledge Base: The particular terms are those used by the author of the grant together with terms from the literature published by this author.[Terry 2003, Terry 2004-A, Terry 2004-B] Each of these ideas, i.e., *term with epidemiology*, was included in the knowledge base. The number associated with each idea indicated the frequency of its use by authors Reporting epidemiologic studies (1996-2004). Overall, the terms – *epidemiology* and *epidemiologic* – were linked with other terms, 68,000 times. Epidemiology was linked with cardiovascular 417 times. Hypertension was linked with epidemiology 191 times. These frequencies have been used to depict those ideas of interest to investigators with the most frequent being designated as more popular.

Idea Categories: Three types of ideas were identified. The first dealt with terms that were not included in the vocabulary. One term, i.e., *onset,* is included in this category. The frequency assigned was zero indicating that the word was missing from the knowledge base. The second category represents terms used by the author in the grant application. All of these terms had been studied and linked with *epidemiology* in the past. The third category includes terms introduced by the author in publications appearing during 2004. Each of those terms also had been studied as ideas and had been included in the knowledge base.

Longevity Studies: The knowledge base contained 17 ideas dealing with longevity. Of the terms used by the author, three had been linked with *longevity* in the knowledge base. Those were – *life, vascular,* and *cardiovascular*. While the ideas have been studied, these ideas have not been studied in the particular subgroup of persons of interest, namely, those offspring of centenarian parents.

This grant application was sponsored by the New England Centenarian Study, a research program going back to the late 1980s. A number of different investigators, interested in geriatrics, had published different findings describing the subgroup of centenarians. The ideas described in the research grant, however, were new to the study as well as to the literature. While established in general epidemiologic studies, these ideas were new to the epidemiology of centenarian offspring.

Chapter Thirteen – Creativity in the Workplace

Introduction

Creativity in the workplace implies that new, effective and efficient solutions to problems will be accomplished within an environment conducive in performing work. These environments cover a wide range of situations from the small area in the corner of a laboratory to the organization's main conference room. At one level, a team could consist of individuals with special skills, experiences, and capabilities. These individuals join to produce a result that requires this collaborative effort. This oriented and focused organization implies that each team member adopts, adheres, and complies with the rules established for or by the team.

An emergency room team is an example of this single-mindedness approach to problem solving. The patient appears with an observable problem. Depending on that problem, the team members carry out specific, detailed procedures in a simultaneous fashion. In that sense, the team acts as a single, multi-armed, multi-tasked entity. As a result, the presenting problem and related ones are met with procedures designed to diagnose, treat, and evaluate the results of the treatment.

This scenario is an example of the wisdom base in action. The necessary information has been prioritized and filtered so that the specific information – diagnostic and personal – can be rapidly obtained. The possible interventions are reduced to the best available in dealing with each presented condition, and surveillance measures are instituted to determine the results. Similar scenarios could be constructed describing defined reaction-action-reaction episodes in sports.

The team appointed to develop some new entity, however, may not act with the precision and conformity exhibited by counterparts in sports or medical care. In those situations, the procedures to be performed were known. The charge was to carry out these tasks expeditiously and effectively. In the creative team, the wisdom base may be a brake on effective progress. Each individual comes with ego and agenda differences. Of greater concern is the observation that each member comes with an individualized perspective regarding the problem and how it should be solved. The time required to transform these different and independent individuals into a cohesive unit may be long. The challenges to ego that emerge during the conditioning process are significant and critical members may elect to drop out.

In addition to the personnel issues that could develop, the workplace environment offers problems. One group may require a quiet secluded setting allowing the individuals to adapt to the serenity and peacefulness so that there are no hindrances to the emergence of creative juices. Another group may require the hum of a busy office with phones ringing and people talking in the background. A third group may require physical contact between the members while a fourth insists on internet communication capabilities. These environmental factors plus the personnel considerations must be tweaked so that the group can focus on the objective, namely, the development of a new solution to an ongoing problem.

Inherent in the formation and operation of a team to accomplish creative work is the assumption that the individuals possess the necessary information and capabilities to transform existing knowledge into a new knowledge generating strategy and beyond. This assumption may be associated with the most challenging barrier to productivity. Individuals do possess personal knowledge bases composed of facts, opinions, and impressions that have been acquired and organized over time. Accordingly, when the individual is recruited to the team, s/he brings this personalized knowledge to the table. More often, than not, that is accompanied by a particular plan intended to solve the problem.

These plans will be aired, discussed, and prioritized by the group depending on the strength of the individuals' convictions and the appeal of the arguments presented. This interaction is considered to be a favorable exercise and has been labeled as brainstorming. The problem is not one of being correct or incorrect. The problem is one of dealing with the specific, realistic problem. The failure to do so is described disparagingly in the form of a humorous statement such as – "A camel is a horse designed by a committee!"

An Alternative Approach: Consider an approach involving a comprehensive description of the problem. This description, text or graphic, consists of a swarm of ideas depicting the world's authors' findings related to the problem. This gestalt view of the problem presents the group with a complete and accurate accounting of what is known regarding the problem. This description differs from the one in the wisdom base because it contains the relevant, possibly relevant, probably relevant, and not so contributors to the problem. This array allows the subject specialists to take a fresh look at the subject and the elements that may be related to the problem. This description constitutes a new learning experience and based on that, possible solutions can be formulated and evaluated. The discussion can be directed toward developing a consensus regarding the critical elements that must be addressed in solving the problem. In addition, a major strength of the team can be realized. That is, the specific insights from members regarding measures to be used, criteria that would be appropriate, and decision-structures that must be considered. These elements fit into the evolving plan in much the same way as adding specific positions to a baseball or football team. The plan cannot move forward without such experience and insights.

This idea-oriented, data-driven approach to identifying the particular solution of merit is also faster and easier to accomplish. The hours and hours of brainstorming involving various personalized views of the real knowledge base would be eliminated, or reduced. There would be individuals with frustrated egos because of the realization that their view of the problem was a filtered one, comparable to 'blind men examining an elephant". However, once the team realizes that their charge is not to adopt an individual's solution but to develop a consensus, quality-controlled path to the solution, they can take personal ownership of the group product.

Wisdom Bases, Knowledge Bases, and Information Overload: In the 21st century, the concept of available information could be changed to one describing the abundance of information. Search engines can identify and retrieve millions of websites in fractions of a minute. Statistical software can perform complex arithmetic operations again in minutes. These technical improvements make the separation of tasks possible and feasible. As such, there are procedures that can be best performed by computer, by technician, and by subject specialist. The overall goal is to enhance lifelong learning by offering methodology to facilitate on-demand, just-in-time, and self-discovery learning. A corollary would involve the enhanced capability for diverse specialists to deal with a problem in a creative fashion. In this sense, the development of an individualized wisdom base may be detrimental. The replacement of the wisdom base with a comprehensive knowledge base together with methods for rapidly accessing, organizing and using the data, could constitute the 21st century contribution to continuing learning. The notion of **what do you know** could be replaced by **can you find the information, organize it and effectively use it.**

Text Mining: Text mining can be accomplished using traditional or computer-supported methods. The traditional ones involved manually identifying possible information sources, screening those for content, and selecting the pertinent ones. Each of these documents would then be read and notes prepared describing the analyst's perceptions of the important issues presented in the text. These would be organized and revised into a new document. These tasks are slow and prone to error if performed manually.

All of the text mining methods – manual or computerized – are designed to strip pertinent information from the text so that those data can be organized and used for some new purpose. The manual method is the most commonly used and involves copying words or phrases from the text. This copying can be done by physically transferring the data to a new record (electronic or paper) or by highlighting the desired information in the original text. If copying involves transfer to electronic records, there are enhanced opportunities to further process the data and to build a repository that allow access by any number of analysts. If the copying is performed manually by highlighting text on the page, the results stay personal and private.

The computerized approaches all involve creating an electronic data record. One software (Idea Analysis^{tm}) was used in this report to capture, edit, store, and retrieve the data in the form of author-presented ideas. The result of these operations is a Scholar's WorkStation dealing with the ideas for a specific subject. These Scholar WorkStations are open-access and can be obtained by sending a request to – learning@tutorghost.com. The major issue is that – separation of the tasks and assignment to software, technical algorithms, and intellectual considerations -- offers a powerful, effective, and efficient way of rapidly accomplishing the act of creating new descriptions or strategies for acquisition of new knowledge.

Data Processing: This function involves the development of data capture instruments, translation of the data to computer records, and organization of these records for different uses. With the introduction of software, data management has progressed so that a 'natural' consequence of information use involves the construction and use of data resources. Once the design of the data records and their relationships to each other are defined, the process of entering, evaluating, and using the data is routine, enabling the analyst to focus on the more creative aspects of information processing.

Statistics: Statistics has come a long way with the assistance of computer software. Calculation of data now involves selecting the appropriate option from statistical program menus. As such, the problem is choosing the appropriate method at the right time rather than emphasizing arithmetic operations.

That shift in operation also is commensurate with a change in emphasis. Earlier text books would emphasize the method and its calculation. With the software, the focus can be on the translation of the information network developed from the literature to a research design capable of providing the desired new information and insights. This design is executed, the data obtained, and findings developed. Those findings must be translated back to text and the body of knowledge updated. To illustrate this, case studies are presented that show the flow process beginning with the literature, formulating a research project, analyzing the captured data, and interpreting the findings.

Multifaceted Focus: The formalization of information processing and knowledge utilization is not an expression of artificial intelligence. Instead, the intent is to standardize those tasks that can be best accomplished by employing consistent, routine operations distinct from those requiring imagination and innovation. These operations are well accepted in disciplines requiring adherence and compliance with methodology. The fact that the computer, the technician and the knowledge expert must co-exist is a reality of modern team science. That sociologic phenomenon has increased as complex, multifaceted problems are addressed.

Efficient Text Management: Suppose text management was considered as a set of defined algorithms, each designed to accomplish a specific purpose. Electronic versions of the scientific reports can be analyzed using software designed to identify:
1. The **vocabulary** used by the authors in describing the topic.
2. The domain used by the author to convey a thought or an idea. That domain is the **sentence**.
3. The **idea** presented by the author within the sentence.

The software would:
1. Segregate each sentence.
2. Identify the nouns, adjectives, and gerunds within the sentence.
3. Form pairs of these informative terms.
4. Build data records containing the pair of informative terms (the idea), the year of publication, the identity of the associated document, and the number of the sentence containing the idea.
5. Store these data records in a data file.

There are advantages associated with this approach:
1. The computer can perform the identification, extraction, and organization in about 0.2 minutes per document.
2. The accuracy in identifying vocabulary can be determined.
3. The completeness in identifying ideas within the sentences can be determined.
4. Once the data records are developed and verified, there is no further need to repeat the process with the same document.
5. With the data records organized as a data file, the emphasis can shift from retrieval and analysis to the higher cognitive functions – synthesis, comparison, evaluation, judgment, and application.

Learning a New Subject: What if the ideas regarding a topic could be arranged by the frequency of use by authors in describing findings related to the topic? The more frequently occurring ideas represent those considered important by a diverse and large number of authors. These ideas, when organized, provide a description of the topic representing its critical features. With this, a new and appropriate description can be developed easily and rapidly.

This description is the result of a knowledge base rather than a wisdom base. Even when frequency of idea citation is used as a criterion for recognizing consensus elements, the description will be more complete than the usual wisdom base. The latter is restricted to the most important. Later chapters contain examples of this distinction. Graphic displays showing tiers of relationships will illustrate the wisdom selective process (inner most tier) versus the knowledge base approach (outer tiers).

The building of this new description employs more than recall of memorized facts. By considering the higher frequency ideas and those other ideas found in the same sentences, an informational web can be developed. This process employs synthesis, comparison, evaluation, judgment, and application. As such, the process involved all of requirements in developing intellectual prowess. Recall of the description would involve essentially a rapid rebuilding of the result with all of the tools and resources considered important in thinking. This **intellectual process** is open and can be monitored. By focusing on the author-provided ideas, the student can more rapidly summarize the findings and create a new description of the topic. In addition, the creative team members can monitor and evaluate the evolution of the solution. Everyone has the enjoyment of being "on the same page". With this description in the form of an information network composed of ideas, gaps and inconsistencies can be easily determined. These idea networks foster the rapid development of the specifics leading to new research.

Ideas and Research: The design of a new knowledge generating approach (i.e., a research study) is illustrated by considering these eight steps.

9. Determine the existence of a problem (*Discovery of an Idea*).
10. Develop a detailed description of that problem (**Problem Description**).
11. Develop an appropriate intervention to correct or eliminate the problem (**Interventions**).
12. Conduct a detailed, quality-controlled process to bring the intervention and the problem together (**Protocol Development**).
13. Capture the findings of this interaction (**Study Conduct**).
14. Analyze the findings against the original description of the problem (**Analyses**).
15. Develop and disseminate the results of the process with emphasis on the modifications necessary to existing knowledge (**Report Preparation**).
16. Ensure that others can benefit by making the development process transparent (**Data Curation**).

By assigning specific tasks to the best qualified performer, the analysis of the subjects and the development of an appropriate description can be accomplished in a short time with little fatigue or error. The assignment process would be:

1. Computerized analysis of the text with algorithms that identify, extract, and organize pertinent data.
2. Technical synthesis of the resulting data to form a variety of possible descriptions of the subjects.
3. Intellectual emphasis on developing criteria, measures, and decision structures so that the syntheses can be prioritized and utilized.

In this system, the human is saved from the tedious, clerical/mechanical functions and is challenged to develop the important elements in a creative process. This shift from perspiration to inspiration is essential as society adapts to a global perspective.

Team Creativity? Can creativity be accomplished by a team of individuals? There are examples where the answer would be yes. One such is the Human Genome Project involving a community of biologic and computer scientists and related disciplines devoted to developing a systematic approach to the study of the problem as well as to the management of the results. In addition to accomplishing the objective, the time involved was shorter than anticipated.

Figure 1. Terms Linked with the Central Idea -- Team & Creativity – From PubMed Bibliographic Database – 1969 to 2011.

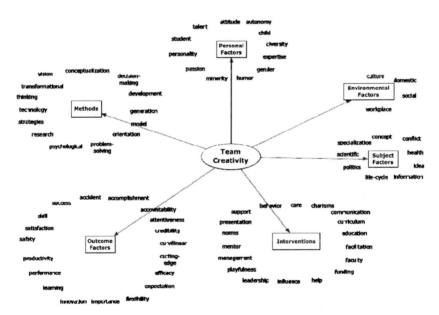

Figure 1 shows the terms forming triadic ideas with the central idea – team & creativity. The contributing reports numbered 177 entered into PubMed from 1969 to 2011. The One-Stop Learning extraction and organization process (Chapter 6) was used to identify the sentences containing the idea – team & creativity. Informative terms in those sentences were identified and organized as triadic ideas. These ideas were further classified into dimensions, i.e., major segments of the subject. These dimensions provide an expansion of the meaning and/or function associated with the central idea. For example, the outcome factor dimension included the ideas linking team creativity with terms expressing a beneficial result. Those included accomplishment, attentiveness, importance, innovation, learning, satisfaction, and success. The methods dimension included conceptualization, decision-making, problem-solving, research, strategies, and thinking. The intervention dimension included team creativity linked with: behavior, charisma, communication, curriculum, influence, leadership, management, and support.

The dimensions shown in Figure 1 illustrate the expanded meaning of team creativity. Each of the ideas could be further expanded. For example, the triadic idea – team & creativity & research – could be translated into specific tasks:

1.   Literature Review with text mining to develop effective organizations of the information leading to an established hypothesis containing a specific idea believed to provide a better or new understanding of the subject.
2.   Protocol Development with detailed construction of procedures involved in recruiting study subjects or material; in capturing, editing, and storing data; in analyzing the data to develop appropriate contributions to the existing knowledge base; and to disseminate those findings.
3.   Conduct the study according to the developed protocol.

These tasks redirect the attention and the effort of the team from broad principles to the needed specifics enabling development of a viable approach in solving the problem posed.

The creative team may require a larger and more diverse group of individuals than is normally considered. Each of the individuals has a specific contribution to make to the final product. These contributions may be intellectual, clerical, or technical. The members of the team may contribute from different locations so that environmental issues associated with the creative process become less relevant. Just as members of a sport team feel the pride and satisfaction of accomplishment through their contributions to the group effort, the members of the creative team can experience these personal emotions. The critical requirement is that all members of the team are thoroughly and completely aware of the process employed and the team's progress in accomplishing the goal.

Effective creativity, performed by one or more individuals, requires a detailed, formalized procedural protocol. That plan spells out the behaviors, the measures, the criteria, the decision-structures to be conducted by each member. The clear message is that group creativity must be based on formalized, disciplined attention to all details. In this sense, the research process becomes an outstanding example of effective system operation.

Bibliography

Allen GD, Rubenfeld MG, Scheffer BK. Reliability of assessment of critical thinking. J Prof Nurs. 2004 Jan-Feb;20(1):15-22.

American Association of School Librarians and the Association for Educational Communications and Technology, Information Literacy Standards for Student Learning", 1998

American Library Association Presidential Committee on Information Literacy: Final Report", 10 Jan 1989.

Arms, W.Y., What are the Alternatives to Peer Review? The Journal of Electronic Publishing. August, 2002 Volume 8, Issue 1.

Association of College and Research Libraries, Information Literacy Competency Standards for Higher Education]", Jan 2000. http://www.ala.org/ala/mgrps/divs/acrl/standards/standards.pdf

Bajic VB. Comparing the success of different prediction software in sequence analysis: a review. Brief Bioinform. 2000 Sep;1(3):214-28.

Berman JJ. Doublet method for very fast autocoding. BMC Med Inform Decis Mak. 2004 Sep 15;4(1):16.

Bermejo-Pérez MJ, Márquez-Calderón S, Llanos-Méndez A. Cancer surveillance based on imaging techniques in carriers of BRCA1/2 gene mutations: a systematic review. Br J Radiol. 2008 Mar;81(963):172-9.

Bernier CL. The indexing problem. *Journal of Chemical Documentation.* 1961;1(November):25-27.

Berry M, Hollingworth T, Anderson EM, Flinn RM. Application of network analysis to the study of the branching patterns of dendritic fields. Adv Neurol. 1975;12:217-45.

Bohm, D. On Creativity. Routledge 1998.

Bratt O. Hereditary prostate cancer: clinical aspects. J Urol. 2002 Sep;168(3):906-13.

Brinn S, Page L. The Anatomy of a Large-Scale Hypertextual Web Search Engine. Computer Networks and ISDN Systems. 1998;30(1-7):107-117.

Britannica Concise Encyclopedia. Britannica Concise Encyclopedia. 2009

Brown, T., Working Party. Peer Review and Acceptance of New Scientific Ideas. Sense About Science, 2004. http://en.wikipedia.org/wiki/Peer_review.

Bruce P, Simon JL, Oswald T. Resampling Stats Users Guide. Virginia: Resampling Stats; 2000.

Buck G, Weiner J, Schuster J, Vena J. Web-based data capture and management in epidemiologic investigations. Proceedings: Fourteenth IEEE Symposium on Computer-Based Medical Systems (Bethesda, Maryland, July 26-27, 2001), Los Alamitos, CA: IEEE Computer Society, 2001.

Busacca M, Somigliana E, Bianchi S, De Marinis S, Calia C, Candiani M, Vignali M Post-operative GnRH analogue treatment after conservative surgery for symptomatic endometriosis stage III-IV: a randomized controlled trial. Hum Reprod. 2001 Nov;16(11):2399-402.

Carretti B, Cornoldi C, Pelegrina SL. Which factors influence number updating in working memory? The effects of size distance and suppression. Br J Psychol. 2007 Feb;98(Pt 1):45-60.

Chalmers I. The Cochrane collaboration: preparing, maintaining, and disseminating systematic reviews of the effects of health care. Ann N Y Acad Sci. 1993 Dec 31;703:156-63; discussion 163-5.

Chang K; SungY; Chen I. The effect of concept mapping to enhance text comprehension and summarization. Journal-of-Experimental-Education. Fal 2002; Vol 71 (1): 5-23.

Chase KA, O'Farrell TJ, Murphy CM, Fals-Stewart W, Murphy M. Factors associated with partner violence among female alcoholic patients and their male partners. J Stud Alcohol. 2003 Jan;64(1):137-49.

Chen J. The Natural Structure of Scientific Knowledge: An Attempt to Map a Knowledge Structure. Journal of Information Science 1988;14:131-139.

Chernichovsky D, Chinitz D. The political economy of healthy system reform in Israel. Health Econ. 1995 Mar-Apr;4(2):127-41.] PMID: 3108317

Chiurchiu C, Remuzzi G, Ruggenenti P. Angiotensin-converting enzyme inhibition and renal protection in nondiabetic patients: the data of the meta-analyses. J Am Soc Nephrol. 2005 Mar;16 Suppl 1:S58-63.

ClusterMed http://www.clustermed.com.

Cochrane AL. Effectiveness and Efficiency. Random Reflections on Health Services. London: Nuffield Provincial Hospitals Trust, 1972.

Collins A. Brown J. & Newman S. "Cognitive apprenticeship: Teaching the crafts of reading writing and mathematics" in Knowing learning and instruction: Essays in honor of Robert Glaser L. B. Resnick Editor. Erlbaum :Hillsdale NJ 1989 pp. 453-494.

Cooney KA, Tsou HC, Petty EM, Miesfeldt S, Ping XL, Gruener AC, Peacocke M. Absence of PTEN germ-line mutations in men with a potential inherited predisposition to prostate cancer. Clin Cancer Res. 1999 Jun;5(6):1387-91.

Cooper GF, Miller RA. An experiment comparing lexical and statistical methods for extracting MeSH terms from clinical free text. J Am Med Inform Assoc. 1998 Jan-Feb;5(1):62-75.

Cotter MP, Gern RW, Ho GY, Chang RY, Burk RD. Role of family history and ethnicity on the mode and age of prostate cancer presentation. Prostate. 2002 Mar 1;50(4):216-21.

Crandall ML, Nathens AB, Rivara FP. Injury patterns among female trauma patients: recognizing intentional injury. J Trauma. 2004 Jul;57(1):42-5.

Croasdell DT. Concept Maps for Teaching and Assessment. Communications of AIS; 2003 12 396.

D'Agostino RB Sr, Massaro JM, Sullivan LM. Non-inferiority trials: design concepts and issues - the encounters of academic consultants in statistics. Stat Med. 2003 Jan 30;22(2):169-86.

DeLong M, Logan JL, Yong KC, Lien YH. Renin-angiotensin blockade reduces serum free testosterone in middle-aged men on haemodialysis and correlates with erythropoietin resistance. Nephrol Dial Transplant. 2005 Mar;20(3):585-90.

Dictionary.com's 21st Century Lexicon. 2011 http://dictionary.com/

Ding W, Marchionini, G. A comparative study of Web search service performance. Proceedings of the 59th Annual Meeting of the American Society for Information Science. Silver Spring, MA: ASIS; 1996:136-42.

Dmowski WP, Gebel HM, Rawlins RG. Immunologic aspects of endometriosis. Obstet Gynecol Clin North Am. 1989 Mar;16(1):93-103.

Dobson V. Pattern learning and the control of behaviour by all-inhibitory neural network hierarchies. Perception. 1975;4(1):35-50.

Druss BG, Marcus SC. Tracking publication outcomes of National Institutes of Health grants. Am J Med. 2005 Jun;118(6):658-63.

Dumais ST, Landauer TK, Littman ML. (1996) Automatic Cross-Linguistic Information Retrieval Using Latent Semantic Indexing. In SIGIR'96 – Workshop on Cross-Linguistic Information Retrieval, pp. 16-23, August 1996.

Eberhart R, Shi Y, Kennedy J. Swarm Intelligence. Morgan Kaufmann, CA 2001.
Egan B, Gleim G, Panish J. Use of losartan in diabetic patients in the primary care setting: review of the results in LIFE and RENAAL. Curr Med Res Opin. 2004 Dec;20(12):1909-17.

Einstein A. Discussion following lecture version of "On the Development of Our Views Concerning the Nature and Constitution of Radiation". Physikalische Zeitschrift 10 (1909)

El-Bassel N, Gilbert L, Witte S, Wu E, Gaeta T, Schilling R, Wada T. Intimate partner violence and substance abuse among minority women receiving care from an inner-city emergency department. Womens Health Issues. 2003 Jan-Feb;13(1):16-22.

ERIC http://www.eric.ed.gov/ 2011

Ericsson K. A. Krampe R. & Tesch-Römer C. "The Role of Deliberate Practice in the Acquisition of Expert Performance" Psychological Review 3 1993 pp. 363-406.

Ericsson K. A. Krampe R. T. & Heizmann S. (1993). Can we create gifted people? In K. A. Ericsson R. T. Krampe & S. Heizmann (Eds.) in The origins and development of high ability (pp. 224-249).

Esnault VL, Ekhlas A, Delcroix C, Moutel MG, Nguyen JM. Diuretic and enhanced sodium restriction results in improved antiproteinuric response to RAS blocking agents. J Am Soc Nephrol. 2005 Feb;16(2):474-81.

Eteläpelto A. 1993. Conceptual Model Construction and Reflection - A Developmental Tool for Expert Knowledge Elicitation. Paper presented at The III European Congress of Psychology Tampere Finland 7.-9. 7. 1993.

Eteläpelto A.1994. Work Experience and the Development of Expertise. In W.J. Nijhof& J.N. Streumer (Eds.) Flexibility in Training and Vocational Education. Utrecht:Lemma 319-341.

Falkman G. Knowledge Based Systems. Center for Learning Systems. 2002. http://www.ida.his.se/ida/research/cls/.

Fallis, D. On Verifying the Accuracy of Information: Philosophical Perspectives. Library Trends, Winter 2004. 52,3;427-446.

Fallows, J. Enough Keyword Searches. Just Answer My Question. NY Times,2005/06/12.http://www.nytimes.com/2005/06/12/business/yourmoney/12techno.html?ex= 1119499200&en=8f6b29f4dac54a51&ei=5070&emc=eta1.

Field CA, Caetano R. Longitudinal model predicting partner violence among white, black, and Hispanic couples in the United States. Alcohol Clin Exp Res. 2003 Sep;27(9):1451-8.

Fincher RM, Work JA. The scholarship of teaching in health science schools. J Vet Med Educ. 2005 Spring;32(1):1-4.

Fink R, Thompson CJ, Bonnes D. Overcoming barriers and promoting the use of research in practice. J Nurs Adm. 2005 Mar;35(3):121-9.

Flanders WD. Review: prostate cancer epidemiology. Prostate. 1984;5(6):621-9.

Floridi, L. Philosophy and Computing: An Introduction. Chapter 4. London, 1999.

Foltz, P. W., Kintsch, W., and Landauer, T. K. (1998). The Measurement of Textual Coherence with Latent Semantic Analysis. Discourse Processes, 25, 285-307.

Fowke JH, Hebert JR, Fahey JW. Urinary excretion of dithiocarbamates and self-reported Cruciferous vegetable intake: application of the 'method of triads' to a food-specific biomarker. Public Health Nutr. 2002 Dec;5(6):791-9.

Fowke JH, Chung FL, Jin F, Qi D, Cai Q, Conaway C, Cheng JR, Shu XO, Gao YT, Zheng W. Urinary isothiocyanate levels, brassica, and human breast cancer. Cancer Res. 2003 Jul 15;63(14):3980-6.

Freda MC, Kearney M. An international survey of nurse editors' roles and practices. J Nurs Scholarsh. 2005;37(1):87-94.

Friedman C, Shagina L, Lussier Y, Hripcsak G. Automated encoding of clinical documents based on natural language processing. J Am Med Inform Assoc. 2004 Sep-Oct;11(5):392-402.

Fuller SS Gilman NJ Weiner RE Stanley D Weiner JM. The literature of decision making – an analytical approach. Proceedings of the American Society for Information Science. 1982;19:100-102.

Fung C, Hitchcock M, Fisher D. Effects of funding family physicians for advanced research training. Fam Med. 2005 Jun;37(6):434-9.

Funk ME, Reid CA. Indexing consistency in Medline. Bulletin of the Medical Library Association. 1983;71(2):176-183.

Furner, J. Information Studies Without Information. Library Trends, Winter 2004. 52,3;463-487.

Gandolfo MT, Verzola D, Salvatore F, Gianiorio G, Procopio V, Romagnoli A, Giannoni M, Garibotto G. Gender and the progression of chronic renal diseases: does apoptosis make the difference? Minerva Urol Nefrol. 2004 Mar;56(1):1-14.

Gauger PG, Gruppen LD, Minter RM, Colletti LM, Stern DT. Initial use of a novel instrument to measure professionalism in surgical residents. Am J Surg. 2005 Apr;189(4):479-87.

Gildea D, Jurafsky D. Identifying Semantic Relations in Text. Chapter 3 in Exploring Artificial Intelligence in the New Millennium. Lakemeyer G, Nebel B., Eds. Morgan Kaufmann CA 2002.

Goldman, A. I. (2001). Experts: Which ones should you trust? Philosophy and Phenomenological Research, 63(1), 85-110.

Gondy L, Lally AM, Chen H. The use of dynamic contexts to improve casual internet searching. ACM Transactions on Information Systems. 2003;21(3):229-253.

Goodyear-Smith F. National screening policies in general practice: a case study of routine screening for partner abuse. Appl Health Econ Health Policy. 2002;1(4):197-209.

Goode EL, Stanford JL, Chakrabarti L, Gibbs M, Kolb S, McIndoe RA, Buckley VA, Schuster EF, Neal CL, Miller EL, Brandzel S, Hood L, Ostrander EA, Jarvik GP. Linkage analysis of 150 high-risk prostate cancer families at 1q24-25. Genet Epidemiol. 2000 Mar;18(3):251-75.

Gordon MD, Linsay RK. Toward Discovery Support Systems. A Replication, Re-examination, and Extension of Swanson's Work on Literature-Based Discovery of a Connection Between Raynaud's and Fish Oil. Journal of the American Society of Information Science, 1996,47(2),116-128.

Govindarajan V, Trimble C. Building breakthrough businesses within established organizations. Harv Bus Rev. 2005 May;83(5):58-68, 152.

Gronroos PE, Irjala KM, Vesalainen RK, Kantola IM, Leinonen VM, Helenius TI, Forsstrom JJ. Effects of ramipril on the hormone concentrations in serum of hypertensive patients. Eur J Clin Chem Clin Biochem. 1997 Jun;35(6):411-4.

Gupta P. Personal Communication 2005.

Gurney, W. Building a Collaborative Network. Soc Work Health Care. 1975-76 Winter;1(2):185-9.

Harnad, S. "The Invisible Hand of Peer Review", Exploit Interactive, issue 5, April 2000. http://www.exploit-lib.org/issue5/peer-review/.

Hearst M. What is Text Mining? <http://www.sims.berkeley.edu/~hearst/text-mining,html, 2003.

Hemilia H. Vitamin C and the Common Cold. Br. J. Nutr. 1992 Jan;67 (1): 3-16.

Hirschman L, Park JC, Tsujii J, Wong L, Wu CH. Accomplishments and challenges in literature data mining for biology. Bioinformatics. 2002 Dec;18(12):1553-61.

Hoelzer S, Schweiger RK, Boettcher H, Rieger J, Dudeck J. Indexing of Internet resources in order to improve the provision of problem-relevant medical information. Stud Health Technol Inform. 2002;90:174-7.

Hoffman E. Defining Information: An Analysis of the Information Content of Documents. Information Processing and Management 1980;16:291-304.

Horowitz RS, Fuller SS, Gilman NJ, Stowe SM, Weiner JM. Concurrence in Content Descriptions: Author versus Medical Subject Headings (MeSH). Proceedings of American Society for Information Sciences. 1982;19:139-140.

Horowitz, RS, Weiner, JM. One-Stop Learning: A text-mining-knowledge utilization process. Session 11 -- Formalized Text Analysis, Proceedings, International Conference on Qualitative and Quantitative Methods in Libraries, May 2009.

Hsu CY, McCulloch CE, Iribarren C, Darbinian J, Go AS. Body mass index and risk for end-stage renal disease. Ann Intern Med. 2006 Jan 3;144(1):21-8.
Huber G. "Organizational Learning: The Contributing Processes and Literature Organization Science 2 (1991): 88-115.

Huberman, M. (1987, June). Steps toward an integrated model of research utilization. *Knowledge,* pp. 586-611.

Iino Y, Hayashi M, Kawamura T, Shiigai T, Tomino Y, Yamada K, Kitajima T, Ideura T, Koyama A, Sugisaki T, Suzuki H, Umemura S, Kawaguchi Y, Uchida S, Kuwahara M, Yamazaki T; Japanese Lasartan Therapy Intended for the Global Renal Protection in Hypertensive Patients (JLIGHT) Study Investigators. Interim evidence of the renoprotective effect of the angiotensin II receptor antagonist losartan versus the calcium channel blocker amlodipine in patients with chronic kidney disease and hypertension: a report of the Japanese Losartan Therapy Intended for Global Renal Protection in Hypertensive Patients (JLIGHT) Study. Clin Exp Nephrol. 2003 Sep;7(3):221-30.

Inspiration 2011. http://www.inspiration.com

Jauhiainen A, Pulkkinen R. Problem-based learning and e-learning methods in clinical practice. Stud Health Technol Inform. 2009;146:572-6.

Jenkins RA, Robbins A, Cranston K, Batchelor K, Freeman AC, Averbach AR, Amaro H, Morrill AC, Blake SM, Logan JA, Carey JW. Bridging Data and Decision Making: Development of Techniques for Improving the HIV Prevention Community Planning Process. AIDS Behav. 2005 Jun;9 Suppl 2:S41-53.

Jenuwine ES, Floyd JA. Comparison of Medical Subject Headings and text-word searches in MEDLINE to retrieve studies on sleep in healthy individuals. J Med Libr Assoc. 2004 Jul;92(3):349-53.

Johnson SB, Aguirre A, Peng P, Cimino J. Interpreting natural language queries using the UMLS. Proc Annu Symp Comput Appl Med Care. 1993;294-8.

Joubert M, Fieschi M, Robert JJ. A conceptual model for information retrieval with UMLS. Proc Annu Symp Comput Appl Med Care. 1993;:715-9. 15.

Justeson J Katz S. 1993. Technical terminology: some linguistic properties and an algorithm for identification in text. Technical Report RC 18906 IBM Research Division.

Kashyap V. The UMLS Semantic Network and the Semantic Web. AMIA Annu Symp Proc. 2003;:351-5.

Kiernan V. Professors are unhappy with limitations of Online Resources, Survey finds. The Chronicle of Higher Education. 2004(April);A-34.

Kipp J, Pimlott JF, Satzinger F. Universities preparing health professionals for the 21st century: can something new come out of the traditional establishment? J Interprof Care. 2007 Dec;21(6):633-44.

Klages M. 2003. http://www.colorado.edu/English/courses/ENGL2012Klages/pomo.html

Landauer TK, Dumais ST. (1994). Latent Semantic Analysis and the Measurement of Knowledge. In RM Kaplan & JC Burstein (Eds), Educational Testing Service Conference on Natural Language Processing Techniques and Technology In Assessment and Education. Princeton NJ: Education Testing Service.

Landauer, T. K., Foltz, P. W., and Laham, D. (1998). Introduction to Latent Semantic Analysis. Discourse Processes, 25, 259-284.

Lane P. C. R. Cheng P. C-H. & Gobet F. (2000). CHREST+: A simulation of how humans learn to solve problems using diagrams. AISB Quarterly 103 24-30.

Lavoie JL, Lake-Bruse KD, Sigmund CD. Increased blood pressure in transgenic mice expressing both human renin and angiotensinogen in the renal proximal tubule. Am J Physiol Renal Physiol. 2004 May;286(5):F965-71.

Lewis EJ, Hunsicker LG, Clarke WR, Berl T, Pohl MA, Lewis JB, Ritz E, Atkins RC, Rohde R, Raz I; Collaborative Study Group. Renoprotective effect of the angiotensin-receptor antagonist irbesartan in patients with nephropathy due to type 2 diabetes. N Engl J Med. 2001 Sep 20;345(12):851-60.

Lewis EJ, Lewis JB. Treatment of diabetic nephropathy with angiotensin II receptor antagonist. Clin Exp Nephrol. 2003 Mar;7(1):1-8.

Liu F, Yu C, Meng W. Personalized Web search for improving retrieval effectiveness. IEEE Transactions on Knowledge and Data Engineering. 2004;16(1):28-39.

Liu X, Shi Y, Giranda VL, Luo Y. Inhibition of the phosphatidylinositol 3-kinase/Akt pathway sensitizes MDA-MB468 human breast cancer cells to cerulenin-induced apoptosis. Mol Cancer Ther. 2006 Mar;5(3):494-501.

Loescher LJ, Lim KH, Leitner O, Ray J, D'Souza J, Armstrong CM. Cancer surveillance behaviors in women presenting for clinical BRCA genetic susceptibility testing. Oncol Nurs Forum. 2009 Mar;36(2):E57-67.

Logan, J. Personal Communication 2005.

214

Lowe, D. Improving Web Search Relevance: Using Navigational Structures to Provide a Search Context. Proc. 6th Australian World Wide Web Conf., 2000. Available at: http://ausweb.scu.edu.au/aw2k/papers/lowe/index.html. Accessed Sept. 8, 2004.

Lunet N, Valbuena C, Carneiro F, Lopes C, Barros H. Antioxidant vitamins and risk of gastric cancer: a case-control study in Portugal. Nutr Cancer. 2006;55(1):71-7.

Malin AS, Qi D, Shu XO, Gao YT, Friedmann JM, Jin F, Zheng W. Intake of fruits, vegetables and selected micronutrients in relation to the risk of breast cancer. Int J Cancer. 2003 Jun 20;105(3):413-8.

Mandel HG, Woosley RL, Vesell ES. Biomedical research funding: view of the National Caucus of Basic Biomedical Science Chairs. FASEB J. 1992;6:3133–3134.

Mandel HG. Funding of Newly Submitted NIH Grant Applications. Science, 1994;266:1789.

Mandel HG, Vesell ES. From Progress to Regression: Biomedical Research Funding. J Clin Invest. 2004 Oct;114(7):872-6.

Mangione S Nieman LZ. Cardiac auscultatory skills of internal medicine and family practice trainees: a comparison of diagnostic proficiency. JAMA 1997; 278: 717-22.

Marinai S, Gori M, Soda G, Society C., Artificial neural networks for document analysis and recognition., IEEE Trans Pattern Anal Mach Intell. 2005 Jan;27(1):23-35.

Markov J. The coming search wars. The New York Times. Feb 1, 2004.

Markow PG. The effects of student-constructed concept maps on achievement in a first-year college instructional chemistry laboratory. Dissertation-Abstracts-International-Section-A:-Humanities-and-Social-Sciences. Apr 1996; Vol 56 (10-A): 3900.

Maron ME. On indexing, retrieval and the meaning of about. Journal of the American Society for Information Science. 1977;28(1):38-43.

Martin JM, Benamghar L, Martin J. About the different steps leading to the quality of medical information (importance of medical computing. Sem Hop. 1979 Nov 8-15;55(37-38):1754-60.

Matsuda H, Hayashi K, Saruta T. Distinct time courses of renal protective action of angiotensin receptor antagonists and ACE inhibitors in chronic renal disease. J Hum Hypertens. 2003 Apr;17(4):271-6.

Matsuda H, Hayashi K, Homma K, Yoshioka K, Kanda T, Takamatsu I, Tatematsu S, Wakino S, Saruta T. Differing anti-proteinuric action of candesartan and losartan in chronic renal disease. Hypertens Res. 2003 Nov;26(11):875-80.

215

McClure JR Sonak B Suen HK. Concept map assessment of classroom learning: Reliability validity and logistical practicality. Journal of Research in Science Teaching 364 April1999475-492.

McFarlane J, Malecha A, Gist J, Watson K, Batten E, Hall I, Smith S. An intervention to increase safety behaviors of abused women: results of a randomized clinical trial. Nurs Res. 2002 Nov-Dec;51(6):347-54.

Medline Plus http://medlineplus.gov/.

Mendola P, Robinson LK, Buck GM, Druschel CM, Fitzgerald EF, Sever LE, Vena JE. Birth defects risk associated with maternal sport fish consumption: potential effect modification by sex of offspring. Environ Res. 2005 Feb;97(2):134-41.

Mervis J. Is the U.S. brain gain faltering? *Science.* 2004;304:1278–1282.

McGrath J, Lawrence V, Richardson WS. Making medical research clinically friendly: a communication-based conceptual framework. Educ Health (Abingdon). 2004 Nov;17(3):374-84.

Microsoft's bCentral Submit it. Search Engine Marketing for Small Business. Available at: http://www.submit-it.com/. Accessed Sept. 8, 2004.

Michalko, M. Cracking Creativity. Ten Speed Press 2001.

Montague R. The proper treatment of quantification in ordinary English. In J. Hintikka J. M. E. Moravcsik and P. Suppes editors Approaches to Natural Language: Proceedings of the 1970 Stanford Workshop on Grammar and Semantics. 1973 Reidel Dordrecht pages 221—242.

Morgan LM. [J Public Health Policy. 1987 Spring;8(1):86-105. Health without wealth? Costa Rica's health system under economic crisis.] PMID: 292787

Muller-Nordhorn J, Willich SN. Angiotensin II antagonists in the treatment of hypertension-effective and efficient? Herz. 2003 Dec;28(8):733-7.

Nathan DG, Wilson JD. Clinical Research and the NIH – A Report Card. N. Engl. J. Med. 2003;349:1860-1865.

Najavits LM, Sullivan TP, Schmitz M, Weiss RD, Lee CS. Treatment utilization by women with PTSD and substance dependence. Am J Addict. 2004 May-Jun;13(3):215-24.

Nakao N, Yoshimura A, Morita H, Takada M, Kayano T, Ideura T. Combination treatment of angiotensin-II receptor blocker and angiotensin-converting-enzyme inhibitor in non-diabetic renal disease (COOPERATE): a randomised controlled trial. Lancet. 2003 Jan 11;361(9352):117-24.

Nakao N, Seno H, Kasuga H, Toriyama T, Kawahara H, Fukagawa M. Effects of combination treatment with losartan and trandolapril on office and ambulatory blood pressures in non-diabetic renal disease: a COOPERATE-ABP substudy. Am J Nephrol. 2004 Sep-Oct;24(5):543-8.

Near JA, Martin BJ. Expanding course goals beyond disciplinary boundaries: physiology education in an undergraduate course on psychoactive drugs. Adv Physiol Educ. 2007 Jun;31(2):161-6.

NIH. Office of Extramural Research. 2004. NIH Competing and Non-competing RPG Awards. Proportion of Awards Devoted to Specific Research Mechanisms. Fiscal Years 1998-2003. http://www.grants.nih.gov

NIH. Office of Extramural Research. Peer Review Policy and Issues. http://grants2.nih.gov/grants/peer/, 2005

NIH Research Portfolio Online Reporting Tools [RePORT 2011] http://report.nih.gov/

Novak JD. Learning creating and using knowledge: Concept maps(R) as facilitative tools in schools and corporations. Lawrence Erlbaum Associates Publishers. xviii 251 pp. Mahwah NJ US. (1998).

Obama B, President of the United States 2009 http://www.whitehouse.gov/assets/documents/2009literacy_prc_rel.pdf

O'Farrell TJ, Murphy CM, Stephan SH, Fals-Stewart W, Murphy M. Partner violence before and after couples-based alcoholism treatment for male alcoholic patients: the role of treatment involvement and abstinence. J Consult Clin Psychol. 2004 Apr;72(2):202-17.

Ontology Google Definitions 2010 [http://www.google.com/search?hl=en&source=hp&q=define%3A+ontology&aq=1&oq=ontolo gy&aqi=n111g10]

Park LA, Palaniswami M, Ramamohanarao K., A novel document ranking method using the discrete cosine transform., IEEE Trans Pattern Anal Mach Intell. 2005 Jan;27(1):130-5.

Parrott DJ, Drobes DJ, Saladin ME, Coffey SF, Dansky BS. Perpetration of partner violence: effects of cocaine and alcohol dependence and posttraumatic stress disorder. Addict Behav. 2003 Dec;28(9):1587-602.

Pascale RT, Sternin J. Your company's secret change agents. Harv Bus Rev. 2005 May;83(5):72-81, 153.

Patipanawat S, Komwilaisak R, Ratanasiri T. Correlation of weight estimation in large and small fetuses with three-dimensional ultrasonographic volume measurements of the fetal upper-arm and thigh: A preliminary report. J Med Assoc Thai. 2006 Jan;89(1):13-9.

217

Paynter RA, Hankinson SE, Colditz GA, Kraft P, Hunter DJ, De Vivo I. CYP19 (aromatase) haplotypes and endometrial cancer risk. Int J Cancer. 2005 Aug 20;116(2):267-74.

Pennebaker J. What our words say about us: Use of computerized text analysis in research and practice. International Society for Quality of Life Research, ISOQOL 2004 Symposium "Stating the Art: Advancing Outcomes Research Methodology and Clinical Applications" June 27-29, 2004.

Piniewski-Bond JF, Buck GM, Horowitz RS, Schuster JH, Weed DL, Weiner JM. Comparison of information processing technologies. J Am Med Inform Assoc. 2001 Mar-Apr;8(2):174-84.

Piniewski-Bond, J and Weiner, JM. Information Literacy and Ideas: An Assessment Using Cervical Cancer Literature. Session 11 -- Formalized Text Analysis, Proceedings, International Conference on Qualitative and Quantitative Methods in Libraries, May 2009

Plum J, Bunten B, Nemeth R, Grabensee B. Effects of the angiotensin II antagonist valsartan on blood pressure, proteinuria, and renal hemodynamics in patients with chronic renal failure and hypertension. J Am Soc Nephrol. 1998 Dec;9(12):2223-34.

Powell AL, French JC. Comparing the performance of collection selection algorithms. *ACM Transactions on Information Systems.* 2003;21(4):412-45.

Praga M, Andrade CF, Luno J, Arias M, Poveda R, Mora J, Prat MV, Rivera F, Galceran JM, Ara JM, Aguirre R, Bernis C, Marin R, Campistol JM. Antiproteinuric efficacy of losartan in comparison with amlodipine in non-diabetic proteinuric renal diseases: a double-blind, randomized clinical trial. Nephrol Dial Transplant. 2003 Sep;18(9):1806-13.

PubMed http://www.ncbi.nlm.nih.gov/pubmed/ 2011
PubMed Online Training 2010 [http://www.nlm.nih.gov/bsd/disted/pubmed.html]

Rappoport A. The state of search. *Searcher:Magazine for Database Professionals.* 2003;11(9):32-37.

Random Number Generator 2011. http://www.random.org

Reckelhoff JF. Gender differences in the regulation of blood pressure. Hypertension. 2001 May;37(5):1199-208.

Reckelhoff JF, Granger JP. Role of androgens in mediating hypertension and renal injury. Clin Exp Pharmacol Physiol. 1999 Feb;26(2):127-31.

RefViz 2004. http://www.RefViz.com

Rehder, B., Schreiner, M. E., Wolfe, M. B., Laham, D., Landauer, T. K., & Kintsch, W. (1998). Using Latent Semantic Analysis to assess knowledge: Some technical considerations. Discourse Processes, 25, 337-354.

Remuzzi G, Ruggenenti P, Perna A, Dimitrov BD, de Zeeuw D, Hille DA, Shahinfar S, Carides GW, Brenner BM; RENAAL Study Group. Continuum of renoprotection with losartan at all stages of type 2 diabetic nephropathy: a post hoc analysis of the RENAAL trial results. J Am Soc Nephrol. 2004 Dec;15(12):3117-25.

Rennie D, Yank V, Emanuel L. When Authorship Fails: A Proposal to Make Contributors Accountable. JAMA.1997;278:579-585.

Rice DC; Ryan JM; Samson SM. Using concept maps to assess student learning in the science classroom: Must different methods compete? Journal-of-Research-in-Science-Teaching. Dec 1998; Vol 35 (10): 1103-1127.

Rice VM. Conventional medical therapies for endometriosis. Ann N Y Acad Sci. 2002 Mar;955:343-52; discussion 389-93, 396-406.

Rinkus S, Walji M, Johnson-Throop KA, Malin JT, Turley JP, Smith JW, Zhang J. Human-centered design of a distributed knowledge management system. J Biomed Inform. 2005 Feb;38(1):4-17.

Rips, L. J., Shoben, E. J., & Smith, E. E. (1973). Semantic distance and the verification of semantic relations. Journal of Verbal Learning and Verbal Behavior, 12, 1-20.

Rivera JA, Levine RB, Wright SM. Completing a scholarly project during residency training. Perspectives of residents who have been successful. J Gen Intern Med. 2005 Apr;20(4):366-9.

Robinson DH; Robinson SL; Katayama AD. When words are represented in memory like pictures: Evidence for spatial encoding of study materials. Contemporary-Educational-Psychology. Jan 1999; Vol 24 (1): 38-54.

Ruilope LM, Aldigier JC, Ponticelli C, Oddou-Stock P, Botteri F, Mann JF. Safety of the combination of valsartan and benazepril in patients with chronic renal disease. European Group for the Investigation of Valsartan in Chronic Renal Disease. J Hypertens. 2000 Jan;18(1):89-95.

Sahai, A. 2005. http://www.imd2.com/.

Salton G Buckley C. Term-weighting approaches in automatic text retrieval. Information Processing & Management (1988). 24 (5): 513–523.

Sandberg AA. Chromosomal abnormalities and related events in prostate cancer. Hum Pathol. 1992 Apr;23(4):368-80.

Savransky, SD. Engineering of Creativity. CRC Press 2000.Shatkay H, Feldman R. Mining the Biomedical Literature in the Genomic Era: An Overview. J Comput Biol 2003;10(6):821-855.

Schau C; Mattern N; Zeilik M; Teague K.W; Weber R.J. Select-and-Fill-in Concept Map Scores as a Measure of Students' Connected Understanding of Science. Educational and Psychological Measurement Feb 2001 vol. 61 no. 1 136-158.

Scharwzennegger A Governor of California 2009 EXECUTIVE ORDER S-06-09

Scheffer BK, Rubenfeld MG. A consensus statement on critical thinking in nursing. J Nurs Educ. 2000 Nov;39(8):352-9.

Scriven M, Paul R. Critical Thinking as Defined by the National Council for Excellence in Critical Thinking, 1987. 8th Annual International Conference on Critical Thinking and Education Reform, Summer 1987

Segura J, Praga M, Campo C, Rodicio JL, Ruilope LM. Combination is better than monotherapy with ACE inhibitor or angiotensin receptor antagonist at recommended doses. J Renin Angiotensin Aldosterone Syst. 2003 Mar;4(1):43-7.

Shapiro JJ, Hughes SK. "Information Literacy as a Liberal Art", Educom Review, 31:2 (Mar/Apr 1996).

Sigurd B, Eeg-Olofsson M, van Weijer J. Word length, sentence length and frequency. Zipf revisited. Sudial inguistica Vol 5 8 Issue Page 37 April 2004.

Silbiger SR, Neugarten J. The role of gender in the progression of renal disease. Adv Ren Replace Ther. 2003 Jan;10(1):3-14.

Sims-Knight JE Upchurch RL. The Acquisition of Expertise in Software Engineering Education. 1997. http://www2.umassd.edu/SWPI/NSF/material.html
Smalheiser NR, Swanson DR. Using ARROWSMITH: a Computer-Assisted Approach to Formulating and Assessing Scientific Hypotheses. Comput Methods Program Biomed. 1998 Nov;57(3):149-53.

Sneiderman CA, Rindflesch TC, Aronson AR. Finding the findings: identification of findings in medical literature using restricted natural language processing. Proc AMIA Annu Fall Symp. 1996;:239-43.

Snell L, Spencer J. Reviewers' perceptions of the peer review process for a medical education journal. Med Educ. 2005 Jan;39(1):90-7.

Sonkaj H, Koenig S, Schmiede, R. How should libraries respond to new forms of publication? Digital Resources for the Humanities; 2003; University of Gloucestershire.

Sparck Jones, K. 1972. A statistical interpretation of term specificity and its application in retrieval. Journal of Documentation, 28(1):11—21.

Spink A. Web Search: Emerging Patterns. Library Trends. 2003;52(2):299-306.

Spink A, Jansen BJ, Czumltu HC. Use of query reformulation and relevance feedback by Excite users. *Internet Research.* 2000;10(4):317.

Standler, RB. Creativity in Science and Engineering. http://www.rbs0.com/create.htm.

Srinivasin P. Text Mining: Generating Hypotheses from MEDLINE. Journal of the American Society of Information Science and Technology, 2004,55(5),396-413.

Stanford JL, Wicklund KG, McKnight B, Daling JR, Brawer MK. Vasectomy and risk of prostate cancer. Cancer Epidemiol Biomarkers Prev. 1999 Oct;8(10):881-6.
Sternberg, RJ. Handbook of Creativity. Cambridge University Press, 1998.

Stanford JL, McDonnell SK, Friedrichsen DM, Carlson EE, Kolb S, Deutsch K, Janer M, Hood L, Ostrander EA, Schaid DJ. Prostate cancer and genetic susceptibility: a genome scan incorporating disease aggressiveness. Prostate. 2006 Feb 15;66(3):317-25.

Stevens PA. Using concept maps for assessing adult learners in training situations. Dissertation-Abstracts-International-Section-A:-Humanities-and-Social-Sciences. Apr 1998; Vol 58 (10-A): 3804.

Stirling D, Evans DG, Pichert G, Shenton A, Kirk EN, Rimmer S, Steel CM, Lawson S, Busby-Earle RM, Walker J, Lalloo FI, Eccles DM, Lucassen AM, Porteous ME. Screening for familial ovarian cancer: failure of current protocols to detect ovarian cancer at an early stage according to the international Federation of gynecology and obstetrics system. J Clin Oncol. 2005 Aug 20;23(24):5588-96

Strachan RA & Roetzel KA. Ancient Peoples: A Hypertext View. 1997 http://www.mnsu.edu/emuseum/prehistory/egypt/hieroglyphics/rosettastone.html.

Stuart GL, Moore TM, Ramsey SE, Kahler CW. Hazardous drinking and relationship violence perpetration and victimization in women arrested for domestic violence. J Stud Alcohol. 2004 Jan;65(1):46-53.

Sumner WG (1906) Folkways, A Study of the Sociological Importance of Usages, Manners, Customs, Mores, and Morals. Project Gutenberg Literary Archive Foundation 2008

Surrey ES, Hornstein MD. Prolonged GnRH agonist and add-back therapy for symptomatic endometriosis: long-term follow-up. Obstet Gynecol. 2002 May;99(5 Pt 1):709-19.
Suzuki H, Kanno Y, Sugahara S, Okada H, Nakamoto H. Effects of an angiotensin II receptor blocker, valsartan, on residual renal function in patients on CAPD. Am J Kidney Dis. 2004 Jun;43(6):1056-64.

Taricani EM. Effects of the level of generativity in concept mapping with knowledge of correct response feedback on learning. Dissertation-Abstracts-International-Section-A:-Humanities-and-Social-Sciences. Dec 2002; 63 (5-A): 1714.

Telimaa S, Puolakka J, Ronnberg L, Kauppila A. Placebo-controlled comparison of danazol and high-dose medroxyprogesterone acetate in the treatment of endometriosis. Gynecol Endocrinol. 1987 Mar;1(1):13-23.

Terry DF, Wilcox M, McCormick MA, Lawler E, Perls TT. Cardiovascular advantages among the offspring of centenarians. J Gerontol A Biol Sci Med Sci. 2003 May;58(5):M425-31.

Terry DF, Wilcox MA, McCormick MA, Perls TT. Cardiovascular disease delay in centenarian offspring. J Gerontol A Biol Sci Med Sci. 2004 Apr;59(4):385-9.

Terry DF, McCormick M, Andersen S, Pennington J, Schoenhofen E, Palaima E, Bausero M, Ogawa K, Perls TT, Asea A. Cardiovascular disease delay in centenarian offspring: role of heat shock proteins. Ann N Y Acad Sci. 2004 Jun;1019:502-5.

Tompkins WJ. Modular design of microcomputer-based medical instruments. Med Instrum. 1980 Nov-Dec;14(6):315-8.

Trimble EL, Harlan LC, Clegg LX, Stevens JL. Pre-operative imaging, surgery and adjuvant therapy for women diagnosed with cancer of the corpus uteri in community practice in the United States. Gynecol Oncol. 2005 Mar;96(3):741-8.

Tucker WB. Evaluation of streptomycin regimens in the treatment of tuberculosis; an account of the study of the Veterans Administration, Army, and Navy, July 1946 to April 1949. Am Rev Tuberc. 1949 Dec;60(6):715-54.

UMLS. Unified Medical Language System. http://www.nlm.nih.gov/pubs/factsheets/umls.html. 2004.

Valente, T.W., & Rogers, E.M. (1995, March). The origins and development of the diffusion of innovations paradigm as an example of scientific growth. *Science Communication,* pp. 242-273.

Valeri A, Drelon E, Azzouzi R, Delannoy A, Teillac P, Fournier G, Mangin P, Berthon P, Cussenot O. [Epidemiology of familial prostatic cancer: 4-year assessment of French studies]. Prog Urol. 1999 Sep;9(4):672-9.

van Bemmel JH, Hasman A, Sollet PC, Veth AF. Training in medical informatics. Comput Biomed Res. 1983 Oct;16(5):414-32.

van der Kuip H, Mürdter TE, Sonnenberg M, McClellan M, Gutzeit S, Gerteis A, Simon W, Fritz P, Aulitzky WE. Short term culture of breast cancer tissues to study the activity of the anticancer drug taxol in an intact tumor environment. BMC Cancer. 2006 Apr 7;6:86.

Velterop J. Necessity is the mother of innovation. Neuroinformatics. 2005;3(1):11-4.

Vena JE, Weiner JM. Innovative multidisciplinary research in environmental epidemiology: The challenges and needs. J Occup Med and Environ Hlth 12(4)353-70, 1999.
Voss D. Better searching through science. *Science*. 2001;293(5537):2024-2.

Wang H, Azuaje F, Black N. An integrative and interactive framework for improving biomedical pattern discovery and visualization. IEEE Trans Inf Technol Biomed. 2004 Mar;8(1):16-27.

Warner AJ. Quantitative and qualitative assessments of the impact of linguistic theory on information science. *Journal of the American Society for Information Science*. 1991;42(1):64-71.

Weber MA. Angiotensin II receptor blockers in older patients. Am J Geriatr Cardiol. 2004 Jul-Aug;13(4):197-205

Weeber M, Vos R, Klein H, De Jong-Van Den Berg LT, Aronson AR, Molema G. Generating Hypotheses by Discovering Implicit Associations in the Literature: A Case Report of a Search for New Potential Therapeutic Uses for Thalidomide. J Am Med Inform Assoc. 2003 May-Jun;10(3):252-9.Epub2003 Jan 28.

Weick KE, Quinn RE. Organizational change and development. Annu Rev Psychol. 1999;50:361-86.

Weinberg BH. Why indexing fails the research. *The Indexer*. 1988;16(1):3-6.

Weiner JM. Issues in the Design and Evaluation of Medical Trials. G.K. Hall, Boston, MA 1979.

Weiner JM, Shirley S, Gilman NJ, Stowe SM, Wolf RM. Access to Data and the Information Explosion: Oral Contraceptives and Risk of Cancer. Contraception. 1981 Sep;24(3):301-13.

Weiner JM. Text Analysis and Basic Concept Structures. Information Processing and Management 19:313-319, 1983.

Weiner JM, Schuster JHR, Horowitz RS, McAfoos WP, Piniewski-Bond J. Fantasies in Processing. 2004, American Literary Press, Baltimore, MD.

Weiner JM. Knowledge Utilization: Paths to Creativity. XXIV Century Press, Wilmington, DE 2005.

Weiner, JM. Differences in Indexing Term Vocabularies and Agreement with Subject Specialists. E-JASL. v.6 no.1-2 (Summer 2005).

Weiner, JM. Epidemiology and Conceptual Architecture, 2006, XXIV Century Press, Gallatin, TN. http://tutorghost.com

Weiner, JM, Piniewski-Bond, J. Pass That Test, 2006, XXIV Century Press, Gallatin, TN. http://tutorghost.com

Weiner, JM. How to Succeed in Graduate Training and Enjoy the Journey, 2006, XXIV Century Press, Gallatin, TN. http://tutorghost.com

Weiner, JM, Editor; Beehler GF, Horowitz RS, Jackman LW, Piniewski-Bond, J, Weiner JM, Weiner, SA. Methods in Knowledge Utilization. (2009) XXIV Century Press, West Lafayette IN, http://amazon.com

Weiner SA, Weiner, JM.Using a Student-Generated Survey to Inform Planning for a User-Focused Learning Commons. Education Libraries Vol 33, No 1, Spring 2010. http://units.sla.org/division/ded/educationlibraries/33-1.pdf

Weiss L; Levison SP. Tools for integrating women's health into medical education: Clinical cases and concept mapping. Academic-Medicine. Nov 2000; Vol 75 (11): 1081-1086.

White HR, Chen PH. Problem drinking and intimate partner violence. J Stud Alcohol. 2002 Mar;63(2):205-14.

Whittemore AS, Kolonel LN, Wu AH, John EM, Gallagher RP, Howe GR, Burch JD, Hankin J, Dreon DM, West DW, Prostate cancer in relation to diet, physical activity, and body size in blacks, whites, and Asians in the United States and Canada. J Natl Cancer Inst. 1995 May 3;87(9):652-61.

Yoo KY, Shin HR, Chang SH, Choi BY, Hong YC, Kim DH, Kang D, Cho NH, Shin C, Jin YW. Genomic epidemiology cohorts in Korea: present and the future. Asian Pac J Cancer Prev. 2005 Jul-Sep;6(3):238-43.

Yoshida K, Kohzuki M. Clinical and experimental aspects of olmesartan medoxomil, a new angiotensin II receptor antagonist. Cardiovasc Drug Rev. 2004 Winter;22(4):285-308.

Yu C, Quadrado J, Ceglowski M, Payne JS. Patterns in Unstructured Data. <http://javelina.cet.middlebury.edu/lsa/out/cover_page.htm, 2002.

Zhang J, Hsu B A JC, Kinseth B A MA, Bjeldanes LF, Firestone GL. Indole-3-carbinol induces a G1 cell cycle arrest and inhibits prostate-specific antigen production in human LNCaP prostate carcinoma cells. Cancer. 2003 Dec 1;98(11):2511-20.

Zheng, W. Molecular Epidemiologic Study of Breast Cancer. CRISP 2005, 2R01CA090899.

Zwicky, F., Discovery, Invention, Research - Through the Morphological Approach, Toronto: The Macmillian Company (1969).

Lightning Source UK Ltd.
Milton Keynes UK
172258UK00001B/57/P